Community and Communication

MULTILINGUAL MATTERS SERIES

Series Editor: Professor John Edwards, *St. Francis Xavier University, Antigonish, Nova Scotia, Canada.*

Other Books in the Series
Beyond Bilingualism: Multilingualism and Multilingual Education
    Jasone Cenoz and Fred Genesee (eds)
Identity, Insecurity and Image: France and Language
    Dennis Ager
Language Attitudes in Sub-Saharan Africa
    Efurosibina Adegbija
Language, Ethnicity and Education
    Peter Broeder and Guus Extra
Language Planning in Malawi, Mozambique and the Philippines
    Robert B. Kaplan and Richard B. Baldauf, Jr. (eds)
Language Planning: From Practice to Theory
    Robert B. Kaplan and Richard B. Baldauf, Jr. (eds)
Language Reclamation
    Hubisi Nwenmely
Linguistic Minorities in Central and Eastern Europe
    Christina Bratt Paulston and Donald Peckham (eds)
Quebec's Aboriginal Languages
    Jacques Maurais (ed.)
The Step-Tongue: Children's English in Singapore
    Anthea Fraser Gupta A
Three Generations – Two Languages – One Family
    Li Wei

Other Books of Interest
Language and Conflict: A Neglected Relationship
    Sue Wright (ed.)
Language, Culture and Communication in Contemporary Europe
    Charlotte Hoffman (ed.)
Language, Democracy and Devolution in Catalonia
    Sue Wright (ed.)
Languages in Contact and Conflict: Contrasting Experiences in the Netherlands and Belgium
    Sue Wright (ed.)
Language Policy and Language Issues in the Succesor States of the Former USSR
    Sue Wright (ed.)
Languages in America: A Pluralist View
    Susan J. Dicker
The Languages of Israel: Policy, Ideology and Practice
    Bernard Spolsky and Elana Shohamy
Managing Language Diversity
    Sue Wright and Helen Kelly-Holmes (eds)
Mass Media in the Asian Pacific
    Bryce T. McIntyre (ed.)

Please contact us for the latest book information:
Multilingual Matters, Frankfurt Lodge, Clevedon Hall,
Victoria Road, Clevedon, BS21 7HH England
http://www.multilingual-matters.com

MULTILINGUAL MATTERS 114
Series Editor: John Edwards

Community and Communication

The Role of Language in Nation State Building and European Integration

Sue Wright

MULTILINGUAL MATTERS LTD
Clevedon • Buffalo • Toronto • Sydney

For Colin, Tom and Anna

Library of Congress Cataloging in Publication Data

Wright, Sue
Community and Communication: The Role of Language in Nation State
Building and European Integration/Sue Wright
Multilingual Matters Series: 114
Includes bibliographical references and index
1. Europe–Languages–Political aspects. 2. Multilingualism–Europe.
3. Nationalism–Europe. 4. Democracy–Europe. 5. European Union.
6. Europe–Politics and government–1989- I. Title. II. Multilingual Matters (Series): 114.
P119.32.E85 W75 2000
306.44'094–dc21   99-048152

British Library Cataloguing in Publication Data

A CIP catalogue record for this book is available from the British Library.

ISBN 1-85359-485-7 (hbk)
ISBN 1-85359-484-9 (pbk)

Multilingual Matters Ltd

UK: Frankfurt Lodge, Clevedon Hall, Victoria Road, Clevedon BS21 7HH.
USA: UTP, 2250 Military Road, Tonawanda, NY 14150, USA.
Canada: UTP, 5201 Dufferin Street, North York, Ontario M3H 5T8, Canada.
Australia: P.O. Box 586, Artarmon, NSW, Australia.

Typeset by Archetype-IT Ltd (http://www.archetype-it.com).
Printed and bound in Great Britain by the Cromwell Press Ltd.

Contents

Chapter 6

Chapter 7

Chapter 8

Chapter 9

Chapter 10

Acknowledgements

I am grateful to all the people who have discussed the ideas of this book with me and commented on various chapters. Numerous people reacted to drafts and conference papers on the subject and made helpful suggestions. I would like to thank them all, but in particular Michael Clyne, John Edwards, John Rex, Dan Smith, Dennis Smith and Bernard Spolsky. I would also like to acknowledge the support of Dennis Ager, Helen Kelly-Holmes and Paul Chilton, my colleagues at Aston, who have given constant encouragement.

My thanks too to the NATO officers, the UN desk staff, the employees at the European Commission, the members of the Committee of the Regions and the MEPs who took time and trouble to answer my questions and find further information for me. Any mistakes or misinterpretations remain, of course, my own.

Introduction

The themes of the book

Three processes which have greatly affected European political development since 1945 are a slow but steady progress towards the abolition of
political and economic frontiers, a tendency for the old nation-states to
fracture, with the communities of which they were composed demanding
some devolution of power, autonomy or even full independence, and
migration on a massive scale.[1]

These three macro-social phenomena have had immense impact on the
communities in which individuals have to operate. If we simply consider
the aspect of communication, we are no longer in the situation where most
children are born into a community of communication which remains
relatively stable throughout their life. The biographies and social settings
of today's children are likely to put them into situations where a far wider
range of language competence will be needed and where communities of
communication are not stable over time and space.

The genesis of this book was a fascination that so much has been written
about these processes, without this linguistic instability always being
considered. In particular, the development of the European Union seems
to raise a number of questions about communication among its constituent
peoples. On a continent where the tradition of 'one language, one state, one
people' is so deeply entrenched, it is surely impossible to consider
European integration without investigating how the linguistic dimension
might affect its chances of success. However, many of the writers on
European integration published in French, German and English devote
little space to the language issue.

Their reasons are probably diverse. Among the pro-European group,
some may be genuinely language blind. Bi- or trilingual themselves with
competence in one of the languages of power in the Union or even
monolingual French or English speakers, they may genuinely see no
difficulty in a plurilingual union because their own repertoire allows them
to interact in all the situations they encounter, and so they underestimate
the linguistic difficulties inherent in integration. It may be that those with

languages that are the *lingua franca*s of Europe prefer to keep the issue in the background and profit from the advantage that such linguistic membership confers, without drawing attention to it. It may be that those who support further European integration recognise the language question as a potentially contentious and divisive issue, best avoided until federalism is achieved. The reasons why the political actors themselves sidestep the question of language is not difficult to discern. Given the affection that national groups feel for their national language and the symbolic importance they attach to it, it would be dangerous to indicate that 'mobility', 'unification', 'harmonisation', all key words in the European project, are likely to undermine the strict divisions between linguistic groups.

The silence among the anti-Europeans is less easily explained. They could evoke loss of national identity in the wake of the possible language shifts which might accompany the free circulation of people and services; they could argue the impossibility of overcoming the democratic deficit in a plurilingual situation. That they largely refrain from employing this line of attack is surprising.

The writers who do address the language issue usually adopt what might be termed a cosmopolitan stance. This group supports and promotes the policy of a plurilingual Europe where a number of the major languages will be taught, learnt and used by European citizens within the networks and institutions of the new polity which is evolving. It could be argued that this is largely an ideological position, part of the ethos of Europe's 'unity in diversity' policy and not related to the language choices that have actually been taking place. Although the cosmopolitans cite precedents to show that such plurilingualism is a well-rooted European tradition, all their examples relate to leisured middle and aristocratic classes at particular conjunctures who had the time, motivation and opportunity to acquire more than their mother tongue. In none of the societies given as models did plurilingualism percolate more deeply to all levels, and the complex conditions which encouraged it are not replicated in the populations of the Member States in the late twentieth century.

In present day Europe, the market is the dominant force in second language acquisition. The personal advantage that the learner can derive from having acquired a second language drives individuals to learn the language which is spoken by the greatest number of speakers and which thus brings greatest returns. On this logic, the motivation for acquiring English or French, perhaps German is clear. The premiss of the 'unity in diversity' policy that all the official languages of the Member States could be taught and learnt was never well founded; a second language needs to be a *lingua franca*; few individuals want to acquire a language that has no such role. National education policies have generally followed voters' wishes that their children learn one of the languages of wider diffusion rather than trying to impose or encourage diversity. Moreover, there is a certain dishonesty in attempting to promote all the official languages of the Member States as potential foreign languages in the various education systems when the policy of plurilingualism has largely broken down in the institutions of the Union and those who wish to play a role in European institutions actually need either French or English. These are the languages of power to which learners want access and the most recent statistics reveal that English is the language which dominates in the various education systems. The citizens of Europe are not, in large numbers, choosing to learn languages for other reasons: proximity, culture, solidarity etc.

The Forces of Linguistic Unification

Whether individuals have particular linguistic skills or not is always one of the factors of inclusion or exclusion in a number of spheres: access to knowledge; employability; participation in the democratic process; active citizenship.

As the European nation states developed, monolingualism and cultural homogeneity within the state were seen as desirable, both from the point of view of the state and the individual. Plurilingual societies were dismissed as the mode of organisation of the old empires, where stratification and differentiation could be accepted. As soon as subjects were members of a national family, participating in national education and national welfare and contributing to defence, then linguistic unification seemed necessary and inevitable.[2] As representative democracy became the norm and as subjects became citizens who must play a political role, the pressure for there to be one single language in which this political process could be enacted intensified. There are few democratic European states which did not attempt to become unified monolingual societies. And, on closer examination, the apparent exceptions do not prove truly exceptional; they largely manage their political life in federal arrangements where the congruence of the political entity and the cultural/linguistic group is achieved below state level.

The other social phenomenon of the nineteenth and twentieth centuries that led to linguistic unification within the state was economic; industrialisation brought workers from different rural areas together into the linguistic melting pot of towns and cities. Governments protected their domestic markets and movement and exchange was greater within state frontiers than across them. Within domestic economies there was more contact than in the past. Journeys, associations, trade, common projects tended to be national rather than transnational. Modernity in both its political and economic manifestations contributed to linguistic uniformity within state boundaries.

Some of the same processes are now at work in the European Union. Citizens of the fifteen Member States are also citizens of the EU. The EU is a fledgling democracy at suprastate level with some of the trappings of a participatory system. The EU is a single market with most of its trade occurring among the Member States. Movement is easy across internal borders; breaching the external borders and gaining access from outside is sometimes more problematic. What is not yet clear is whether a single European market and European political institutions will have a similar linguistic effect to that produced by a single national market and national political institutions. How Europeans will manage their communication needs within these new political and economic contexts is not yet clearly fixed.

The early evidence, however, suggests that English, the *lingua franca* which has accompanied and permitted the process of globalisation, may play the same role in Europeanisation. Because English is the language which dominates as first foreign language in the Member States education systems it is becoming the working language of many of the EU's transnational networks and teams. The penetration of English in some societies is so far advanced that there is presently some anxiety about the development of national languages. What will happen if, for example, advanced science and technology are always described in English? Will certain languages become less appropriate for use for such subjects because the terminology and usage for the domain is never developed? Is a diglossic situation developing in some areas? At the moment there is no evidence that any speakers of any European languages are actually shifting to English. English remains purely an additional language increasingly employed as the European *lingua franca* and gradually replacing French in that role. There is, at present, no replication of the language shifts and linguistic unification of the nationalist era.

Language Renaissance

There does appear, however, to be some undoing of this unification. A number of European states have come under pressure from autochthonous minority groups to devolve power to subnational levels of governance. Provinces and regions which had seemed securely incorporated into nation states have demanded some autonomy. It seems feasible to explain this trend as a corollary of Europeanisation. The umbrella of the Union permits groups which would have been too small to constitute a viable polity in the Westphalian system to envisage distancing themselves from the tutelage of the nation state in which they were incorporated. This is true both for those which are already inside the Union and for those which would join. The Union provides both economic and political protection, even if the present European security and defence identity stems more from NATO than from internal structures. As these processes develop, the influence of the national capitals is eroded from both above and below as political power appears to be realigning at three levels: the regional, the national and the supranational. Although national governments remain the most powerful at the present time, they have lost their power monopoly.

A similar and parallel process has occurred in linguistic practices. Within the Union, regional languages, long suppressed have reappeared in public life. Welsh, Basque, Catalan, Galician and Gaelic are once again official languages and their speakers able to use them in their devolved assemblies and parliaments, to learn them or through them in their education systems, to be heard in them in their courts. Among the applicant states to the Union, there have been even more complete reversals of linguistic fortune. For example, Russian has been ousted from political and public life in Estonia, Latvia and Lithuania where the autochthonous languages have replaced it as the language of power.

It remains to be seen what the complementary language practices in these small states and autonomies will be. Speakers of languages which are restricted in area and number of speakers need a language of wider diffusion to allow them access to the outside world. Whether this will continue to be the language of the state to which they were traditionally linked or a language playing a more extensive *lingua franca* role is not yet clear. There is also the possibility that some groups may attempt to develop trilingualism although the precedents for this are not legion.

Whatever solutions are found to the communication needs of the new Europe it does appear inevitable that fewer Europeans will be monolingual in the language of their nation state. The pressures from above and below all militate against this.

The Pattern of the Book

These themes together with a consideration of some of the ways language and political power intertwine in nation states, in international organisations and in super- and supra-national entities constitute the content of the book. The first chapter surveys theories of nationalism, focusing on linguistic nationalism, civic nationalism and the invention of tradition. It divides theorists into nationalists, modernists and post-modernists and notes how they position language in their paradigms.

Chapter 2 presents a number of case studies which highlight the role language played in the formation of the nation states of Europe. There are two principal European models. In the assimilatory nation state, boundaries were set by conquest and dynastic marriage and inheritance. The linguistically disparate states within these boundaries were unified after the creation of the state. To secure these aims, rulers and ruling elites employed various policies and strategies, and, in the European context, they have generally been successful. In the other model, which could be termed 'blood and belonging' (Ignatieff, 1994), the state is created to be the homeland of a linguistically and culturally homogenous group. Those who are not considered to be of the blood or from the language group may be excluded from citizenship and may even be persecuted.

Chapter 3 discusses the opinions of the contending schools in the debate and challenges some accepted wisdom. It suggests that the worst excesses of linguistic nationalism may be at the root of a general refusal to recognise the fundamental importance of language in group formation. It observes that humans cannot change linguistic group easily or quickly and that language remains a defining characteristic of human groups. It concludes with the reflection that western Europeans have certain preconceptions about political structures, including the expectation that these structures will coincide with their community of communication and that they will be able to understand and contribute to political debate within the polities to which they belong.

Chapter 4 notes that globalisation has often brought anglicisation in legal, political, economic, defence and cultural domains and provides further evidence of this trend. The economic reasons for acquiring English are increasing and the proliferation of cultural sources, caused by the new technologies, is a further source of anglophone domination.

Chapter 5 traces the history of the European Union to see how a Euro-polity is emerging. This Euro-polity is *sui generis* but replicates nonetheless many attributes of the nation state. The national experience is, after all, what the various European populations bring to their new venture. In one significant way, however, there is no parallel to be drawn. The EU is officially plurilingual and there is complete rejection of the concept of a single community of communication.

Chapter 6 exposes the consequences of plurilingualism for democracy. The tradition of democracy in Europe is very diverse but in all its varieties, information, association, debate and the voicing of opinion have been central. Democracy is inextricably bound with language, and one wonders how it can be managed without a community of communication. Achieving meaningful, plurilingual democracy is a challenge that has not yet been taken up. It is perhaps the greatest obstacle to overcoming the EU's democratic deficit. To accomplish worthwhile democracy across language divides will require the same kind of conceptual leap that was necessary in the move from participatory to representative democracy.

Chapter 7 focuses on communication in the institutions of the EU and finds that the commitment to plurilingualism is breaking down, even where translation and interpretation are readily available. English and French have emerged *de facto* as *lingua franca*s but, since this is not official policy, a number of unplanned and unwanted effects have arisen. The fiction that the institutions are plurilingual means that linguistic reality is not recognised and those unable to work in French or English are marginalised. The existence of two *lingua franca*s reinforces other fractures within the EU, particularly an undesirable north-south cleavage.

Chapter 8 examines regionalism within the EU and finds a resurgence of self-confidence and energy in subnational entities. Two processes seem to be at work. The first is a return to the nationalist ideal that political entity and linguistic/cultural group should be congruent. The second is an enthusiastic participation in transnational European networks. These two phenomena are, of course, linked: the European Union umbrella makes it possible for a small entity to overcome the disadvantages of being small in the realm of the market, of defence or of diplomacy. Regional languages may benefit from a parallel process. If a situation emerged where social promotion, economic advantage and access to political power required mastery of a global and/or European *lingua franca*(s) as well as one's mother tongue, speakers of regional languages would be no more disadvantaged than speakers of national languages. The individual's rational choice of language would be influenced by where the balance of power and influence was to be found: retained by the nation state; devolved to subnational groups; relinquished to supranational organisations.

Chapter 9 considers language and identity and asks whether any of the strategies employed in the nation building era have resurfaced in the European project. The conclusion is that there are many parallels already in existence or envisaged: common defence, commitment to some redistribution of wealth and resources, invention of tradition, reinterpretation of history to highlight common origins and influences, shared journeys and networks within a geographical space. However, policies on language are different, and the desire to safeguard linguistic and cultural diversity dominates the need to build a community of communication where the common political project can be elaborated and played out.

Chapter 10 concludes that the present EU strategy of promoting plurilingualism is admirable in its idealism and concern to maintain equality between groups, but utopian; not all of us will become polyglots. Europeans are at a crossroads: without a community of communication, the European Union must remain a trading association run in an autocratic way by bilingual patrician technocrats; with a community of communication, the European Union could develop democratic structures and legitimacy and give meaning to its policies of free movement. In theory, the achievement of such a community would not be difficult; personal bilingualism and social diglossia would cater for European communication needs and conserve all the ancestral languages of Europe. In reality, such a policy, which touches at the very heart of personal and group identity and advantages one language above all the others, could never be adopted formally. However, history demonstrates that communities and individuals usually achieve the communication networks they need, whether this happens in a planned or an unplanned way.

The Problem with Language

Language is an immensely emotive subject. It is a carrier of identity and any undermining of a variety is experienced as an attack on fundamental group values. It can be a weapon of exclusion, used, as in linguistic nationalism, to justify a particularly virulent variety of racism. The emotive and racist dimensions of language to be found within the nationalist tradition may explain why it has been neglected in some of the scholarly work on European integration and globalisation. It can only be a distaste for the subject which can explain why it is possible to read books about EU policy-making, about EU citizenship, nationality and migration, about EU political parties, about European networks and the information society, about doing business in Europe, about almost any aspect of European unification without the authors discussing what effect the multilingual nature of the entity must have on developments.

The neglect may also stem from a scholarly distaste for *engagement*. Much of the literature on the spread of language and language domination has been written in the *engagé* tradition. In particular there is a French school which is activist. The work of Hagège, Druon, Calvet and de Broglie, for example, includes a robust defence of French and an attack on the way that English has become the main communication medium within international regimes, multinational corporations and transnational movements. In the

Anglo-Saxon camp, there has been an attempt at a structuralist, positivist reading of English hegemony, with the language portrayed as a neutral medium for international exchange.[3] This has to be dismissed as an analysis which ignores the basic facts.[4] The spread of English is, like all preceding examples of language dominance, proof of growing political and economic power, and cannot be presented as value-free.

There is in all of this the great danger of the researcher being seen as partisan; everyone is a member of a community of communication; allegiance is inevitable; access to information is defined by the language(s) one understands. To make my own position clear, I realise that as a mother tongue English speaker with French and German as second languages, I run the risk of interpreting from certain perspectives and of acquiring information from a limited range of sources.

Notes

1. This book deals with two of these three phenomena. Migration is the process which is omitted. It has, of course, had an immense impact and no European state, except perhaps Iceland, has been untouched by the vast movement of peoples in the second half of the twentieth century. Migration touches language because it breaks down the homogeneity of the communities of communication created by national governments, introducing large numbers of bilinguals into largely monolingual societies, and because it has been accompanied by racist backlash and reaffirmation of nationalism among autochthonous groups. However, the migration aspect of the language issue will not be treated in this work. It is a story which touches the issues dealt with here at many points but which remains largely parallel. It is an immense subject which deserves a book of its own for an adequate treatment.

2. Immigration in the post war period reopened this issue. States, such as the Netherlands, the United Kingdom and France, where homogenising policies for autochthonous minorities had succeeded to a large degree found themselves faced with new allochthonous minorities to incorporate. Assimilatory policies for migrants followed the model of assimilatory policies for autochthonous minorities.

3. For a discussion of those in the Anglo-Saxon world who take this line see Pennycook (1994). Siguan (1996) gives the view from continental Europe.

4. In August 1997, Claude Allègre, the French education minister, suggested that the French should cease 'de considérer l'anglais comme une langue étrangère'. The subsequent storm in the press insisted that it was 'naïf de ne pas donner un sens politique à la domination de l'anglais' (*Le Monde*, 1 December 1997, p. 15).

Chapter 1

Definitions. Theories of nationalism and the role of language. The nationalists and linguistic nationalism. The modernists, industrialisation and democracy. The post-modernists and the invention of tradition

Nationalism: A Contested Concept

The nation state has been the key allegiance for most Europeans during the past two centuries. The concept that the territory of the state has unchanging boundaries and that the people(s) who live within these boundaries are a cohesive nation, different from those who live in neighbouring states, continues to be widely accepted as a self-evident truth by most Europeans, as any survey of their national media will reveal.[1] The jingoism of the age of high nationalism may have waned, but the continuing power of national sentiment still provides an important focus of identity for many people.

However, at the end of a century in which nationalism is taken to have been a major factor in all the inter-state wars on the continent as well as in many intra-state conflicts, it would be inconceivable that nationalism should continue to attract unquestioning support. Various international movements, from the desire for international socialism to the wish for European integration, have some of their genesis in a rejection of nationalism. Many intellectuals and scholars have shown a dislike for the concept and the feelings generated by it, seeing themselves as cosmopolitan and untrammelled by this affiliation. Scientific enquiry into the subject is coloured by disapproval and has been sporadic (Hutchinson & Smith, 1994). Much current theory in the Anglo-Saxon and French worlds takes a critical perspective.[2] It is understandable that there should have been a clear rejection of nationalism in certain quarters. Kedourie's 'dark goddesses'[3] are not confined to the Indian context; nationalism has been a dark force in the European context too.

These two attitudes towards nationalism coexist in a situation of increasing globalisation. The growth of supra-national trading blocks, of trans-national companies, of new forms of media and communication technology, of international peace-keeping forces have led to much talk of the demise of nationalism. But, to adapt Mark Twain, one might say that reports of its death have been exaggerated.[4] Nationalism remains one of the most potent organising forces on earth, and not only in the obvious examples furnished by the struggles of the constituent states of the former Soviet Union and former Yugoslavia. In western Europe too, new political entities are forming according to the organising principles of nationalism. The three autonomies in Spain are a response to demands for national self-determination from the Catalans, Basques and Galicians; the 1994 Belgian constitution gives the Flemings greater independence; Scottish and Welsh devolution are fuelled by the same national aspirations.

The Difficulties of Definition

Nation and nationalism are difficult to define. The ideas have taken many forms, even when we limit ourselves to nations and states within the confines of Europe. There are numerous schools of nationalist theory. According to A. D. Smith (1995) their definitions fall mainly into four categories. Firstly, those who have espoused nationalism and are its apologists argue that nations are part of the 'natural order', that the modern nation evolves from an enduring descent group, that nations are ubiquitous and ancient. Secondly, there are the perennialists who agree on the primordial nature of nationalism but deny that it is predestined; one may choose one's nation and the nation may build on past traditions, changing them as required and desired. Thirdly, the modernists tend to discount the role of the past and tradition in nation building, and treat it as a recent and necessary phenomenon, a socio-political fact, a function of development necessarily linked to industrialisation, urbanisation, democracy, mass education and the concept of 'progress'. Lastly, the post-modernists claim that nation building is social engineering and that nationalism is no more than a cultural construct. In their interpretation, history, myth, ritual and symbol are invented to promote a spurious identity. The construction of a narrative of the past allows a group to imagine that it belongs together. While not totally agreeing that a clear division exists between the modernists and post-modernists, I shall use these categories to group the various theories of nationalism.

Further disagreement in scholarly definitions of nations and nationhood stems from the fact that the study of nationalism is, by definition, inter-disciplinary and specialists from the numerous cognate areas have tended to prioritise different aspects. This causes problems as Hutchinson and Smith recognise in their introduction to an anthology of key texts on nationalism:

(T)here is little agreement about the role of the ethnic, as opposed to the political, components of the nation; or about the balance between 'subjective' elements like will and memory, and more 'objective' elements like territory and language; or about the role of ethnicity in national identity. (Hutchinson & Smith, 1994: 4)

Confusion among non-specialists results partly from the imprecise way the terms 'nation' and 'state' are used. The former is often substituted for the latter, blurring the distinction between the two and suggesting that they are synonymous, with all that implies for non-recognition of cultural diversity within state boundaries. At the highest levels of *international* relations the distinction is not respected; the United Nations ought more accurately to be termed the United States, were this label available for use. However, at a very deep level of consciousness, we acknowledge the difference between the political components and the more subjective elements. We readily understand the concept of a stateless person. On the other hand, that a person should be nationless makes no sense to us given the collective experience of the last century. Gellner points out that belonging to a nation is actually just as contingent as belonging to a state, but that this is rarely recognised:

A man must have a nationality as he must have a nose and two ears; a deficiency in any of these particulars is not inconceivable and does from time to time occur, but only as the result of some disaster, and is itself a disaster of a kind. All this seems obvious, though, alas, it is not true. But that it should have come to *seem* so very obviously true is indeed an aspect, or perhaps the very core, of the problem of nationalism. Having a nation is not an inherent attribute of humanity but it has now come to appear as such. (Gellner, 1983: 6)

When, where and how ethnic groups began to acquire the self-awareness that propelled them to nationhood and a political project is also a matter of considerable dispute. One group sees the late Middle Ages and the Hundred Years War (1337–1453) as the first stage of the process in Europe (Duby, 1987; Seton-Watson, 1977). Seton-Watson writes:

In 1200 neither a French nor an English nation existed, but in 1600 both were important realities. (Seton-Watson, 1977: 8)

Liah Greenfeld argues that, when in Tudor England the term 'nation' came to be applied not just to the elite but to the people,

(T)his semantic transformation signaled the emergence of the first nation in the sense in which the word is used today and launched the era of nationalism. (Greenfeld, 1992: 6)

Another school takes the French revolution (1789) as the starting point (Seton-Watson, 1977). Gellner (1983) is persuasive in his argument that the industrial age with its need for a literate and socially/geographically mobile work force makes nationalism and culturo-linguistic homogeneity inevitable.

Many scholars in the Anglo-Saxon political science tradition question the very endeavour of definition. They ask whether it is possible to arrive at a formula which adequately describes all the situations in which groups define themselves as nations. Seton-Watson is

> driven to the conclusion that no scientific definition of the nation can be devised; yet the phenomenon existed and exists. (Seton-Watson, 1977: 5)

Hobsbawm asks 'What is (a) nation?', then concludes, unequivocally:

> . . . no satisfactory criterion can be discovered for deciding which of the many human collectivities should be labelled in this way. (Hobsbawm, 1990: 5)

To identify this 'satisfactory criterion' might indeed be a difficult task. Nonetheless, it seems illogical that although theorists (Hobsbawm included) appear to be able to say that a specific situation is **not** an example of nationalism or nation, they cannot say what **is**. There must be a concept with parameters into which certain groups do or do not fit.

A Working Definition

So, while recognising that any attempt to propound a normative concept for the constitutive elements of the nation would be doomed to failure, I am going to attempt, nevertheless, an amalgam of the definitions available and suggest what factors are present when people associate as a nation. My desire here is to try and understand what people *believe* to be the organising principles of the associations that have brought us to the collectivities which we call nations. The interest here is that it is these *beliefs* which provide the context in which all new political experiments will be played out. The variety of components and causal factors in the various nation building projects that Europe has witnessed are part of the various national consciousnesses and the shared national experiences. We may see a rejection of the methods of nation building in the configurations of state groupings or supra-national polities of the future. On the other hand, they may be remembered and reused.

There is general consensus that nationalism has political, economic, moral, cultural and linguistic dimensions, although the relative weight and absolute necessity of each of these elements is contested. Theories of nationalism state, with varying degrees of emphasis, that peoples have a right to self-determination, either within their own nation state or some self-governing unit within another nation state; that the nation will safeguard the economic interests of its own people and may exclude outsiders from trade and employment; that in its defence, or even simply to further its own interests, the nation has the right to employ violence and to ask its members to sacrifice their lives; that nationality is the primary form of identity and takes precedence over all others; that the nation should be a community in which all members can communicate with each other, a 'community of communication'. For all forms of nationalism, sovereignty is invested in the people, but this does not necessarily imply democracy. In some nationalisms, the 'people' may be taken to be 'incarnated' in a leader or a ruling class; in others, the 'people' may not include all of the people resident in the state.

Language

Having acquired a working definition of nationalism, a venture that is in itself controversial, let us move into the next contentious area – the role of language in nation state formation. The various theories of nationalism differ greatly on the function of language in the processes of nation building and the four main schools of thought accord very different weighting to the need for a community of communication, to underpin the process. Ethnolinguistic nationalism makes language a mythical and mystical unifier; only those who share the linguistic world view can participate in the nation. The perennialists argue that the linguistic world view can be acquired. The modernists see linguistic unification as a by-product of industrialisation and the development of democracy. The post-modernists see language as discourse, the tool **and** the product of the creative process which constructs the nation, but have little to say on language difference. It seems that most theorists play down the importance of a single community of communication, seeing 'one language one people' as an essential element in the 'blood and belonging' tradition but not in other forms of nationalism. Only the apologists for nationalism argue that language is an essential component in nation building. The primordialists, the perennialists, the modernists and the post-modernists each give a different role and a different weighting to language, as this brief overview of their theories shows.

Ethno-linguistic Nationalism

According to the ethno-linguistic variety of nationalism, the nation is a natural, preordained entity, existing since time immemorial, possessing its own particular attributes:

> Each nation has a beauty that belongs to it; each nation should be satisfied with the beauty peculiar to it; none deviate from its nature nor from the temperament peculiar to it. (Ehrensvärd, quoted in Kohn, 1946: 418)

Many of the early theorists and defenders of ethno-linguistic nationalism were German. In the *Sturm und Drang* reaction to the ideas of the mainly French Enlightenment a mythical, anti-intellectual tradition of nationalism was born. The German Romantics argued that it was the *Volk* with its common roots and pre-existing characteristics – language, culture, history and religion – which created the nation. Among the first writers in this tradition were Klopstock (1724–1803) and Voss (1751–1826). Turning aside from the rational humanism and optimistic universalism promoted by the chief theorists of the Enlightenment, they lauded Germany's mythical, mystical and irrational past and evoked a time when the German nation, unfettered by the constraints of civilisation, was a glorious and heroic tribe. This *Urvolk*, supposedly the repository of a particularly 'German' vitality, imagination, seriousness and simplicity, represented primeval force and unspoilt nature. Klopstock rediscovered ancient Nordic and Germanic myths and legends, Voss portrayed Charlemagne as the 'bad' German who had sold out to Rome, 'put the chain of slavery on true Germans and ordered Saxons to worship statues and idols instead of Wotan's invisible godhead' (Kohn, 1946). Other *Sturm und Drang*, writers such as Möser (1720–1794), painted an idealised and sentimental picture of a supposed golden era of innocence.

Formulations of the idea that language and thought are inextricably linked appeared in the work of Herder (1744–1803) and Hamann (1730–1788). In *Über den Ursprung der Sprache*, Herder argued that the ancestral language of a people was essential to its continued well-being, that it was a collective achievement and, thus, the means of accessing the group's authentic core. It ensured the group's cohesion and identity both in the present and into the future. As a corollary to this, he argued that each nation was unique and that for a group to preserve its specificity and survive as a discrete entity it must preserve its own language and culture; that difference in language reflects the natural divisions between nations; that linguistic diversity was, *per se*, good and any reduction of it catastrophic in its consequences for those who lost their link with the past. Herder opposed the cosmopolitanism and universalism of the Enlightenment:

> (He) was the first to insist that human civilisation lives not in its general and universal, but in its national and peculiar manifestations. (Kohn, 1946: 429)

From such speculative philosophy, it was a short step to the very Sapir-Whorfian[5] notion, that national consciousness must be bound to national language – that a group which shares a common language shares a unique way of viewing the world. Von Humboldt (1767–1835) and Fichte (1762–1814) were the main exponents of such views. Fichte asserted that:

> the foreigner can never understand the true German without a thorough and extremely laborious study of the German language, and there is no doubt that he will leave what is genuinely German untranslated. (Fichte, quoted in Edwards, 1985: 26)

He provides some of the clearest theoretical statements of belief in the indissolubility of language and national identity:

> Weit mehr die Menschen von der Sprache gebildet werden , denn die Sprache von den Menschen. (Fichte, 1905: 60)

Fichte took from Herder the premise that loss of language equals loss of identity and, extrapolating, evolved a doctrine of German superiority based on the belief that the German language was far closer to the *Ursprache* than other languages such as French, which had been adulterated with Latin elements. The argument that German and its speakers were demonstrably superior was to be used and abused by later theorists and activists and it is to this disreputable strand of ethnolinguistic nationalism that we can trace some of the subsequent reluctance to recognise the importance of language in nation building (Hutchinson & Smith, 1994; Breuilly, 1982).

This reluctance is, however, a twentieth century phenomenon and was not true of nineteenth century theorists. The almost mystic association between language and people fitted well with the Romantic mood. The idea had wide currency in many sectors of society, particularly in central and eastern European, anti-imperialist movements. At that time, the peoples of that part of the continent were, in the majority, under the rule of the Tsarist, Ottoman or Habsburg empires. Poles and Balts under Russian domination, Serbs under Turkish rule, Croats and Hungarians under the Habsburgs, all saw in German ethno-linguistic nationalism a model for their own liberation. Significantly, the leaders of these proto-nations were not always speakers of the vernaculars of the peoples they represented, although they quickly realised the necessity of becoming a member of the relevant speech community. They also recognised the importance of language planning, to prepare their various vernaculars for the role of national language. Together with a 'national' history for the people, an ancestral language was seen to be a prime requirement of nation-building.

> There is not a new nation in Europe, which has not been preceded by fifty to eighty years of philology and archaeological studies. (Fournol, quoted in Fishman, 1972: 158)

The evidence would lead us to believe that, if there were some who accepted Herderian beliefs that a nation was a predestined entity defined by its language, culture, history and religion, there were others who recognised the gap between such a description and reality, and set out to supply the missing elements. And, if so many of the proto-elites were receptive to the appeal of this brand of nationalism, it was partly because it coincided with their ambitions for political freedoms and economic development. Independence from these empires appeared to nineteenth century nationalist revolutionaries the only route to political and economic improvement. Ethno-linguistic nationalism had two advantages. Firstly, it was an organising principle that was relatively easy to harness and promote. The people understood it and could be manipulated to respond to its emotional appeal. Promoting the national language fitted neatly with promotion of oral and written nationalist imagery. Each fed on the other. Secondly, it tended to produce a political unit of manageable size and cohesion where political reform could be envisaged. The theory of ethnic cohesion might be more or less liberally interpreted, depending on whether economic advantage was at stake. Nineteenth century theory held that a state must be of a certain size in order to survive as an economic unit.[6] Slight difference in ethnic composition and language might be overlooked if it proved beneficial to the founding group. We shall see in Chapter 2 how ethno-linguistic nationalism and theories of blood and belonging contributed to the unification of Germany and the appearance of Romania as a sovereign state.

The challenge to ethno-linguistic nationalism stemmed from ideas of universalism and republicanism deriving from the Enlightenment and the philosophers of the French and American Revolutions. This is not to say that either the French revolutionaries or the America secessionists rejected nationalism, merely that most American and French philosophers eschewed ethno-linguistic exclusivity. In fact the assimilatory policies towards both autochthonous and allochthonous minorities adopted by these two Republics have illustrated that nation building can be effected successfully with linguistically heterogeneous populations.

Some authorities hold that the naivety of ethno-linguistic nationalism has been widely recognised and for that reason has withered (Edwards, 1985).[7] However, the situation has evolved since the early 1980s when Edwards was writing. Linguistic nationalism has resurfaced in Europe – and with some virulence (Clyne, 1997). The new nations of Europe, e.g. Serbia, Croatia and the Baltic states, have institutionalised ethnic majority domination. They use language as a determiner for in and out groups. Ignatieff's (1994) account of his journeys in Croatia and Serbia illustrate the detail of how this is happening in former Yugoslavia. The new language legislation in the Baltic Republics has enshrined the practice in law (Ozolins, 1994, 1999; Rannut, 1991).

Modernism and Civic Nationalism

The modernists' thesis is that various social developments, happening on a world-wide scale, have made the nation state inevitable as a form of political organisation (Gellner, 1983). The most important of these were the economic transformation from agrarian to industrial society and the political development from absolutism to democracy. Both have interacted with the growth of nationalism and helped establish it as the dominating political principle of the last two hundred years. In civic nationalism, citizenship is a right for all. One becomes a citizen by being born within the state boundaries (*jus soli*) or by acquiring citzenship after immigration (naturalisation). It is an inclusive form of nationalism, in contrast to the exclusiveness of the *jus sanguinis* of ethno-linguistic nationalism.[8]

From Agrarian to Industrial Society

In the modernist interpretation, the social organisation of agrarian society was not favourable to nationalism; its focus was both more international and more local. At its apogee, agrarian Europe typically organised itself as a three class system: a ruling aristocratic class owned the land and was the locus of military and political power; two international clerisies (Orthodox and Catholic) held the monopoly in spiritual matters and also wielded significant temporal power; the masses, tied to the land, were agricultural producers, whose status was usually a form of serfdom (Bloch, 1940; Duby, 1987; Gellner, 1983). No aspect of European society in the agrarian period fostered 'national' allegiance, in any modern sense of the word.

For the secular power elites, identity was linked to class. Land and population were the property of this class and could be conquered, inherited, acquired by dynastic marriage. No state boundaries were rigidly fixed. Territory could change hands either through force or contract. The highest echelons of this class could become part of the ruling elite in any region of the continent. Most members of the aristocracy married and inherited locally, but at the apex of this class, marriage, inheritance and feudal relationships happened on a pan-European scale. This made it psychologically easy for the group to see itself as a single polyglot ruling class who knew each other, who used one or more of a limited number of prestige language varieties, and who were horizontally differentiated from the peasant masses. They were the self-reproducing 'nobility of Christendom',[9] forged in common endeavours, such as the Crusades, as well as by an intricate system of feudal allegiance. The peasant class and nobility from one locality might fight as a unit, but the impermeability of the ruling class and the chasm between classes would prevent a single identity becoming predominant.

The Christian clerisy was also an international class, transcending frontiers and owing allegiance to a supra-national entity. The Church, split between its Orthodox and Catholic branches, was a great temporal as well as spiritual power. It organised itself on a continental scale. Unlike the aristocracy, it was not impermeable from below. In the Catholic church the celibacy required of the priesthood meant that in each generation the group had to be replenished from outside. In general, positions of power and influence were filled by recruitment from the aristocracy, but peasants could enter the lower echelons. The clerical class underwent a common training, acquiring a single belief system in the medium of a single sacred language. Even at the lowest levels the clergy constituted a bilingual elite, with some degree of literacy in Latin. The allegiances and identity of this class were bound to be 'international'.

The peasant class, the great mass of people, had a very local identity. Anchored to the village, to the farms, their experience did not allow them to see themselves as part of a wider culture. They spoke language varieties which had very restricted speech communities. This did not hamper them in their daily lives; they rarely moved except when pressed by war, crusade or pilgrimage. Language for the great majority was oral, literacy almost non-existent. Outside the immediate community, they would have looked to their lord, their clergy to be their bridge to the outside world. In the feudal organisation of the agrarian era they were insulated from wider society.

Where a commercial class started to develop and towns grew in importance and influence, this division of society started to break down. However, for a very long period agrarian society had patterns of allegiances that were both wider and more narrow than those in the age of nationalism. The communities of communication in such societal organisation are more easily managed than the larger communities of the nationalist era, where language tends to become politicised, a focus for loyalty, as well as the single medium for the communal life of all the classes of the nation.

The advent of the industrial age introduced a new form of social organisation that seemed, as Gellner (1983), Deutsch and Foltz (1963) and Kohn (1944) have argued, to make a move towards nationalism likely, perhaps inevitable. Firstly, industrialisation caused geographical mobility; the workforce moved from the scattered patterns of habitation demanded by agriculture to the high density settlement required by industrial processes. Peasants became workers. People living together in larger groups in urban settings acquired different social identities; the tight network of inward looking peasant communities began to break down. Secondly, industrialisation demanded social mobility. Technological, entrepreneurial elites could not always be drawn from the old ruling classes. Innovators and risk-takers had to be recruited wherever they could be found; the demand for technological and economic progress outweighed the requirement to protect privileged groups. Elites had to become more permeable for the process to work, and some measure of egalitarianism and meritocracy developed. Thirdly, industrial society needed to educate the whole population to permit the most efficient use of its human resources. Agrarian society could train its young by lengthy apprenticeships. Since techniques were unlikely to change, individuals were able to invest immense time and effort in acquiring skills and crafts. This allowed the provision of education to be the business of individuals; they replaced themselves by training apprentices. Industrial society, on the other hand, was undergoing constant change as its members strove for technological progress and the economic advances it promised them. Workers in such a society had to be flexible; they needed a long generic education to give them the basis for further advances in knowledge and then shorter and more specific vocational training. Such training might happen on several occasions in their working life to allow them to accommodate change. Gellner (1983) has argued that when education becomes generic and caters for very large numbers for very long periods, it is bound to become a matter for the state. This is the only entity able to command the resources necessary for such an undertaking. Linguistically this had far-reaching implications. State education in the state language is one of the most powerful means of unifying a linguistically diverse population.

Urbanisation, a less rigidly stratified society, an educated and literate population: all these things contributed to the conditions in which nations and national consciousness could develop. This happened in a number of ways, but the linguistic dimension was always central. The state education system promoted a standardised language. Whatever dialect or language individuals might speak, they acquired literacy in the official language(s) of the state. A state-wide community of communication came into existence, making possible written or spoken contact between all its members. Other factors reinforced the process: industrialisation and a conscript army provided the contact between dialect groups necessary for a standardised language to become the *lingua franca*. Also, as Anderson (1983) has argued, print capitalism both created and served a limited national market. The state now had a community of communication with less intra-group difference than before. At the same time, the standardisation of national languages created breaks in the dialect continua. Each national language group found that there were higher linguistic boundary fences between it and the contiguous groups outside than had existed in the past.

Meanwhile, horizontal differentiation weakened. The hierarchy of the old aristocratic system had to accommodate those who rose through merit, enterprise and education. The middle class was growing in size and power. Peasants and the rural poor also acquired an element of choice in their lives; they could stay on the land or move to the new factories, thus creating the new social category of urban and/or industrial working class. This may have been a bleak choice, but it existed where none had existed before. So, there was movement between classes; each society possessed fewer rigid internal divisions than in the past. Where the individual could move was, however, circumscribed. The communities of communication provided by national education systems allowed people to circulate easily within their own community. As industrialisation progressed, belonging to the appropriate community of communication became important even for those who did the lowliest tasks, for 'work' in such a society consisted less in actually handling and transforming materials and more in managing the machines which replaced humans. Such processes became 'conceptualised' and work which had previously been rooted in the physical became more language-bound. Anyone unable to communicate easily in the standardised state language was restricted to jobs where people worked like machines and did basic repetitive tasks. All this influenced individuals to remain within the community of communication to which they belonged – in effect, the state (and, in the nineteenth century European context, the colonies of that state). To move across language boundaries was always possible but inevitably less likely.

The usual result of industrialisation was that industrial areas became a linguistic melting pot where a variety of the standardised national language took root; on the other hand, the populations remaining on the land, engaged wholly in pastoral and agricultural pursuits and untouched by industrialisation, usually remained linguistically conservative and resisted the standardisation of their language variety.

From Absolutism to Democracy

Industrialisation brought new patterns of political organisation. In the agrarian age, the state had a very narrow territorial and legal definition. Basically, it meant the land and the ruler of the land. The masses were simply workers on the land, the lower ranks of the army. Their rights were not enshrined in law; only the power of moral norms established by religion for their society could protect them.[10] The ruling elites had little regard for the opinions, desires, requirements of this group, although they might concern themselves with its religious adherence.[11]

The ideas of the Enlightenment and the lessons of the French Revolution changed this radically. Eighteenth century philosophers believed that everything should be questioned and could ultimately be explained. As a corollary to this, they rejected anything that could not be proved. This tradition of doubt and questioning toppled the hierarchies and certainties of earlier times; everything could be questioned. The divine right of kings gave way, challenged by philosophies of equality and legitimacy. Rousseau, rejecting the embodiment of the state in the sovereign, was among the first to link state with people. Ultimately, there was a philosophical acceptance of the individual's importance as part of the collective whole; s/he was no longer subject but citizen; the locus of political power was no longer a single ruling class but the 'people'. This is most clearly seen in the ideas of the French Revolution, but all European nationalisms – left-wing and right-wing, religious and secular, aristocratic and petit bourgeois – paid lip service to the rights of the citizen and claimed legitimacy through the support of the people.

The citizens of the nation state increasingly obtained rights enshrined in law; the obligations to the person of the monarch which had always existed evolved to become duties to the nation. These rights have been mainly representation through the electoral process and protection by a formal legal system; the duties have been largely conscription and taxation. In this definition of nationalism, the nation is a political entity and membership has a legal meaning. However, the linguistic and cultural dimensions become clear as soon as we consider how such rights and duties will actually work in practice. Participation in the electoral process demands that there be some kind of dialogue. The population is no longer governed solely by decree; there must be some consensus, which has to be negotiated; some common language is necessary. A community of communication allows the easiest execution of the process. Similarly, access to a legal system is regulated through language. Justice can be done with the help of translation and interpretation, but layers of mediation distance the individual from the system. Both political representation and legal protection are further reasons which make acquisition of the standardised language useful and advantageous for the individual.

In the duties that the new European nation states demanded of their populations, they remained closer to the practices of the old empires and absolutist monarchies. Taxation and soldiering were not new concepts in the way that electoral participation in the democratic process was. However, the general acceptance of conscription in place of professional, mercenary armies of earlier periods was innovative. This accompanied and stimulated the growth of patriotism, the increasing commitment to the nation state and the intensifying sentiment of national identity which have been the hallmark of much of the nineteenth and twentieth centuries. In linguistic terms the conscription army had far-reaching effects; all young men underwent the experience. In the national armies of Europe, they were exposed to the medium of the national language. Conscription became another promoter of linguistic consonance with state borders.

In broader terms conscription was even more significant. Nineteenth and twentieth century nationalisms in Europe have been categorised by the fervent patriotism that nationalist leaders have been able to stir up and which, of course, feeds back into the movements, making them ever more potent. In its strongest formulation, nationalism is the philosophy that holds that one's country is worth dying for. It is the prime locus of identity for the modern age. And it replaces the old allegiances – to religion, to the feudal lord, to the king appointed by God.

These processes appeared first in western Europe. The Civil War in Britain was an early attempt to question the concept of divine right and establish the ideal of legitimacy through parliament; the French revolution established the idea that people could be citizens and not subjects; industrialisation and urbanisation were to take place firstly in Britain, then in the Netherlands and France. In Chapter 2 patterns of nationbuilding which are peculiar to western Europe will be explored through a close study of the French.

Late Modernists? Post-modernists?

In this most recent reading of nationalism, the nation is a community imagined by its constituent members. This community is constructed and accessed through the cultural artefacts, the symbols and the representations it produces. It is a very language bound process since it is mostly through and in the cultural representation of *texts* that the collectivity is created and apprehended – texts which may use the medium of film, the novel, the theatre, the print media, television, the radio.

The concepts of 'invention of tradition' and 'imagined communities' were developed by scholars, such as Hugh Trevor-Roper and Benedict Anderson, who would not see themselves as in the mainstream of post-modernism, However, it can be argued that they use typically post-modernist techniques of deconstruction to reveal the realities of identity formation. Their explanations make clear the manipulations of which we had always suspected the traditional ethno-linguistic nationalist leaders. Disentangling image and fact in the organising principles of nationalism, they assess how language, history, geography and culture have been drafted into the nation building process.

Imagining

Anderson (1983) defines nation thus:

> (I)t is an imagined community and imagined as both inherently limited and sovereign. It is imagined because the members of even the smallest nation never know most of their fellow-members, meet them, or even hear of them, yet in the minds of each lives the image of their communion. (Anderson, 1991: 6)

As Anderson readily admits, this is not a new concept. Gellner, Seton-Watson and others had already revealed the role of invention and imagination in nation building in their dismissal of claims that nations are predestined, pre-ordained, pre-existent to self-consciousness. It was a key idea in Renan's 1882 seminal essay, *Qu'est-ce qu'une nation.*

Nor is the concept of imagining limited to nation. Anderson argues that it is part of an ongoing process: Christendom is and was an imagined community. Medieval Europe conceived of itself as an entity, particularly when pitched against the 'infidel'. The locus of identity was both universal and local. For example, the artefacts produced by medieval society, the representations of saints, martyrs and biblical figures, were common to the whole continent, although the execution and the models would have been rooted firmly in the locality. Jewish figures have the features of Languedocian peasants in the frescos and carvings of Albi cathedral, of East Anglian serfs in Ely and Lincoln. Anderson terms this the juxtaposition of the cosmic-universal and the mundane-particular. Across Europe there was, and still is, enough commonality in religious artefacts for the traveller to recognise a community.

The advent of the Reformation, followed by the development of the secular society of the Enlightenment and finally the French Revolution brought this particular imagined community to an end. Anderson argues that new and different communities arose, organised according to the geographical areas throughout which a certain standardised language could be understood. The introduction of printing in vernacular languages aided both the standardisation of such print languages and the growth of literacy in them. Print capitalism required a certain size of readership for its productions to be both possible and profitable; it could not survive in too small a language community. Its principal productions, after the bible and religious works, were the political treatises, tracts and newspapers which permitted national groups to conceive of themselves as unique and homogenous societies. Readers of a new literary form, the novel, recognised members of their society existing in chronological time parallel to them. The novel made them aware of multiple destinies linked by simultaneity in the 'homogenous space' which is the nation (Anderson, 1983). Language has a key role here; choice of one vernacular rather than another determines the audience and the view point of the audience. For those who belong to the same community of communication, the novel or the newspaper acts as a means of socialisation and as an agent of recognition and solidarity; for those from outside the community, the novel and the newspaper become a means of apprehending a society to which they do not belong.

Cultural heritages and the forms of life articulated in them are reproduced when members of the group wish this to happen. When culturally differentiated groups are in contact there is always the choice of appropriating and adopting the cultural ways of others, if to do so is advantageous or attractive. To conserve traditions, to retrieve forgotten common cultural practices, to refuse 'foreign' influence is to choose to reaffirm group distinctiveness and group solidarity, to combat dilution of group markers.[12] We can note how there are differing strengths of imagining, of attachment to cultural difference between groups, with some groups being more or less permeable to influence. We should also remark that when a cultural production is language-bound it serves to reinforce the homogeneity of the group and mark difference; where it is not language bound it is more easily available to outsiders, more likely to cross boundaries and be adopted and adapted outside the group.

Inventing

We should not be misled by a curious, but understandable, paradox: modern nations and all their impedimenta generally claim to be the opposite of novel, namely rooted in the remotest antiquity and the

> opposite of constructed, namely human communities so 'natural' as to require no definition other than self-assertion. Whatever the historic or other continuities embedded in the modern concept of 'France' and the 'French' – and which nobody would seek to deny – these very concepts themselves must include a constructed or 'invented' component. And just because so much of what subjectively makes up the modern nation consists of such constructs and is associated with appropriate and in general fairly recent symbols or suitably tailored discourse, . . . the national phenomenon cannot be adequately investigated without careful attention to the 'invention of tradition'. (Hobsbawm, 1983: 14)

Hobsbawm argues that nationalists have always taken an utilitarian approach to history, harnessing the power of belief in common origins to build national consciousness and cohesion. The story of the origins of the nation – in some cases based loosely on known facts, in others the result of pure invention – establishes a common past for the group and promotes a feeling of and a desire for present social cohesion. It has been used extensively to legitimise the authority of the state.

Scottish nationalism is a particularly rich seam to mine for examples of this invention of tradition. In one example, late eighteenth century Scottish historians, principally James and John Macpherson, set out to rework the history of the Gaels in Scotland. It had always been believed, and all evidence suggests that it is true, that Irish-speaking Celts had colonised the Highlands and Islands. However, the Macpherson version of early Scottish history makes Celtic Scotland the 'mother-nation' of the Gaelic tradition and Ireland the cultural dependency (Trevor-Roper, 1983). These claims of an unbroken tradition of Caledonian nationhood with the Scots as the founding nation appealed immensely to the Highland Scots. The Macphersons' 'discovery' of the 'lost' literary works of the poet Ossian, 'the Celtic Homer', helped to prove this claim. This fraud suggested that the Celtic literature of Scotland predated that of Ireland and was, therefore, the source of the rich Celtic tradition. Discovery of the 'works of Ossian' promoted a sense of immense national pride and they became known and admired throughout Europe. These fabrications and forgeries fulfilled their perpetrators' goals; the previously despised Highlanders were transformed into the *Urvolk* of Scotland, removed from their cultural dependency on Ireland and given status in Lowland eyes (Ferguson, 1998).

In the next century, concepts of Scottishness were again linked to Highland 'tradition'. The kilt and the clan tartans were produced in large quantities by cloth manufacturers, promoted among and adopted by Lowlanders, by the Scottish regiments in the imperial army and by the

British (German) royal family. They were soon symbolic of the whole 'Scottish nation' and presumed erroneously to date from ancient times (Trevor-Roper, 1983). In fact, Trevor-Roper argues, they were a contrivance based in small part on the actual ancient Highland costume, in large part on what Romantic tradition would have liked it to be, but mostly they were an invention exploited commercially by textile industrialists and for political ends by those wishing to foster a separate Scottish identity.

The recalling, refurbishing and reinventing of tradition has continued and continues. In 1995, two films retold the story of the struggles of two Scottish heroes against the English aggressor (Rob Roy in the film of the same name and William Wallace in *Braveheart*) These films, international productions funded by international finance, were clearly not made in the service of a narrow nationalist project. However, they did appear at a time when devolution of some political power to a Scottish assembly seemed to be closer to realisation that at any time in the recent past.[13] Whether by chance or by design, such films clearly contribute to the insider's socialisation into group identity and to the outsider's awareness of that identity. *Braveheart* in particular conforms to the traditions of history in the service of nationalism in the way it retells the struggles of a feudal past in terms of the nationalist principles of self-determination and self-government. The treatment of the theme of liberation is very much in the tradition of Woodrow Wilson's principles of the self-determination of nations and largely ignores the reality of the feudal-dynastic struggles of medieval Scotland.

The Scots are, of course, not the only group to have a long tradition of invention in the cause of nationalism. Hutchinson (1987), using examples from the Czech Republic, France, Romania and Ukraine, shows how most nationalist historians are mythmakers in the same mould.

The Mainstream Post-modernists

Post-modernism can be seen as a negative reaction to the Western tradition of rationalist thought, to claims of progress and perfectibility, and to the essentialist ideas of certainty of meaning. Lyotard rejects the ideologies and philosophies of history, the big ideas with capital letters – 'Progress', 'Emancipation'. Derrida attacks the production of meta-narratives to explain human actions. His techniques of deconstruction prompt us to peel away the layers in any construct. In his interpretation, reality can only be a cultural, linguistic and historical imagining. Foucault attacks the conventional presentation of history as a linear sequence of events, a story which makes sense. For him, the narrative presented by those with power is a fabrication, legitimising the possession of that power and repressing and ignoring all the underlayers and setting up structures of exclusion for all the social categories which do not fit the social identity constructed by the dominating episteme. History, in this interpretation, becomes an overlapping and interactive set of 'legitimised' and 'excluded' stories. It is in this sense that I have grouped Hobsbawm and Anderson with this tendency.

Kristeva, writing on feminism, sees the very notion of identity as challenged in the context of the late twentieth century. New theoretical and scientific space causes us to reexamine the human condition. Questions of identity must be posed anew. On nationalism, she is categorical; it is 'primal shelter to compensate for personal disarray' (Kristeva, 1993: 2). She accounts for the rebirth of nationalism as a 'redrawing into the family' after the wounds inflicted by the apparent bankruptcy of ideology in the post-communist era. However, in the way that she returns in several essays to support the Montesquieu tradition of the *esprit général* and in her belief that the 'cult of origins is a hate reaction' she proves herself to be in the mainstream of French tradition, renewing the fight against Herder and the *Volksgeist* and rallying support for universalism – of the French kind.

Nationalism must be opposed to post-modern theory since it relies on a model of linear, purposeful evolution where continuity allows the gains of one generation to be passed to the next, and on a self-recognised group identity which allows such gains to be shareable among its members. Post-modernity counters the concept of unilinear history, dismisses modernity's instrumental and technical rationality and challenges its will to power. In parallel, the globalisation of culture intertwined with evolving forms of media and communication makes defining the group in limiting terms ever harder.

However, despite various attacks on the intellectual basis of nationalism, it seems to have lost none of its general attraction as a philosophy. At the end of the twentieth century it is latent in most parts of Europe and has surfaced in some places with a sometimes alarming virulence and in its most aggressive forms. And even those who would reject the nationalist label have internalised, knowingly or not, many of the norms, beliefs and attitudes associated with the idea. These constitute some of the prejudices and expectations which Europeans bring with them to current supra-national, international and transnational ventures on their continent.

Notes

1. The fact that there are virtually no states in Europe (with the possible exception of Iceland) where there is congruence between a nation defined as a single ethnic collectivity and state territory does not appear to have obstructed the spread of this belief. In Chapter 2 the processes that have permitted this are discussed.

2. See for example the discussion of this in Tom Nairn (1997) *Faces of Nationalism*, London, Verso. See also E. Hobsbawm (1990) *Nations and Nationalism since 1780*, Cambridge University Press; Pierre Birnbaum *et al.* (1991) Nationalismes, special edition of *Pouvoirs* 1991, p. 57; Noelle Burgi *et al.* (1994) *Fractures de l'Etat-nation*, Paris, Kimé; Hélène Carrère d'Encausse (1978) *L'empire éclaté*, Paris, etc. Serious journalism in the West usually takes the same perspective, as the treatment of nationalism in Eastern Europe post 1989 shows. Journalists often adopt Hans Kohn's (1946) stance; ethnic nationalism is wrong, but civic nationalism is necessary.

3. Kedourie was describing the revival of the cult of Kali, the goddess of destruction, in the service of Indian nationalism: 'How can we explain these fervent appeals to dark goddesses, garlands of human heads and dripping blood?' (Kedourie, 1970: 76).

4. See for example Alan Milward (1992) *The European Rescue of the Nation-state* for a discussion of this.

5. This theory holds, in its strongest form, that thought is inextricably linked to the language in which it is expressed and is based on the work of the American linguist Edward Sapir (1884–1939) and his pupil Benjamin Lee Whorf (1897–1941). Some scholars present Herder, von Humboldt, Fichte, Sapir and Whorf as part of the same tradition (Crystal, 1987).

6. For example List F. *Das nationale System der politischen Okonomie*, 1841.

7. The political dimension of Herder's ideas was to evolve much further than he had ever envisaged. He focused almost entirely on the *Kulturnation* as opposed to the *Staatsnation*. However, the dangerously racist implications of the philosophy were ultimately exploited by the fascists and this association has served to discredit linguistic nationalism completely.

8. *Jus soli* is the principle which underpins the French tradition. 'The availability of French citizenship to the children of immigrants on condition of their education in, and identification with, French culture expresses the idea of the French nation as a daily plebiscite (Cesarini & Fulbrook, 1996: 5). *Jus sanguinis* is the principle underlying acquisition of German citizenship. The ethnic basis of citizenship in Germany has been challenged and is now being reviewed. It still characterises, however, the German system (Horrocks and Kolinsky (1996). Britain has 'a weak notion of citizenship and a confused definition of nationality' (Cesarini & Fulbrook, 1996: 5) deriving from both *jus soli* and *jus sanguinis*.

9. See for example Baldesar Castiglione *Etiquette for Renaissance Gentlemen*, 1528, who asked how he should choose the most perfect model 'from all the various customs followed at the Courts of Christendom'. Pim den Boer argues that this identification of Europe with Christendom is a relatively late development. He suggests that it occurred in the fifteenth century (Wilson & Dussen, 1993).

10. The first step in the emancipation of the masses was the abolition of serfdom and slavery. According to Voltaire, writing in 1756, the Middle Ages may be considered as the beginning of this process, but change was slow and it took many centuries for the mass of Europeans to emerge from their various enslavements to become the *people* .

11. There was usually pressure for the subjects of the ruler to profess the same religion as he did – *cuius regio, eius religio*.

12. See Hutchinson (1987), Smith (1991a, b) on the politics of cultural nationalism.

13. In 1995 the British Labour Party promised legislation to make such an assembly

possible in their next administration. Within months of Labour coming to power in 1997, the Scottish people voted on this subject in a referendum. They chose devolution and a parliament with limited tax-varying powers. In May 1999 they voted for their first parliament since 1707.

Chapter 2

The role of language in nation state formation. The three European models: assimilation, blood and belonging and fragmentation

Much of the literature on nationalism divides Europe into old historic continuous nations and new nations born of movements for national unification or from secession from multi-national empires (Seton-Watson, 1977; Breuilly, 1993; Greenfeld, 1992 etc.). I have used this approach, highlighting the linguistic dimension, and dividing the continent into states whose borders were set by conquest or inheritance and whose elites attempted to weld the heterogeneous populations within those borders into a cohesive, monolingual nation, and states whose borders were determined to reflect the belief of the population within that they already possessed some commonality and basis for association, in particular a 'community of communication'. The historic continuous nations fall mainly into the first category and those resulting from movements of unification or secession mainly into the second. In both categories the same organising principles prevail: similarities of language, culture, religion, and beliefs of common history and shared ancestry are used to construct national identities. However, although these elements are always present in some way in the equation, it is essential to labour the point that ultimately it is the political ambition of dynasties and power elites which has proved the decisive factor in nation state formation rather than any natural congruence of nation and state.

Ethnies and Proto-nations

Weber (1948) and his followers make a distinction between ethnic group (ethnie) and nation, differentiating between a collectivity that, while recognising itself as a group, has a very weak feeling of ethnic solidarity, and a collectivity which defines itself as a group, wishes others to recognise it as such and has a political project. The first group has little group consciousness; the second is highly self-aware. The process of acquiring self-awareness has been termed a period of proto-nationalism, but not all communities with a sense of belonging together progress any further than this stage:

> The number of national movements with or without states is patently much smaller than the number of human groups capable of forming such movement by the current criteria of potential nationhood. (Hobsbawm, 1990: 77)

If a group possesses enough elements for it to imagine itself a distinct community then this is proto-nationalism; nationalism proper occurs when and if there is a political project. This project is usually concerned with territory; the group or leaders of the group desire to maintain as exclusive the territorial space which houses the nation or to acquire such, in other words to achieve the congruity of the political and the cultural nation.[1] Not all communities with a sense of belonging together aspire to nationhood in this sense:

The congruence between *ethnie* and sovereign state rarely occurs naturally. Realisation of the four main aims of most nationalist leaderships: the nation's awareness that it is a nation, the nation's desire to have political control over its own affairs, the nation's agreement to a social contract with the state government, and the acquisition or maintenance of territory for the exclusive use of the nation will require manipulation by political elites somewhere in the process and struggle will be endemic. There is always conflict in the construction of the nation state – either resolved through force of arms or politically. In Europe, in each of the three processes which eventually achieve this resolution, such conflict has been inherent. In the first category, the founding *ethnie* rules a larger territorial space than that inhabited by its members and sets out to assimilate culturally and linguistically all other groups within its boundaries. Conflict is usually between the centre and the periphery as the dominant group attempts to eradicate linguistic, cultural and religious differences. Such nationalism is usually inclusive as long as those who are to be included do not demand recognition of such differences.

In the second category, the state is constituted by a number of groups who perceive their similarities – linguistic, cultural and religious – to be greater than their differences and who exclude those who do not share those similarities. In the final category, the founding *ethnie* defines itself in very narrow terms linguistically, culturally and religiously and the resulting state is likely to be small. In the last two categories, there is typically a belief that the constituent groups share blood ties. Conflict occurs because the enmeshed nature of European populations makes it difficult for such groups to achieve congruence of nation and state without driving out those who do not belong. In extreme cases, genocide and 'ethnic cleansing' have resulted from the desire of ethnic nationalists to achieve a culturally homogenous state, the nation state in its most rigorous definition. All cases of such nationalism are exclusive.

And a final point; there is no necessary linear progression from a group's awareness of itself as nation to its political organisation as a nation state; indeed in many instances, particularly among states formed according to the first pattern, the construction of a national identity for *all* citizens is likely to post-date the emergence of the 'nation' state.

Assimilation[2]

In this form of nation-building, the majority group sets by conquest and annexation the boundaries of its territories and subsequently determines to assimilate minorities within its boundaries into the nation. One of the key policies in the process is to achieve linguistic, religious and cultural homogeneity from elements of the population deemed to be disparate. A number of western European states, e.g. Britain, France, Spain, have followed this pattern. France has been arguably the most successful in applying assimilatory policies and continues to do so. Even at the end of the twentieth century, French policies on immigration and regionalism can be seen to be in this tradition.

The creation of the French state within its present boundaries has been a very lengthy process (Mordrel, 1981). However, in the very nationalist pedagogy which still dominates the history, geography and civics syllabi of the French education system, the Hexagon is presented as a natural entity:

> the contours of which seem to have been sketched out in advance of the achievement of unity, as the result of a long series of obstinate struggles. (Longnon, quoted in Johnson, 1993: 35)

Maps of Roman Gaul or medieval France in text books show how the state boundaries of France are taught as preordained. This is to interpret with hindsight; past populations of much of present-day France would not have given their allegiance in this way, and certainly not before the 17th century (Mordrel, 1981).

Pre-Roman Gaul had no natural cohesion. The north was predominantly Celtic, the south predominantly Iberian and Ligurian. Roman Gaul was not governed as one unit and its limits did not coincide with modern frontiers. In the massive movement of peoples at the end of the Roman Empire, the *Völkerwanderung*, a number of German tribes colonised the territory. The

Franks in the north, the Visigoths in the south and the Burgundians in the east were all equally vigorous and expansionist. In the early medieval period there seemed no good reason to imagine that it would be the Franks who would eventually dominate the Hexagon. At first they were masters of a relatively small territory. Under the kingship of Clovis they extended their fiefdom by conquest. Under Charlemagne the whole of what is now France came under Frankish rule – as did parts of present day Belgium, Germany, Italy and Spain etc. On Charlemagne's death, the empire was divided into three. After the Middle Kingdom was eliminated at the Treaty of Verdun (843), two kingdoms were created which romantics like to see as the basis of contemporary France and Germany (Keating, 1988). However, they were both too large to survive in the circumstances of the ninth century and soon fractured.[3] The brief existence of the Western Kingdom fuelled claims for Frankish (French) suzerainty over wider areas than their power base – which they eventually established in the Ile-de-France (Dunbabin, 1985; James, 1982).

The Franks had the great advantage of dynastic continuity – from Hugh Capet in 987 to the execution of Louis XVI in 1792, the line moved either in the direct line of descent or through close collaterals. This allowed a policy of constant and, in the long term, successful expansionism; territories were acquired by force, marriage and purchase, and retained. Even on the one occasion when there was disputed succession (when Edward III of England, claiming the throne through his mother, contested Philip de Valois' claim to be the heir through a collateral male line) the war which resulted benefited French expansionism. Firstly, the French acquired territory in the south-west and expelled the Anglo-Norman kings from most of their mainland possessions. Henceforth, these latter would be English, confined to their island and no further threat. Secondly, the hundred years of war instilled what has been seen as the first stirrings of a nationalist consciousness in the French (Guizot, 1826). Perhaps to have had one single enemy over such a long period prompted the polarisation necessary for group self-awareness.

French expansionism continued; marriage and inheritance brought Provence and Brittany into the kingdom. A number of invasions of the Italian peninsula brought parts of the area briefly under French tutelage but gave no long-term territorial acquisitions. The conquests of Louis XIV took the frontier of the French state to its present north-eastern and south-western boundaries, although, in pursuing this 'plus digne et plus agréable occupation des souverains',[4] Louis left a colossal debt and an impoverished country. His successor, Louis XV added Lorraine in 1766 and Corsica in 1768.

At first the Republic was non-expansionist, concerned only to create a new order on French territory. However, the threat from the surroundings kingdoms, both real and imagined, coupled with a missionary zeal to propagate the Revolution soon changed this policy back to expansionism. Much of Europe came under French domination for a period, although the only lasting acquisition from that episode was to be the Comtat Venaissin, formerly the property of the Vatican. The French state's final acquisition was Nice and its territory, which joined the French state in 1860 after a deal had been struck between Napoleon III and Victor-Emmanuel. In all fairness it should be said that this deal was ratified by a plebiscite of all adult males.

Language in the Service of Unification

As France extended its borders, the population within became more linguistically diverse. The Franks had adopted the Vulgar Latin of Roman Gaul. The language varieties which emerged in the north of the Hexagon were basically Romance with a Celtic substratum and a Germanic superstratum. The peoples of the south-west whom the French conquered in the crusades against the Cathars in the early thirteenth century spoke a variety of dialects of Occitan, a language which was much closer to its Latin roots than French had remained. The acquisition of Provence through inheritance in 1481 brought more speakers of Occitan into the state, although their varieties varied quite considerably from those spoken in the south-west. The acquisition of Brittany through marriage in 1491 added Celtic speakers to the linguistic mosaic. The accession of Henri IV of Navarre to the French throne brought in the Basque speakers from that Pyrenean kingdom. The wars of the seventeenth and eighteenth centuries gave the king subjects who spoke varieties of German, Dutch, Catalan and Italian. More Italian speakers (of a different dialect on the Occitan-Piedmontese continuum) arrived with the annexation of western Savoy and Nice.

The ruling dynasty had a policy of combating diversity from a very early period. The reign of Louis XI (1461 –1483) was a period of much territorial gain. These acquisitions were to be anchored into the French state in a number of ways. Louis set out to concentrate power in Paris, building up military, administrative, commercial, fiscal and financial structures for the whole of France, administered from the capital. This can be seen as the beginning of the policy to make the infrastructure of France highly centralised.[5]

The first step in the process of creating linguistic homogeneity within the population was the language law of 1539 (Villers-Cotterêts) in the reign of François I, whereby French became the language of the law courts throughout the kingdom and all laws were formulated in it and promulgated through it. Before this *ordonnance* became law, a language shift from Latin to the various vernaculars of the French state had already started to take place. Occitan, Picard, Burgundian etc as well as French were employed in the courts and in official documents. François I's first reaction to the linguistic situation was to recognise that this shift had taken place and to permit the use of his subjects' various mother tongues in the courts. However, after a very short period of reflection, he reversed his decision and decreed that all official business would be carried out in *langage maternel françois*.[6]

The sixteenth century saw the production of a number of grammars of French (Palsgrave, 1530; Dubois, 1531; Meigret, 1550). Latin was abandoned for French in a number of scientific works (Cartier, 1545; Nostradamus, 1555). There was already a strong literary tradition in a number of the vernaculars of the French state, but French literary production gained ground steadily, naturally profiting from its association with royal power and the role of French in social advancement and admittance to the elite. Printing made these works available to a wider public. Codification, printing and prestige were the three strengths of French: standardisation made it accessible to non-speakers; numerous works published in it made it widely available; the king and court made it desirable. *L'Académie française*, a learned society to oversee the normalisation, development and protection of French, founded by Richelieu in 1635, advanced the process. Political power was further centralised by the Bourbons after the dissident nobility had been defeated in *les Frondes*, the civil wars of the mid-seventeenth century. French was inextricably bound up in this development, as both an agent and a beneficiary of centralisation and absolutism.

Religion in the Service of Unification

The second agent in the homogenisation process was religion. A widespread belief that the subjects of a monarch must share his religious allegiance was the norm in Christian Europe until industrialisation. Before the Reformation, such a requirement was most likely to concern the Jews. Subject to persecution in much of Christian Europe, they were expelled from France in 1394.[7] The other threat to religious unity came from the various heresies based on Christianity. In the eleventh and twelfth centuries, Manicheanism in the guise of various sects and groups spread across Europe. Among these were the Cathars, persecuted in the French north. In the south, in the lands of the Counts of Toulouse and Béziers, they were tolerated. The Pope urged that the Cathar heresy be eradicated and called for a crusade. His desire to maintain Catholic universality fitted well with the ambitions of the northerners to acquire lands which they had long coveted. The conquest of the south-west (1213) was at first the affair of individuals but then the initiative passed to the crown. The king of France enlarged his kingdom, ensured a religiously homogenous people and proved to be the defender of papal interests. In this, the crusade against the Cathars was neither the first nor the final time that the French monarchy was strongly identified with the defence of Catholicism.

After the Reformation, achieving congruence between the beliefs of ruled and ruler became more problematic. Catholic hegemony in France was challenged by rising numbers of Huguenots and bitter religious wars which lasted several decades (1562–1598). Patriotism and religious belief were often at variance. At first the Catholic monarchy benefited from traditions of loyalty and the Huguenots appeared the outsiders, the threat to the state. During the reign of Henri IV, the Guises, the Catholic party, worried at the earlier Huguenot orientation of the king, turned to Catholic Spain for support. A polemical work written during this period, the *Dialogue du Maheustre et du Manant*, illustrates how religion was the first loyalty of the individual, taking precedence over the ties of birthplace, over loyalty to one's sovereign:

> J'aime mieux être Espagnol catholique pour vivre en ma religion et faire mon salut, que d'être Français hérétique, à la perte de mon âme. (Lebrun, 1980: 94)[8]

Finally, the *Révocation de l'Edit de Nantes*, in 1685, put an end to any tolerance of religious diversity; the French Protestants had a choice either to accept the religion of the monarchy or to leave the country.[9]

The Revolution and Republicanism as a Unifying Force

In the aftermath of revolution there was a demand for decentralisation, particularly from the south. The Girondin party proposed a federal structure for France in which regions would retain some autonomy and maintain their languages. In the struggle between the Girondins and Montagnards, the former lost and the revolution became yet another agent of centralisation.

Linguistic unification was seen as a prime requirement in a participatory political system which derived its legitimacy from the people and which would not be achieved unless the revolutionaries could create a community of communication. Although French had spread geographically throughout the territory of the Hexagon, by the year 1789 it had not yet extended to all social groups. The language census carried out in 1790 at the request of the Convention led its organiser, the Abbé Grégoire, to conclude that it was possible that only three million French citizens (out of a population of perhaps 25,000,000) had French as a mother tongue (Walter, 1988). However, in the areas where the revolution was accepted enthusiastically, the Ile-de-France variety of French tended to oust the original dialect or language within a short space of time. The parts of France which rejected the revolutionary philosophy most decidedly were also those areas where the regional language and religion were most jealously guarded. Conservatism was for *all* the old ways; rejection included the French language as well as the revolutionary message.

Linguistic unification was thus symbolically as well as practically necessary for revolutionary success. The message of the revolution was carried by French; the propagation of universalist ideas demanded that the target groups speak French.[10] The key method of linguistic unification was to be the provision of primary education in French for every child. The revolutionaries could not achieve their aims in the short term – through lack of finance, too few French speaking primary teachers and the diversion caused by the imperial wars. However, the revolutionary armies and then Napoleon's *grande armée* proved to be a linguistic melting pot. At Valmy on 20 September 1792, the French army fought shouting the revolutionary battle cry 'Vive la nation'. Loyalty to nation overcame provincial particularisms. The requirements of military command encouraged one language. When the soldiers went back to their various regions many took French with them.

Eventually, through the compulsory and free schooling, introduced in the Third Republic by Jules Ferry, all children received primary education through the medium of French. The education system set out quite consciously to turn the disparate elements of France into a nation. In Eugene Weber's famous phrase, the plan was to turn 'peasants into Frenchmen'. The canonical history texts of Lavisse and Michelet were powerful agents for identity formation and the republicanism which permeated the whole curriculum replaced religion with civics. The histories used in French schools, from 1860 to the present day, dwell on the periods when all the French shared a destiny (e.g. after the invasions of Charlemagne, after the Revolutionary Wars in the 1790s). There is a neglect of other actors in the national space which allows French history to be presented as if it were the story of one group.

This secular national school system,[11] in which all teachers were agents for the spread of the French language and a republican spirit, often promoted a virulent anti-clericalism and so pushed Catholicism into a liaison with regional conservatism. In the nineteenth and twentieth century, the areas in France which have the highest proportions of practising Catholics are also those where the regional languages have survived best: the Basque country, Brittany, the Belgian border, Alsace, the inland regions of Languedoc (Lebrun, 1980). Rejection of republicanism, secularism and French went hand in hand. At the same time, the nineteenth century saw the growth of a virulently right wing French nationalism linked to Catholicism.[12]

A number of other policies in the Third Republic were designed to promote national cohesion and linguistic unification: government employees – railway workers, teachers, civil servants – were often sent to work in another region; conscription for all young men completed what the education system had set in train. Regiments were not organised on a regional basis and socialised the conscripts to acquire both the French language and French identity.

In the Fourth and Fifth Republics the move to monolingualism and monoculturalism has continued. The use of the languages of the autochthonous minorities has fallen sharply since the revolution; where they have survived, they are spoken only in the private and family domain. Significantly there are no reliable statistics on language use since French censuses do not include questions on it. However, one may safely assume that, given the French medium education system, there are no monolingual speakers of any of these languages in France today. The very few concessions made to the autochthonous minority languages have been insignificant and are of recent date, at a time when it is unlikely that they will have any real effect.[13]

To understand why these policies were so successful and why the non-French speakers, with minor exceptions, accepted language shift, we have to recognise the importance of economic advantage, gained in exchange for relinquishing regional specificity and identity, and acknowledge the immense power of the republican ideal. These two factors ensured the success of centralising policies and linguistic unification.

Immigration

In the twentieth century France has accepted large numbers of incomers in successive waves of immigration: Italians, White Russians, Spaniards, Armenians, Poles, Eastern European Jews, Portuguese, Moroccans, Algerians, Tunisians, Vietnamese, Cambodians, Laotians, Africans from a number of West African states. It has been relatively easy for first generation immigrants to acquire citizenship. For second generations, born on French soil, citizenship was, until recently, an automatic right. Newcomers are expected to assimilate linguistically and culturally. The attitude of the state towards immigrants is revealed by the practices of INSEE, the government agency for social, economic and demographic data collection. Censuses do not ask for details of racial or ethnic origins, other than place of birth and even then very little use is made of this set of statistics in government studies (Hargreaves, 1995). The effect is to obliterate the different origins of French citizens. As many as 10,000,000 French citizens may be the children or grand-children of immigrants. Yet, as there is no indication of this in government statistics, this remains an unverifiable claim. The same attitude and expectations are revealed in the language of academics and policy-makers. The conceptual framework in France is *intégration*; the French overwhelmingly reject the Anglo-Saxon concepts of 'race relations' or 'ethnic minority'. This desire to be 'blind' to immigration seems to me to be totally in accord with the centuries of assimilatory policies described above.

The autochthonous and allochthonous groups who have refused to assimilate or integrate to the French state have been seen as a menace and have caused great feelings of resentment from the majority population. For example, it is clear that recent Corsican demands for autonomy have been received with some hostility by mainland France and that this hostility stems not just from the violence employed by the separatist faction, but also from the very ideas themselves.[14] In the past, Jewish demands for recognition of difference is, at least in part, at the root of the France's former anti-semitism. The reluctance to assimilate of minorities professing Islam may explain to some extent the race relation problems of recent years and the growth of organisations such as the *Front National*. This more recent rejection of assimilation has contributed to a new legal development. For a time it was no longer true that to be born on French soil automatically gives the right to French citizenship. In 1994, the French state began to ask children of non-French nationals to make a declaration that they wish to be considered French.[15] This request for an act of 'loyalty' may be seen as that Government's response to sections of the allochthonous population who have rejected the policy of total assimilation.

It goes without saying that the French have not striven to maintain the languages of allochthonous minority groups any more than they did to maintain autochthonous languages. Where classes, such as Arabic for second generation immigrants, exist, these have usually been funded and staffed by the states from which the migrant groups originated.

The Other Continuous Nations

The United Kingdom and Spain are examples of other states where a similar policy of assimilation has been tried, although arguably with less success. Autochthonous groups, such as the Catalans, Basques, Galicians have successfully resisted the homogenising policies of the centralising Castilian state and have regained a certain political, linguistic and cultural autonomy. The Celtic lands once governed from London have either achieved full independence or limited autonomy: Eire is now a separate sovereign state; the fight for autonomy in Northern Ireland is unresolved; the Welsh have Welsh-medium education and media; the Scots have maintained clearly differentiated identity from the English and separate institutions. The last two achieved limited political autonomy with their new assembly and parliament for which the first elections were held in May 1999.

For nation states in this category one may summarise thus – the philosophy which underlies membership of a nation is territorial – you are here, therefore you are 'X' or must become 'X'.

Blood and Belonging

In this category, groups which perceive themselves to possess a common culture and language come together to make a political state; 'blood' and language are the criteria for association. More accurately one should say that it is usually the leaders or would be leaders of such groups who persuade the group of their consanguinity. This describes accurately, if simplistically, German and Italian unification. Both states emerged from groupings where the main organising principles were a belief in the possession of a common cultural and linguistic heritage. 'Language' in each territory can, however, only be described as a dialect continuum not a unified language. Dialectal diversity did not prove a stumbling block and both the politicians and intellectuals who were the architects of unification and the populations who acquiesced in it accepted the ambiguity of terming diverse dialects a single language. A written standard provided a common national language in each case and permitted the continued existence of very dissimilar spoken varieties of the language in the different regions of the state.

Germany unified along linguistic lines although not all German speakers were included, and, of course, given the mosaic of peoples in Europe, a number of non-German speaking enclaves found themselves within its borders.

A group of Germanic peoples settled the east, the centre, the north and ultimately much of the west of the European peninsula in the first millennium of our era. The German linguistic continuum stretches from the islands off the west coast of the continent – the British Isles, Iceland, the Faeroes – eastwards far into the former USSR. This presented problems to the collectivities in the central belt as they embarked on the process of nation-building; one of their key problems was to define the limits of the 'German nation'. There was never any question that the German speaking Swiss would be a part of a Greater Germany. The Swiss peasants and burghers had struggled against the feudal tutelage of the Holy Roman Empire and left it in 1499 (reaffirmed in 1648). The Dutch had once been within the States General belonging to the Empire, but had distanced themselves both culturally – through the development of a written vernacular based on a Lower Franconian dialect – and economically – establishing one of the first European nation states founded on mercantilism and early capitalism.

In the central belt of the German dialect continuum, a German state had seemed a possibility at a very early period. The *regnum teutonicorum* was an established fact from the coronation of Otto 1 as emperor in 962. Waever (1990) argues that a recognisable national identity existed in the tenth century and that it is possible to see Otto's empire as a proto-national state. However, the process stumbled as the political power of the constituent principalities grew to the detriment of the emperor's. The Holy Roman Empire had been in the first instance the legacy of the Roman Empire. From the fifteenth century it was known as *das heilige römische Reich deutscher Nation*, the addendum showing the identification of empire with the German peoples. It continued to be a very decentralised power structure, bound partially by cultural factors. In 1438 the accession of the Habsburg dynasty to the imperial crown changed the focus of the entity, since the Habsburgs possessed territory throughout Europe.

The Reformation fractured the German speaking world. Charles V's agreement, at the Peace of Augsburg in 1555, to the principle 'cuius regio eius religio' ensured that the religious differences between the German princes would extend to their subjects. The Thirty Years War (1618–1648) deepened the fissures. Originally a conflict between the northern Protestant princes and the Catholic Habsburgs, the war spread to include other European states. The battlefield was the central German-speaking belt of the continent and the suffering in these lands was monumental; more than half the population died as a result of the fighting and the famines resulting from it. The short term legacy of the war was poverty and suffering, the long term legacy entrenched polarisation between Catholic and Protestant. The Treaty of Westphalia (1648) reaffirmed the principle of religious cohesion within the state and mixed populations of Catholic and Protestant became a rarity.

So, prior to the nineteenth century, the area which was to become Germany was a collection of over 350 small states and cities, still known collectively as the Holy Roman Empire, but with a lack of internal cohesion. Customs barriers, a lack of a common currency or a common system of weights and measures divided these states economically; an acceptance of multi-state particularism (*Mehrstaatlichkeit*) divided them politically; the religious cleavage persisted. There was no consensual feeling that these political entities and their populations – and only these – constituted any kind of cohesive whole. At the same time, the absence of any central power favoured the idea that anyone whose mother tongue was one of the German dialects and who partook of German culture in some way could be defined as German.

Thus nationalism proper starts in Germany in the eighteenth and nineteenth centuries with no clear political power base but a very clear sense of who might belong to the nation. The theorists and popularisers of German nationalism gave, as we have already noted, immense weight to the role of language, which together with culture and blood were held to be the critical factors for nationality and membership of a putative German state. Such linguistic criteria meant that the German *Kulturnation* was perceived as a very extensive collectivity. These theories and beliefs were adopted wholeheartedly throughout the nationalist movement. Karl von Hase, a member of the *Burschenschaften*, the student nationalist movement which started in Jena, illustrates how the concepts of language, culture and blood are accepted as the key variables in a speech he made to the Youth of the Free Universities of Germany in 1820:

> Germans are we all together! . . . that wonderful people from the Weichsel to the Vosges, from the North Sea over the Alps to Carpathia made *equal through speech, customs and descent*, all citizens of the Reich – a unified people of brothers . . . . (von Hase, 1820, cited in Gorman, 1989: 28, my italics)

For others it was the economic advantages which were the principal argument for national unification. The *Zollverein* set up between Prussia and Hesse-Darmstadt in 1828 and expanded in 1834 to include much of the German-speaking world – except Austria, Hanover, Oldenburg and Brunswick – was a powerful agent for unification. However, even for those wishing to unite for pragmatic reasons, language and identity retained an emotional appeal. Nineteenth century German economists, such as Friedrich List, while citing improved economic performance as the main reason for a united Germany, still enthused over the special mystic relationship between the nation and its language.

The revolutions and rebellions of 1848 seemed at first as if they might play a decisive role in the formation of a German state. In the wake of the February Revolution in Paris a number of rulers and governments in the German states were toppled or weakened. After a flurry of constitutional and electoral activity, a national German parliament met in Frankfurt charged with producing a constitution for a united Germany. The great problem was to define Germany. Was it to be *Grossdeutschland*, including Austria, or *Kleindeutschland* without Austria? The Austrians, under the leadership of Schwarzenberg, saw unification as a chance of achieving Greater Austria rather than Greater Germany. This ambition and the conservatism of the Austrians were repellent to the Frankfurt assembly and it gave enthusiastic support to the *Kleindeutschland* solution, with Prussia offered the leadership. The victory of the counter-revolutionary forces in 1849 was the end of this democratic version of German unity and when unification eventually came, although it was under Prussian leadership, it was not in the form envisaged by the Frankfurt assembly. Engineered by Bismarck it was 'a revolution from above' and again excluded Austro-Hungary which posed too great a threat to Prussia's hegemony (Schmidt, 1993).

The Prussian victory over Austria in 1866 set the seal on the exclusion of the southern German speakers from the German state. Political considerations had furnished the primary reasons for Prussian-Austrian rivalry, but there had also been the cultural dimension. Both the Prussians and the other north German states had been wary of the large number of non-German speakers Austria would have brought to a new Reich.

Finally, in the same period, the annexation of Schleswig-Holstein and Alsace-Lorraine brought, by conquest, further German-speaking populations into the Reich. In 1871 the North German Confederation became the German Reich; the state, thus formed, was a victory for the Prussian *Junker* class to which the German bourgeoisie allied itself in reaction to the threat of democracy glimpsed in the events of 1848 (Schmidt, 1993). Militarisation, anti-democratic political institutions and attitudes, a high-jacking of the national ideal by the forces of reaction were bound to mean that the philosophy of 'blood and belonging' would thrive.[16] The concept of citizenship and assimilation as key tools in nation-building would not gain a toe-hold until the democratic elements of German society achieved some power (Winkler, 1993).

This state was not the 'nation state' of the Germans. It was, as A. J. P. Taylor (1988) said, simply the state that was possible, not necessarily the one that was desired. Pan-Germanism did not die as a concept. Movements both in the German Reich and in the Austro-Hungarian Empire kept the idea alive. At the end of the First World War, the defeat of Germany and Austria had a profound effect on feelings of national identity; the treaties of Versailles and Trianon fragmented the German nation physically but forged a psychological national cohesion, promoted by the shared experience of the 'nation as victim'. Many of the German speakers who were incorporated into other states – e.g. Alsatians into France, Bohemian and Moravian Germans into Czechoslovakia, East Prussian Germans into Poland – felt great resentment which was reflected in attitudes in Germany proper. The discontent engendered by an awareness that the German nation extended far beyond the German state helped pave the way for the nationalism of the radical right. There is also the view (Waever, 1990) that the legacy of romantic, ethno-linguistic nationalism, fostering as it did a belief that the state and culture were organically and mystically linked, was partially responsible for a climate in which the idealisation of the irrational, the heroic, the apocalyptic could arise and, lead, ultimately, to Hitler and Nazism. In among the range of philosophies linked to fascism we can find the continuing traditions of ethno-linguistic nationalism: a commitment to the *Volksgemeinschaft*; a desire for the early annexation of the German-speaking populations of Austria and Czechoslovakia; a belief in a different status for conquered German-speakers in Slav states; the harnessing of tradition and history in the nationalist cause.

Germany was only a nation for seventy-nine years (1866–1945) before its division. In that short period it had passed from absolutism, to empire, through the brief interlude of the Weimar Republic to ideological totalitarianism. After the Second World War, the constitution imposed by the victors sought to provide the mechanisms to keep the state in check; there was the rejection of a centralised government and power was shared among the *Bund*, the *Länder* and the *Gemeinde*. 1945 proved a rupture: the old Herderian Romanticism was eclipsed; the concept of *Kulturvolk* underwent a crisis of confidence in the shadow of Ausschwitz (Habermas, 1996; Arendt, 1962); the Hegelian concept of the strong state disappeared; there was a revulsion for nationalism in West Germany and seemingly little nationalist reaction to the victors' partitioning of the country to ensure its future weakness. This anti-nationalism was manifested in enthusiasm for the European Union and an apparent wish to unload as much as possible of the responsibilities and apparatus of statehood onto it (Pfaff, 1993).

However, the idea that belonging to the nation comes first and foremost from biological ties had not been totally eclipsed. During the 1980s Waever (1990) sees a harking back in German political thinking to the Romantic concepts associated with 'nation', in particular among the Greens.

On 9 February 1984, the Bundestag declared that the German nation continued to exist, though fractured, and that the ultimate goal was unity. As communism collapsed in the late 1980s one of the first outcomes was a call for the reunification of the two Germanies, despite nearly a half century of separate development. After the fall of the Berlin wall, the SPD, others on the left and intellectuals (Habermas, 1996; Grass, 1990) called for a referendum on the reuniting of the two Germanies, to show that there could be choice, that there was no such thing as the primordial nation, that reunification was not a preordained historical necessity. The referendum did not take place[17] and by the end of 1990 the two Germanies were reunited. Commentators felt that 'blood and belonging' was reasserting itself:

> Essentially, there were no civic grounds for German unity only ethnic ones. There was no particular reason for Germans to unite in one state other than the fact that they were Germans. In other words it was the ethnic factor which fuelled this move. (Schöpflin, 1995: 58)

As migration across the frontiers of the former Warsaw Pact countries became slightly easier, ethnic Germans in ever increasing numbers exercised their right to 'return' to Germany. The law permits those of German origin, even those whose families left the German heartland in the far distant past, to continue to have rights within the modern German state – and even when they are no longer German-speaking. In the collapsing communist world this right appeared immensely attractive.

The states in which ethnic Germans live are often incensed by the primary claim of cultural 'nation' over state and citizenship in the German context. German actions in this area are often experienced as unwarranted, even intolerable, interference in the internal affairs of the state. A clear example of this occurred in 1995, when the German government offered the 700,000 strong German minority living in the Polish region of Silesia the right to a German passport alongside their Polish passport. The Polish government expressed its indignation vehemently (*The European*, 17–23 February 1995, p. 4).

At the same time those born on German territory of parents who are not of German origin cannot easily claim citizenship. For example, the children of Turkish *Gastarbeiter*, even where they are linguistically and culturally 'German' have traditionally been excluded.[18] The vocabulary for this is quite revealing – the ethnic German immigrants from Eastern Europe are called *Aussiedler*, the immigrants from Turkey, from Greece, from other parts of Asia, from Africa are called *Ausländer*. Germany enacts policies towards incomers which are both praise- and blameworthy. On the one hand, the country habitually admits a larger number of asylum seekers than any other comparable country. On the other, German policy makers and large sectors of the German public have traditionally believed that national and cultural homogeneity is essential and have refused, until very recently, to make obtaining citizenship easier for groups who would cause continuing linguistic and cultural diversity (Horrocks & Kolinsky, 1996).

It is, however, interesting to note that among German speakers there is no pressure for language standardisation on the French and English model. The heterogeneity of German dialects is largely accepted in their spoken forms. Both in the former German Federal Republic and in the German Democratic Republic there was tolerance of the retention of dialectal difference and this continues in the new Germany. Some dialects tend to be stigmatised. For example, Saxon accents are associated, stereotypically, with stupidity, but, apart from this kind of pressure, there is no movement towards normalisation of the spoken language, and a large degree of change across the dialect continuum is tolerated.

This form of nationalism is totally opposed to the previous model, where nationality and citizenship derived from birth and presence in and occupation of a space. For nation-states in this present category, the philosophy which underlies membership of a nation is genetic. One is born 'X', one cannot *become* 'X' because membership of the nation can only be inherited. The rational way to form a state is to regroup all those of the blood. Minorities cannot be assimilated and the radical solution has been to expel, in extreme cases to eradicate, those who are not of the 'blood'. Language is important here because it is a more salient marker than blood and the concept of language as mother tongue is key in this model.

A Hybrid

Romania provides another example where language was the organising principle of a state. Here a Latin language cut off from contact with other Romance languages survived for centuries to become, in the nineteenth century, the main marker of a national group and the basis for nationhood. At the same time it is a state that attempts to assimilate on the French model.

Although the province of Dacia was part of the Roman Empire for less than two centuries and never heavily colonised by the Romans, Latin was, nonetheless, rooted firmly enough in the population to withstand the linguistic effects of incursions by Goths, Gepidae, Avars, Bulgarians, Slavs and Magyars. There is an argument that Romanian cannot possibly have retained its character in this situation and that the region must have been repopulated by Romance speakers at a later stage, but this is countered by the existence of a diversity of dialects in Romanian. The development of such variety suggests very strongly the existence of the language in the area over a lengthy period (Stevenson, 1983).

The Romanian-speaking areas were rarely an independent political entity. The separate principalities of Wallachia and Moldavia were under Turkish suzerainty from the beginning of the fifteenth century until the mid-nineteenth century, interrupted only by very short periods of Russian occupation and an even shorter period of independence, when they were brought together as one kingdom under Michael the Brave in the early seventeenth century. In the early nineteenth century Romanian intellectuals, fired by prevailing nationalist philosophies, set out to:

> motiver un peuple sans histoire nationale pour l'idée nationale sur une base purement linguistique. (Stefanink, quoted in Calvet, 1993: 61)

The national movement was based negatively – on a rejection both of Turkish suzerainty and of links with Slav and Hungarian neighbours – and positively – on awareness of group singularity defined most precisely by language. None of the other organising principles of nationalism could be co-opted to allow the Romanians to constitute themselves as a collectivity with precisely the boundaries dictated by language criteria, separate from the surrounding Slavs and Hungarians. There was no internal cohesion from a single, separate tradition, no common past from which to draw: Wallachia, Moldavia and Transylvania had each experienced a distinct history. There were no high boundary fences in terms of religious allegiance; the Romanians had no reason to differentiate themselves from their Slav neighbours for they were all members of the Orthodox Church.

Romance identity fed off association with the French, perceived as the most prestigious of their Romance kin. In the early nineteenth century Romanian intellectuals maintained close links with France, spoke French, wrote in French, found in the French Republic a political model, in French literature the ideal standard. They also adapted French strategies for harmonisation of a linguistically disparate state: Ion Radulescu founded the Literary Society in 1827, the education system was reorganised and centralised, a national theatre was opened, a Romanian-medium press created, foreign works of literature were translated into Romanian. As well as fulfilling their primary aims each of these initiatives also served to promote a standard for the diverse Romanian dialects (Calvet, 1993).

As well as the standardisation necessary to produce a single written form, a conscious latinising of the language took place. Romanian had borrowed heavily from the Slav languages and in its early written form used the Cyrillic alphabet. Words adopted from Slavonic languages and

Hungarian were replaced by those with Romance roots (e.g. libertate replaced slobozenie); neologisms were coined by analogy with French (e.g. timbru/timbre; natie/nation).[19] The first Romanian book in Roman script appeared in 1779.[20]

The nationalist project was a political success in the sense of achieving territorial autonomy. The 1848 revolutions in Moldavia and Wallachia were repressed, but, in 1859, the two regions were joined under Alexander Cuza into what was *de facto* a semi-autonomous province, although, nominally, still under Turkish rule. Having chosen to support the winning side in the Russian-Turkish war of 1877, Romania was then granted independence at the Congress of Berlin in 1878. After the First World War and the demise of the Austro-Hungarian Empire, Transylvania was joined to the other two provinces and Romania gained not only the remaining Romanian speakers in the region but also a large Hungarian minority.

To say that Romania is a state that has formed itself according to linguistic criteria is only true in the broad sweep (Calvet, 1993). In the detail of reality there were, of course, linguistic minorities intertwined geographically with the Romanian majority, as is usually the case in Europe. Apart from the significant Hungarian minority, a legacy of the annexation of Transylvania according to the provisions of the Treaty of Trianon in 1920, there are, or have recently been, also German, Ukrainian, Romany, Russian, Serbo-Croat, Yiddish, Tartar, Slovak, Turkish, Bulgarian and Czech speakers on the territory of the Romanian state. Romania's recent policies – both under the Communist and post-Communist regimes – have aimed to assimilate non-Romanian speakers. The majority's refusal to permit difference and the feeling that disadvantage is entrenched for those not of ethnic Romanian origin has led to deep dissatisfaction among the minorities. The Hungarian speakers of Transylvania, in particular, are resisting linguistic and cultural assimilation, look to Hungary for the locus of their identity and allegiance[21] and are agitating for some kind of recognition. The situation is unresolved and still potentially explosive.

Fragmentation

The third category is in one sense the reverse process of the previous two models; not union or incorporation into a larger state but fragmentation into ever smaller units until the constituent groups are satisfied with the congruence of *Kulturnation* and *Staatsnation*. Fragmentation which we might term Balkanisation, if the term had not acquired so many layers of negative connotation, found its clearest expression in the reconstruction of Europe which took place in the name of the fourteen principles of national self-determination formulated by Woodrow Wilson in the treaties which brought the First World War to an end. A number of small nation states were created from the ruins of the Russian, Turkish and Austro-Hungarian empires, ostensibly on the principle of cultural cohesion. However, borders did not always satisfy ethnic criteria since one of the aims of the treaties was also to weaken the losers, Germany, Hungary, Austria and Turkey.

The process of fragmentation continues; it may be violent as independence movements struggle to achieve autonomy and irredentist movements fight to redraw boundaries as in ex-Yugoslavia or the Caucasus, or it may be reasonably peaceful as groups rewrite constitutions to uncouple the destinies of constituent parts of states, as the 1994 constitution has done for the Dutch-, French- and German-speaking populations of Belgium and the 1993 constitutional reforms did for the Czech and Slovak Republics. This redrafting of constitutions and redrawing of boundaries is also a form of Balkanisation, albeit without the traditional connotations of conflict that the word has acquired.

In a different sense this process is in accordance with the other two models, in that once again we witness the belief that the cultural nation and the political nation should be congruent, that a political entity should also be a community which shares beliefs, values, history and traditions and whose members should, through a common language, communicate with each other. This model is, however, reductionist. Groups who are different are not assimilated; slight differences of language or cultural practice are not ignored. Indeed the opposite may be true. For example, where the group imagines itself to be different from another but where the languages of the two are very similar, the small differences between the language varieties will be stressed rather than the similarities and the mutual intelligibility.

The differences between varieties in the Serbian-Croatian-Bosnian dialect continuum were minimised in the time when Tito's aim was to forge a socialist whole from diverse ethnic identities. Now in the midst of conflict, differences are accentuated and underlined. Even as the shelling of Sarajevo, Mostar and Tuzla was taking place, Bosnian linguists were publishing a Bosnian language dictionary to mark the status of Bosnian as a language distinct from Serbo-Croatian; Serbs were insisting that the dialect of Serbia proper be spoken in Bosnian Serb territory to underscore the cohesion of 'Greater Serbia'; Croats were working on corpus planning, ridding their language of all 'foreign', Turkish-derived elements.[22]

The perception of the similarities between the Czech and Slovak languages has evolved in a similar way. Czech and Slovak are adjacent in the Slavonic dialect continuum and thus their speakers could imagine themselves part of a single community of communication if they so wished. However, the two groups possess none of the other elements which contribute to a perception of shared nationhood. The Czechs of Bohemia and Moravia have no common history, weak religious ties, no shared culture and traditions to give them feelings of community with the Slovaks.

Bohemia and Moravia were peopled by both Slavs and Germans in the sixth and seventh centuries. The Czechs were converted to Catholicism in the eighth century and the growing power of the Holy Roman Empire brought them under the suzerainty of the Habsburgs from the late thirteenth century. In the late Middle Ages, the reformer, Jan Hus, channelled Czech grievances against the Catholic church and against German domination of the clergy and the aristocracy (Klíma, 1993). This early dissenting movement paved the way for Czech Protestantism. The Catholic Habsburgs determined to stamp this out. Czech defiance led to the defeat of the battle of White Mountain (1620), was one of the reasons for the Thirty Years War and resulted in the almost complete destruction of the Czech nation. The Czech nobility were forced to relinquish their lands, which were redistributed to new landlords from Austria and other German-speaking lands. The peasantry remained Slav-speaking. The gentry and the town were almost fully Germanised (Lewis, 1987). The Habsburgs incorporated Bohemia and Moravia back into the Catholic Empire; the Jesuits charged with the Counter-Reformation oversaw religious conformity; the German-speaking nobility ensured cultural assimilation. Seen as a safe region for investment and with natural resources, the area became the focus for industrialisation in the nineteenth century Austro-Hungarian Empire. At the same time Slav nationalism flourished and found expression in art, literature and music (Bideleux & Jeffries, 1998).

Slovakia, on the other hand, was conquered by the Magyars in the tenth century and remained under Hungarian rule from that period until the twentieth century. The Slovaks, a peasant people, uneducated and illiterate, were largely left alone by their rulers. There was little investment in the country, the towns were less developed than in the Czech lands; there was little industry. Slovakia became Catholic along with the Magyars in the early 11th century and remained so.

The Czechoslovakian state was formed in the post World War I peace conferences, mostly through lobbying from the Czechs, Masaryk and Benes, and the Czech government in exile. Masaryk, the academic, based his vision on Hussitism, humanism and democracy. Benes, the politician, wanted geographic security, a country with mountain frontiers, that could be defended. Fear of a resurgence of the Austro-Hungarian Empire, concern over the number of Hungarian speakers in the new state, led the leaders of the Slovaks to agree to union for security reasons. The institutions of the First Republic favoured the Czechs who expected, and assumed, a dominating role in the partnership.

In the period 1938–1944, the Czech lands of Bohemia and Moravia were incorporated into the III Reich. Slovakia became independent, although under a puppet regime. In 1945, this independence was seen as 'ill-gotten gains' (Nairn, 1997) and Slovakia returned to Czechoslovakia. In the same period, the mass expulsions of the German speakers from the state made it linguistically more homogenous, particularly in the north.

After the Second World War, the communist regime that took power in 1948 adopted a new constitution that recognised some Slovakian autonomy in theory but which in practice centralised power in the traditional communist fashion. The Slovakian people were the keenest supporters of federalism and decentralisation. Despite some tinkering by the regime of the Slovakian leader, Husák, post 1968, institutions remained obdurately centralised. The Slovaks were granted some rights in education, language and culture. However, in line with centralising doctrines, pragmatic official reaction to linguistic differences was that these were insignificant and that the language could for most purposes be treated as a single entity.

The Slovakian desire to secede which grew in momentum in the late 1980s and early 1990s was accompanied by an increasingly vociferous movement to have Slovak treated as a separate language and for the differences rather than the similarities to be underscored. The Slovaks' desire for independence on ethno-linguistic grounds was matched by the Czechs' feeling that they would be economically better off without Slovakia and that accession to the EU might be easier (Nairn, 1997). In this example, peoples who share a very similar language and who have retained this language through long periods of foreign domination have not found in their linguistic similarities enough common ground to overcome the difference in the other organising principles of association. History had made the Czechs look north, the Slovakians turn south. Early urbanisation and industrialisation for the Czechs contrasted with a long and widespread agrarian tradition in Slovakia. An awareness of different histories and religious traditions had contributed to an inability of the power elites of the two groups to obscure difference and build one entity. Language was the weak and unregarded common ground. It is a powerful example of how language on its own is not a sufficient cause for nationalist feeling.

Even after the division of Czechoslovakia on 1 January 1993, absolute congruence of *ethnie* and political entity has not been realised totally; in the south of the Slovakia there are substantial numbers of Hungarian speakers, a legacy of the 1920 Trianon treaty. Ethnic tensions between Slovaks and Hungarians are a problem and friction has been noted. For example, the constitution of the Slovak Republic which became law on 1 October 1993 requires Slovak citizens to register their family names according to Slovak transcription. Hungarian speakers have been incensed by this, considering it a symbolic offence against their ethnic identity (Szépe, 1994).

Language as the Defining Criterion in Fragmentation

The Baltic States are further examples of fragmentation to achieve the congruence of nation and state in the wake of the fall of communism. They demonstrate the tenacity with which peoples hold to their cultural, linguistic and religious specificity through centuries of incorporation in other political entities. Furthermore, they provide a contemporary example of how language is being used explicitly as the marker of the group in a fragmentation process. Thirdly, they show once again the virtual impossibility of achieving absolute political and cultural congruence in the mosaic of Europe.

The peoples of Latvia, Estonia and Lithuania are thought to have settled in the territory of the present-day Baltic Republics some four thousand years ago. They predate the Scandinavians, German and Slavs who have ruled over them for most of the past eight hundred years and, most remarkably, have retained their very different languages and cultures whilst in contact with and under the domination of groups using other languages.[23]

The three republics are very different in terms of language, culture, religion and history. From the late fourteenth century, Estonia and a greater part of Latvia were ruled by the Teutonic knights who established a German-speaking land-owning ruling class. This ascendancy survived the dissolution of that order, the Reformation, a short period of Swedish rule and the absorption of the territories into Russia after the Treaty of Nystad in 1721. The power of the German-speakers was not totally eclipsed by russification and only disappeared when German speakers were evacuated in the autumn of 1939, after the Molotov-Ribbentrop pact. The Lithuanians, on the other hand, resisted the Teutonic knights and were allied to Poland from the early fifteenth century, uniting formally in 1569. This coalition was one of the great powers of the area, ruling at one time from the Baltic to the Black Sea. When Poland was partitioned in the eighteenth century, Lithuania suffered the same fate. However, by the beginning of the nineteenth century, all three peoples were part of the tsarist empire. In addition to these very different experiences the three groups can be differentiated by language and religion. Estonian is a Finno-Ugric language, in the same phylum as Finnish; Lithuanian and Latvian are Baltic languages, separate from Slavonic. Lastly, there are religious differences: the Estonians and the Latvians are Lutheran, the Lithuanians are Catholic (Hiden and Salmon, 1994).

At the end of the First World War, all three peoples sought and gained independence; the republics were constituted along national lines and for the first time the ethnic Latvians were together in a political entity. Each of the states had significant minorities: Russians and Germans in Estonia and Latvia; Poles and Jews in Lithuania; Gypsies in all three states. In the early years of independence there was a certain tolerance of minorities and some positive policies for cultural diversity. However, with economic difficulties, came a growth in nationalist parties and a move to various forms of authoritarian dictatorship in the three states. Minority interests came under attack. In August 1939 the Molotov-Ribbentrop pact gave the Republics to the USSR; in June 1940 they became Soviet Socialist Republics. Although the process was enforced and the legitimatising referenda were rigged, there was some support for the Soviets – a reaction to the years of right-wing dictatorships. In Stalin's view, however, the Balts were unreliable. Deportations and liquidations started almost immediately. In 1941, German forces crossed the frontiers. Once again this foreign incursion was not totally without support among those sections of the population in opposition to the Soviets. Once again elements in the population were persecuted; this time the Jews and communists. Thousands died in pogroms, concentration camps and in the fighting.

In 1945, only states which had existed before World War Two were returned to sovereignty. The Baltic States did not appear to be eligible in a strict reading of this requirement. It was argued that the Baltic Republics had joined the USSR by plebiscite and should remain within it. The allies, needing Stalin, agreed. The Baltic populations, on the whole, did not. Guerrilla resistance led to defeat, more deaths and further deportations.

Between 1945 and 1990 the USSR nearly succeeded in extinguishing the separate identities of the Baltic Republics, not through a direct attack on language and culture (the USSR permitted and financed education in the languages of the various republics and encouraged the maintenance of cultural tradition) but through massive immigration from Russia itself, with the express purpose of the russification of the area. The highly industrialised areas of Estonia and Latvia were the main destination. This immigration, together with the very low birth rates among the Estonians and Latvians, led to a situation in the 1980s in which the Latvians were nearly a minority in their own country, 'a disappearing nation' (Zalik, quoted in Hiden & Salmon, 1994: 134), counting for only 52% in the 1989 census.

In the late 1980s, nationalist movements in Latvia, Estonia and Lithuania began to claim a measure of autonomy within the USSR. At first demands were for cultural self-determination, including cuts in immigration. This led to the republics instituting language laws (Estonia January 1989, Latvia January 1989 and Lithuania June 1989). The Estonian legislation made Estonian the state language and required all official and sales personnel to be able to operate in that language within four years. The other states had similar requirements. Then a demand for economic independence, including some power to act to control the massive ecological damage resulting from heavy industrialisation, became the focus of discontent. Finally, the call was for full political independence. In 1989, on the fiftieth anniversary of the secret protocol, the incorporation of the Republics into the USSR was declared illegal and in March 1990 Lithuania declared independence. After an attempted Russian military crackdown in 1991, Latvia and Estonia too proclaimed their independence from the former USSR (August 1991), perhaps worried by the possible consequences that could have resulted from the anti-Gorbachev coup.

At the moment of independence, the populations of these three states were mainly of mixed Baltic and Russian descent. In Latvia, as a whole, 41% of the population were Russian-speaking, in Estonia 34.3% and in Lithuania 11% (Hiden & Salmon, 1994). Massive Russian immigration to industrial areas had resulted in many of the major towns becoming predominantly Russian-speaking. After independence, the autochthonous populations sought to re-establish Baltic culture and language as the norm in these states and to exclude those of Russian origin from gaining citizenship. In Estonia, only those people who were citizens at the time of the illegal annexation in 1940, or direct descendants of such, were to be admitted to citizenship. This, of course, excluded the Russians. However, this was not exclusive linguistic nationalism. Citizenship could be earned if individuals were prepared to give proof of their acceptance that the new republic was to be a political expression of the autochthonous ethnies' culture and language. Thus state citizenship depended on a cultural, and most importantly a linguistic, qualification for those of Russian origin who wished to remain. They must demonstrate their readiness to acquire the national language and pass examinations to prove they have reached a certain level of linguistic competence. Estonia waives the five year residency qualification for very able Estonian speakers who wish to settle and take citizenship. The Estonians expect to regain monolingualism in public life within a generation (Rannut, 1994).

In Latvia, the issue was more complex.[24] In 1991, Latvia adopted citizenship laws which based eligibility on the individual's (or his/her family's) citizenship in 1940. It thus appeared that half a million or more

Russian speakers could be potentially stateless and that Europe might witness once again the population exchanges or expulsions which have marked nation state building in other Balkanisation situations. A bill requiring applicants for naturalisation to show 16 years residence, knowledge of Latvian and Latvian history as well as an oath of loyalty was discussed in parliament. The discussions dragged on until 1994. This delay and the difficulty of registering residence caused grave concern and Russia appealed to Human Rights organisations for support. In reaction, the Conference on Security and Cooperation in Europe met with the aim of assuring the stability of populations within state boundaries in this area. At the beginning of 1993, CSCE (later OSCE) long-term missions began operations in Latvia (and in Estonia) to promote stability and understanding between the majority and minority communities (US Department of State, 1994; Birkavs, 1997). In June 1994 a law was passed which only allowed a small quota to apply for citizenship each year. In July an amended law increased the numbers.

The Russian speakers lobbied vigorously. There were some ugly incidents between protesters and police. The Western press took a keen interest, seeing in the language element of the naturalisation process the old demons of ethno-linguistic nationalism and blood and belonging. Western organisations, including the EU and the Council of Europe brought pressure to bear on the Latvian government. Unwilling to cede the point, the very nationalist prime minister, Guntars Krasts, referred the question to a referendum. However, in October 1998, the Latvians voted by a small majority (52.54%) to accept amendments to the law which would make citizenship easier and quicker to obtain. The carrot on offer was fast track talks on EU membership.

In the Baltic States the tension between the Balts and the Russians is not caused by linguistic difference; it is, of course, the result of power relationships between conquerors and conquered. Nevertheless, language is important because it is the salient marker that defines the groups and has been chosen as a criterion for access to citizenship.

Finally, economic factors have clearly been present in the various Baltic independence movements but have never been decisive. In the 1919 movement, it was clear that independence along national lines would be disadvantageous in the short term (Hiden & Salmon, 1994). In the 1990 movement, there was clear economic motivation, a desire to disengage from the USSR economy, perceived to be in danger of imminent collapse. However, although there was a feeling among Western commentators that these republics were too small for successful economic independence, there was never any possibility that the three republics would constitute themselves as one group (Hiden & Salmon, 1994). A number of schemes for cooperation exist but nothing more. In this instance, culture, language, history and religion have proved their power as primary organising principles for state formation.

Thus, in summary, we may say that the reductionist (fragmentation/ Balkanisation) model is close to the culturally inclusive (Blood and Belonging) model and that linguistic and cultural unity is sought in each (sometimes religious unity as well). However, the latter ignores minor variance in order to unify groups into a larger whole, whereas the former tends to exaggerate any slight difference in order to break away from a larger entity.

We can also add that the congruence of polity and cultural group remains largely fictive in the European mosaic and that, in the interests of safeguarding national sovereignty, the wider European community has, until the recent events in Kosovo, usually reacted disapprovingly to the processes of *Balkanisation* and *Blood and Belonging*, seeing them as 'nasty', 'reactionary' ethno-nationalisms; in contrast the civic nationalism of the assimilatory model is often approved (Kohn, 1946).

Notes

1. A famous definition of nationalism is that given by Gellner: 'Nationalism is a political principle which holds that the political and national units should be congruent' (Gellner, 1983: 1).
2. In recent policymaking in France and the UK there has been a fine distinction made between assimilation and integration, with the former defined as the requirement that minority groups conform to majority norms and the latter as a negotiated accommodation whereby both groups accept the need for some change (although the minority group is expected to accommodate most). I use assimilation here because it was the reality for the time span of which I write and because it might be argued that integration, as I have defined it, is far from being a reality in either France or the UK.
3. The inheritance practices of the Franks which caused a tripartite split among Charlemagne's heirs was one reason, gigantism and the diffculties of communication and transport in the 9th century another.
4. In a letter to the Marquis de Villars 8 January 1688.
5. Braudel (1986) reminds us that although this is undoubtedly true, internal customs barriers existed up to the Revolution and territorial privileges were the norm rather than the exception.
6. Schiffman (1996) suggests that the contemporary effect of the ordonnances of Villers-Cotterêts was limited. It acquired significance subsequently.
7. The clearest case of Jewish persecution for political as well as religious and commercial purposes is probably Spain. After the fall of Granada in 1492 and the final victory over the Muslims, Isabella of Castile and Ferdinand of Aragon demanded that the Jews in their kingdom either convert or leave, believing that religious unity would reinforce political unity.

8. It is widely recognised that the power of printing served the Protestant cause and that bibles and other religious works translated into the various vernaculars furthered the development of the vernacular. The uses of the press were recognised by the Catholic hierarchy too. French Catholics brought out twenty editions of the bible in French between 1487 and 1524; *livres d'heures*, lives of the saints and other religious productions in French constituted the majority of books printed in France in the course of the fifteenth century.

9. Similar attempts to achieve religious 'homogenisation' took place in other countries. In Britain the population was under pressure to convert three times – from Catholicism to Protestantism to Catholicism to Protestantism – following the demands of successive Tudor monarchs. The Peace of Augsburg (1555) had introduced the idea of *cuius regio eius religio*, the philosophy that would have subjects follow the same version of Christianity as their ruler.

10. In the Convention there was much debate about whether the revolutionary message should be translated into the other languages of France or not. There were many who argued 'that it was wrong to bargain with jargons' (Schiffman, 1996: 109).

11. From 1905, although the achievement of a secular education system had its roots in a strong anticlerical movement which started decades earlier.

12. Maurice Barrès played a major role in the nationalist revival that swept France between 1905 and 1914. His cult of 'blood and soil' was sometimes at odds with Catholicism and he wrote 'I am firmly opposed to the error, the betrayal, of confounding religion and nationalism' (quoted in Soucy, 1972: 145), but he employed Catholicism in the fight against the Protestant Prussian 'occupation' of Alsace-Lorraine (cf. Colette Baudoche). Together with Charles Maurras and Action française (1908–1944), he symbolised cultural traditionalism and conservative nationalism in France. Violently anti-democratic and anti-republican, the followers of these two men often found themselves in the same camp as the anti-democratic and anti-republican strand in the Catholic Church.

13. For a discussion of the limited effect of the Loi Deixonne which permitted the teaching of some autochthonous minority languages in schools, see D. Ager (1990) *Sociolinguistics and Contemporary French*, Cambridge: CUP and (1996) *Language Policy in Britain and France*, London: Cassell. The French signed the Council of Europe's Charter for Minority Languages in May 1999. There is some suspicion that this may not benefit autochthonous minorities in any concrete way since, at the time of writing, Cerquiglini's reporting group were recommending the inclusion of 76 languages. This is likely to draw the teeth of the measure. Furthermore, in June 1999 the Conseil Constitutionnel judged the signing unconstitutional. The matter is at present unresolved. See below (Chapter 8) for further discussion.

14. Public reaction is clear from opinion polls (e.g. IPSOS 9 February 1998 reported in *Evénement du jeudi*). Government opinion is shown in Juppé's speech, refusing to allow the Corsicans to designate themselves a people (17 July 1996) and in Chirac's speech after the murder of Claude Erignac, the Corsican préfet, reaffirming the indivisibility of the French nation (7 February 1998). See also debate in Sénat 6 February 1996.

15. *Le code de la nationalité*. Law passed 22nd July 1993 and applied since 1st January 1994. From this date onwards children born of non-French nationals wishing to acquire French nationality had to make a *déclaration de volonté* between the ages

of 16 and 21 either at the *tribunal d'instance* or at their *préfecture*. Conviction of any serious crime (i.e. any crime meriting six months sentence or more) precluded this. By September 1994 25,000 young people had requested French nationality. After Lionel Jospin's victory in the legislative elections in 1997, this policy returned to the political agenda, provoking a debate about choice and rights in the matter (cf. Bernard, P., 1997 'Immigration, nationalité, intégration' in *Le Monde* 13 November 1997). In 1998 the law was amended and new legislation came into force on 1 September 1998. The situation is now (1999) that all those born to foreign nationals on French soil who have at least five years residence on French territory by the age of 18 have an automatic right to French citizenship at that age. There is no longer an obligation to ask for it. It may, of course, be refused.

16. 'Bismark's famous exhortation to the German people, over the heads of their particular political leaders, to 'think with your blood' was a (similar) attempt to activate a mass psychological vibration predicated upon an intuitive sense of consanguinity' (Connor, 1994: 37).

17. It has been argued that the March elections in Eastern Germany were a form of referendum. Cf. Hella Pick 'March elections were referendum on unity' in *The Guardian* 31 January 1990.

18. The *Reichs-und Staatsangehörigkeitgesetz* which was the law until 1999 predated the First World War and was based firmly on *jus sanguinis* and the principle of descent. Until the 1970s nationality could only be passed through the paternal line; then the mother also had the right to pass German nationality to her children. In the last decades there was a relaxing of the law to allow naturalisation for spouses of German nationals and *Ausländerkinder der dritten Generation*, although the process was still difficult and there were certain restrictions: e.g. dual nationality was forbidden for those holding a German passport (Fietz, 1995). This position was reaffirmed in the Bundestag on 27 March 1998 when an attempt to amend the law was defeated (WDR 27 March 1998). In Spring 1999, however, a new law moved the German system a step towards *jus soli*. Now children born to foreign nationals, one of whom has been resident for eight years in Germany has automatic right to German citizenship. There are some provisos (e.g. there must be no criminal record). Dual nationality is still officially unacceptable and between the ages of 18 and 23 the holder of German nationality by birth and another nationality by descent must choose one or the other. There are provisions for exceptions, as in the case where the other state will not permit renunciation of citizenship (e.g. Iran) or where the renunciation of citizenship would entail loss of inheritance (e.g. Turkey).

19. Romanian adaptation from the French has continued up to the present day. Manoliu argues that borrowings and calques from the French represented 'an act of covert political protest' in the communist era (Manoliu, 1994: 96). Romania is part of *Francophonie* despite the fact that French has no official role in the state apart from being a favoured foreign language in the education system.

20. In this the Romanians do not follow the general rule in eastern Europe, noted in Siguan (1996). Usually Catholic and Protestant groups use the Latin alphabet (e.g. Poles, Czecks, Slovaks, Slovenians, Hungarians and Croats) and Orthodox groups uses the Cyrillic alphabet (e.g. Bulgarians, Ukrainians, Serbs, Russians and White-Russians).

21. Students from the Hungarian-speaking minorities of Romania go in large numbers to the universities of southern and south-eastern Hungary, e.g. Pécs.
22. Cf. R. Katicic (1997) Undoing a 'unified' language: Bosnian, Croatian, Serbian. In M. Clyne (ed.) *Undoing and Redoing Corpus Planning*, Berlin: Mouton de Gruyter.
23. For a comprehensive history of the Baltic Republics see Hiden & Salmon (1994), Lieven (1993), Clemens (1991), Ozolins (1999). These authors treat the issue of language and nationalism at length.
24. See Ozolins (1999) for a full discussion of the Latvian situation.

Chapter 3

Language as a key organising principle of nationalism. Contending schools in the debate. The linguistic realities of multilingual states

The discussion of the theories of nationalism and the examination of the various case studies of nation building have revealed the varying roles that language plays in the process of unification. We have seen that the function of language changes according to circumstances and that a common language may contribute to or result from nation state building. It has become clear that the issue of language has always to be addressed in the context of nation building and that it is more central to the issue than many allow.

The various philosophies of nationalism and the case studies have demonstrated the predictable features of nationalism. Groups tend to acquire self-awareness, to mobilise feelings of solidarity, to see themselves as discrete entities and to be treated by others as such, through a mixture of delimiting factors which may include some or all of the following: shared language; belief in common ancestry, the sharing of a common living space; a single set of laws; shared customs and traditions; shared religion; shared history; a sense of shared destiny; a common project. None of these factors is in itself an essential element of the definition and there are examples of groups who see themselves as nations who do not have one or the other. However, what is necessary is that there are enough elements from the list for the group to *imagine* itself to be a distinct community (Anderson, 1991) and for there to be a psychological bond which joins the people and differentiates it in the subconscious conviction of its members (Connor, 1994). Thus the definition of 'nation' is both objective and subjective; we can predict some of the features which will be shared by a 'nation' and we know that when a 'nation' exists it will have defined itself as such. We bear in mind too that the self-definition of such a group may have little to do with rational calculation by all its individual members and may have much to do with manipulation for political ends, including the invention of tradition and ritual to promote solidarity and the erection and reinforcement of boundaries to delineate in-groups and out-groups.

In this chapter I want to investigate further the role of language in group formation, both as a factor in its own right and in the way it interacts with the other factors. Some theoreticians of nationalism underestimate or misrepresent the role of language in nation formation. There are good reasons for this as I hope to show.

Contending Schools of Thought in the Language Debate

It seems axiomatic that there must be a common idiom within a group, for, without this fundamental tool for association, most of the other elements in group formation would not be possible. It is unfortunate that many of the clearest expressions of this point come from highly discredited sources. We have already seen how ethno-linguistic nationalism was adopted enthusiastically by extremist nationalisms and ultimately by fascism, and thus lost credibility. Even those parts of the doctrine which may be considered so banal as to be self-evident – the idea that nation building requires a common idiom, that language and culture are closely bound – are not accepted unquestioningly because of their association with the more fantastical notions proposed by the theorists of linguistic relativity and linguistic nationalism.

Stalin's theorising on the inextricable relationship of language and nation appeals as basic common sense:

> (A) national community is inconceivable without a common language . . . There is *no nation* which at one and the same time speaks several languages. (Stalin, 1973: 58, my italics)

In all the European examples that are quoted to contradict this – for example, Belgium and Switzerland – there is a tendency to accommodate the linguistic cleavages within loose federalism structures. However, a discredited source such as Stalin (moreover, the essay was written partly as anti-Semitic polemic, to make the point that, lacking territory, the Jews could not be a nation[1]) will not be readily accepted by those who argue that language is not an essential element in nationalism.

Stalin makes a further crucial point that 'shared language' does not imply that the language need be exclusive to the group; those who see themselves as different may speak the same language or varieties of the same language:

> (T)his does not mean that there cannot be two nations speaking the same language! (Stalin, 1973: 58)

Stalin's second point is easily illustrated. The Scots show how language has no need to be exclusive. They share language with their southern neighbours, the English, without this having a diluting effect on group identity; they retain a clear perception of different identity, different culture, different history; they see themselves as a distinct nation.

The fact that common language surfaces as a central tenet in many right wing nationalist movements with racist proclivities further contributes to a desire to dismiss it as an essential organising principle. Language interacts with racist ideology in the following way. Where group formation hinges on the concept of blood and belonging there are difficulties of recognition in the European context. On a continent where large scale movements of people have taken place over millennia, where conquest and economic migration have brought about complex interbreeding, any claim from a group that it possesses a common ancestry is purely fictive (Sahlins, 1976). In such biologically complex societies, where the concept of 'racial purity' makes no sense and where intra-group physical variation may be as great or greater than that between groups, group recognition on physical criteria is, despite all racist or nationalist rhetoric, unreliable. Thus a cultural diacritic such as language becomes the salient marker of group difference and minor variations of dialect and accent which allow members of an exclusive group to recognise each other as such are emphasised. This role of language in the 'blood and belonging' brand of nationalism – the variety which provokes the most disgust in a Western intellectual tradition that insists on the near pathological character of all nationalisms – seals its fate (Geertz, 1963). Language will not be treated dispassionately.

There are currently three approaches to the language question. A number of well respected authorities, far less controversial than Stalin, subscribe to the view that a capacity for communication is essential for building communities, particularly modern democratic communities. For some in this group, this capacity develops as a by-product of modernity and industrialisation and appears concurrently with nationalism; for others, the capacity stems from linguistic unification, planned and executed by nationalising elites. A second group argues that language is simply one among a number of elements which may or may not define a particular national group. They argue that language can be adopted or abandoned where the individual wishes to join or leave the group. A third set of scholars downgrades the importance of language and denies that it is essential to the nationalising process. Some of the divergence in views stems from the dual role that language plays in national mobilisation. Those who see language as fundamental to the process are mainly interested in the communicative functions of language; those who dismiss it, usually do so because they are considering language in its symbolic function. Edwards (1985) points out the importance of disentangling the symbolic function of language from the communicative. A certain imprecision in the use of the word allows some commentators to slide from one definition to the other and make claims about language which appear to relate to both domains, whereas they are only proven for one.

Language as the Basis for Association and Cooperation

Karl Deutsch sees language as a social glue – members of a group can communicate, share ideas, share traditions, share language-borne culture, trade easily, learn from each other when they share a language:

> Peoples are held together 'from within' by this communicative efficiency, the complementarity of the communicative facilities acquired by their members. (Deutsch, 1966: 97)

The defining criterion of a 'people' in his model is this complementarity of communication. Communicative facility underlies cultural community and allows social action. Negatively, it may well demand the assimilation of some sub-sets and the suppression of diversity to weld a heterogenous group into a homogenous whole.

Central to much of Jürgen Habermas' thought is the idea that the 'community of cooperation' necessary for the modern democratic state derives from consensus formation. It is only through the capacity of the individual members of that community to communicate that consensus can be negotiated:

> When parents educate their children, when living generations appropriate the knowledge handed down by their predecessors, when individuals cooperate, i.e. get on with each other without a costly use of force, they must act communicatively. There are elementary social functions which can only be satisfied by means of communicative action. (Habermas, 1994: 146)

The promotion of vernaculars is necessary for the contrastive self-identification that nationalism demands according to Joshua Fishman (1972). He argues that elites and masses alike could extrapolate from linguistic differentiation to socio-cultural uniqueness and thence to political independence. He discusses language both as a medium of nationalism and as a message of nationalism. To illustrate the first process, he shows how the elaboration, codification and dissemination of vernaculars to promote them as languages of power (language planning) is a key tool of nation building. To exemplify the second, he examines the symbolic primordiality of language, its embodiment of ethnicity and its use as a diacriticon of identity. In this claim that language embodies the authenticity of the group, he approaches some of the earlier writers on language and nationalism.

Pierre Bourdieu dissects the process of language standardisation in nation building and finds that the political will to unification contributes to the construction of a state language which linguists then accept as a natural phenomenon (Bourdieu, 1991). A national consensus is built in the schoolroom where in a Whorfian/Humboldtian sense the pupils are brought to moral and intellectual integration in a medium common to all.

Language as a By-product of Modernity

Gellner (1983) recognised that nationalism was a feature of modernity and industrialisation, and not – or not simply – a Romantic, primordialist reaction to it. As noted above, the rapidly undertaken business of industrialisation required a common culture and language to allow it to succeed and that culture tended to be rooted in the demotic variety of the language.

Anderson is another who sees the linguistic unity we witness in nations and nationalism as an outcome of the processes of modernity and not as a pre-existing cultural phenomenon which required a nation state as its political expression. Print capitalism with its desire for large markets is, as we have seen, a force for language standardisation and may reinforce the efforts of the state to achieve the same ends. Anderson's imagined communities develop symbiotically with a common language of literacy. In the national press a medium evolves which links large numbers in a daily ritual of newspaper reading. The recreational consumption of novels reveals parallel lives within the nation. The same stories in the same language are a potent force for the creation of consensus and feelings of community. For Anderson, national sentiment develops largely through stories shared in a national language.

Nairn (1997) suggests that this modernist thesis should not be stretched too far. The diversity of pre-national social formations constitutes an archaeological layer underneath the policies of nation building. He agrees that language is the required cultural instrument of industrialisation and that 'tongues' will be elevated into high cultures in the processes of modernisation and industrialisation, but he then makes the judicious point:

> Yes, but was their original constitution and variation of no importance for grasping the way things then evolved? The 'spell' of community always depended not just on language but on the proliferation of tongues

which always entailed incommunicability, privacy and falsehood, as well as understanding, common sense and truth. (Nairn, 1997: 14)

Is it not this spell of community which modernity has failed to diffuse and which keeps resurfacing in requests for the recognition of linguistic and cultural difference, in demands for autonomy or in struggles for secession?

The Question of Choice

Within the writings of the second group, there is widespread agreement that language is only one amongst many elements and not necessarily the most important. Language appears in the list of possible elements present when groups coalesce. No claim to primacy is made for it. It is observed that there is nothing preordained or predestined about language use; societies and individuals always have the possibility of adopting or abandoning a language. Ernest Renan's seminal essay on nationalism has the clearest expression of this last point:

> L'homme n'est esclave ni de sa race, ni de sa langue, ni de sa religion, ni du cours des fleuves, ni de la direction des chaînes de montagne. (Renan, 1882: 906)

There are a number of other writers who express the same view. The German nationalist, Bauer, stated:

> (I)n the last resort it is simply which nation an individual feels himself to be a part of which is decisive, not which one he physically or linguistically, or otherwise, belongs to. (Bauer, 1918 translated and cited by Bruckmüller, 1993: 197)

Liah Greenfeld claims that a nation can form without a language:

> (T)here are important exceptions to every relationship in terms of which nationalism has ever been interpreted – whether with common territory or common language, statehood or shared traditions, history or race, none of these relationships has proved inevitable. (Greenfeld, 1992: 7)

A.D. Smith regrets that scholars

> persist in regarding language as *the* distinguishing mark of ethnicity, a standpoint that leads to gross simplification and misunderstanding. (Smith, 1986: 27, my italics)

He includes language among the various symbols of collective life – dress, etiquette, diet, art, music, rituals, and the like which serve to differentiate members of an *ethnie* from outsiders, but suggests that because language is highly manipulable and that the borders of a speech community are notoriously difficult to agree, it cannot be taken as the most important criterion for group formation.

John Armstrong (1982) finds shared meanings and shared experiences allow individuals to feel themselves to be part of an *ethnie* or a nation. He provides a list of domains in which such sharing may take place. Where sacred texts, languages, religious shrines and tombs, styles of dress, art and architecture, music, poetry, dance, legal codes, city planning, forms of hierarchy, crafts and modes of warfare are held in common then individuals will recognise community; where these are not shared, there may be barriers to association and solidarity.

Fredrik Barth (1969) discusses the same features within an ecological approach to ethnic diversity, He makes the point that any cultural pattern for exploiting biotic niches will necessarily include a means of protecting that niche. This leads to the need to develop boundary markers. Any cultural difference can be used to distinguish between ethnic groups, but, of all the cultural differences which can be employed, language is one of the most impenetrable, least easily acquired and thus most effective in this role.

The Relative Unimportance of Language

In this camp – which is heavily Anglo-Saxon – there is a certain dismissiveness towards language. Mostly this is expressed by an absence; language is barely mentioned in some authors' discussions of nationalism.

Other scholars set out to demolish the claim that language is one of the fundamental organising principles of nationalism. Eric Hobsbawm is particularly trenchant. Writing of the pre-nationalist era, he states unequivocally that:

> Special cases aside, there is no reason to suppose that language was more than one among several criteria by which people indicated belonging to a human collectivity. And it is absolutely certain that language had as yet no political potential. (Hobsbawm, 1990: 63)

Writing of groups in general he ask why language should be a criterion of membership 'except perhaps where language differentiation coincides with some other reason to mark oneself off from some other community?' (Hobsbawm, 1990: 56). Where there is only one language in a society then its members do not reflect on language and do not use it as a group criterion. Where there are a number of languages coexisting, bi- or multilingual speakers may identify with more than one speech community, switching among languages to suit the situation and interlocutor and dismissing altogether any mystical identification with a 'mother tongue'.

Hobsbawm does not target language alone His argument is that all the so-called objective criteria which are used to define nations are riddled with ambiguities and imprecisions and open to misuse. He argues that attempts at definition are doomed:

> (T)he criteria used for this purpose – language, ethnicity or whatever – are themselves fuzzy, shifting and ambiguous, and as useless for purposes of the traveller's orientation as cloudshapes compared to landmarks. This, of course, makes them unusually convenient for propagandist and programmatic as distinct from descriptive purposes. (Hobsbawm, 1990: 6)

According to Paul Brass, language is not important to most people. He maintains that:

> Many illiterate rural persons, far from being attached emotionally to their mother tongue do not even know its proper name . . . (M)any people, if not most people, never think about their language at all and never attach any emotional significance to it. (Brass, 1994: 84)

Dell Hymes (1968), writing about pre-national groups, puts the case against using language as a primary criterion for mapping cultures. According to his argument, to do so would be to assume that ethnological units exist discretely, that communication discontinuities match other socio-cultural boundaries, that language is the only relevant communication medium and that cultural-linguistic boundaries persist in time.

Gellner joins this group in a limited way when he makes the point that although a nation state might need a language this does not mean that the corollary is true and that a language needs a nation state. Gellner argues that there are approximately 8000 languages in the world, 200 states and about 600 nations aspiring to acquire their own state.[2] This leads him to a ratio of one actual nation for every nine linguistic groups that do not aspire to nation status. He holds that this weakens the argument that shared culture and language are fundamental elements of nationalism.

Elie Kedourie (1960) demanded to know why having one's own language should entail having one's own government. He makes the very defensible point that:

> (R)ace, languages, religions, political traditions and loyalties are so inextricably intermixed that there can be no clear convincing reason why people who speak the same language but whose history and

circumstances otherwise widely diverge should form one state. (Kedourie, 1960: 79)

and cites the United States and Great Britain to show that groups who share language, culture and religion often see themselves as two nations. He also wonders

. . . why people who speak two different languages and whom circumstances have thrown together should not form one state. (Kedourie, 1960: 79)

Critique

For me the idea of community seems inextricably linked to the idea of *community of communication*. Indeed the latter tends to tautology since a community must communicate to be a community in any meaningful sense. While not subscribing to the linguistic nationalist thesis and not believing that language is anything other than a construct, I would nonetheless suggest that language constantly organises experience and that experience constantly generates new language and causes a review of old. Where two sets of speakers interpret experience there are likely to be two sets of experience, if only in minor matters of emphasis and choice. In this way, slightly differentiated national views become established. Thus the Habermas/Deutsch view of language as social glue seems eminently defensible. At the same time Hobsbawm's and Kedourie's reservations cannot be brushed aside; language has been used in a programmatic way to build national groups and for propagandist purposes of exclusion and inclusion. However, far from proving the case that language is unimportant, this seems only to show the opposite. The language issue is far more complex than some authors claim, and while open to manipulation and misrepresentation, no less central because of that.

The argument in the second half of this book rests on the belief that 'nations and nationalism' have brought most Europeans to expect to be members of a community of communication congruent with their polity, and that the social glue of a common medium is the bedrock of association in European nation states. So perhaps it is now essential to examine the main arguments of those authorities who would contest this assertion.

The Definition of Language in Europe

The first task is to define what is meant by language. Leaving aside the situation of tiny populations living totally hermetic existences, in the jungles of Borneo for example, and speaking languages which are not comprehensible to outsiders, even those in closest geographical proximity, the general rule is that human language is organised in a number of language phyla. These phyla are much fewer in number than the 8000 which Gellner quotes. In Europe, for example, there are only nine: Celtic, Italic, Germanic, Slavonic, Baltic, Finno-Ugric, Basque, Albanian and Greek. Within each phylum there are dialect continua and a degree of mutual intelligibility which result in linguistic change in the traditional spoken idiom being gradual over distance.[3]

How these phyla fracture to become national languages is not a linguistic but a political decision. Thus we have the example of the Danish, Norwegian and Swedish 'languages' on the one hand. These three form part of the North Germanic continuum, possess a degree of mutual comprehensibility but have differing standardised written norms because they are associated with three different states.[4] On the other hand, there is the example of the various German 'dialects'. In their spoken form the varieties of German spoken in Germany proper arguably exhibit similar degrees of difference and mutual comprehensibility. The German dialects have, however, only one written standard and are considered one language, because they are associated with one state. In dialect continua, mutual comprehensibility is often a question of individual choice; speakers may choose to grant comprehension to those who are not distant from them on the continuum, or they may choose to withhold it. The choice is not usually concerned with linguistic matters. The effort needed to communicate will be made if the interlocutor is considered part of the same group or part of a friendly, neighbouring group. The attempt will not be made and comprehension will usually be refused if there are old enmities, continuing divisions, rivalries.

The definition of language is central to Gellner's thesis. When he argues that a 'language' group does not need its own state, we have to ask what is meant here by language. Language difference will *tend* to lead to separate nationalisms and to demands for separate nation states more readily where communication fractures along the breaks between continua. On the other hand, language shifts to the dominant state language take place more easily where the dominating and dominated idioms originate from the same phylum. In purely linguistic terms accommodation is less problematic and language maintenance of the dominated idiom more unlikely. Language difference within dialect continuums can be accommodated. Where nation states have been formed across the fissures between dialect continua we note two tendencies. Firstly, there is the indigestibility of minorities incorporated into states from other dialect continua. Secondly, those few states which have formed with a balance of power between two or more profoundly different linguistic groups have tended to exhibit centrifugal tendencies in the long term or survive through loose federal arrangements. This is the case for Belgium and Switzerland.

Minority linguistic groups in France illustrate the first phenomenon. Over a third of the French state was once Occitan speaking. Occitan speakers (from the same phylum as French) have assimilated linguistically and there are now very few left. However, French Basque speakers, Breton speakers and German speakers (from different phyla) have retained their languages to a much greater extent.[5] Scotland which had four ancestral languages: early Welsh, Gaelic, Inglis (Lallans) and Norn,[6] is another example. The original linguistic diversity of the Scottish population has been largely forgotten – to the extent that even the names of these languages are not widely known; most Scots will have only heard of English and Gaelic and see only the cleavage Highland and Lowland. The language difference which is recognised is between the two language phyla – Celtic and West Germanic. Within each phylum difference is accepted as simple dialectal variety.

However, this apparent rule falters in other examples. Where groups decide for other reasons that they do not wish to be a single political unit, mutual comprehensibility of the languages of the groups is never a weighty argument against separate development. In the Spanish context, those 'minorities' on the same dialect continuum as the Castilian speakers did not assimilate more easily than those who were not. Catalan speakers (from the same Romance phylum as Castilian) and Basque speakers (from a separate phylum entirely) have been equally committed to acquiring autonomy/independence. In terms of language maintenance the Catalans have actually been more successful.

Kedourie's argument that there is no reason why a nation should not be multilingual is no longer supported by the examples he gives to prove his point. He cites the example of French- and English-speaking Canada to show that bilingual nations are possible. With hindsight this has proved a particularly unfortunate choice. Quebec, given in 1960 as an illustration of linguistic accommodation, has come by the end of the century to exemplify the opposite. A 1982 European parliament report on multilingualism, under the chairmanship of K. Nyborg, founders in the same way. Besides Canada, the list of states cited to show that multilingual polities can function includes the USSR, Yugoslavia, Sri Lanka, Israel, Czechoslovakia, Romania and Belgium. In the intervening years all of these countries have witnessed dissension between linguistically differentiated groups and different degrees of separation, achieved by conflict or by negotiation. Where linguistic difference is not accommodated, association is not secure.

An understanding of dialect continua and the subsequent development of national languages also modifies the argument that Hobsbawm develops to show how the importance of language has been overplayed. He states that before universal primary education imposed a standard national form, there would not have been one single idiom which would have had currency throughout the territories which were to become the various European nation states. This being so, he concludes that common language was not a key element in group formation. This is only a partial truth. Dialect continua are not composed of sets of dialects with clear cut boundaries; within them language is indeed 'fuzzy'. Until codification and standardisation of national language academies slowed the pace of linguistic change across time, and national frontiers brought about the customs posts which artificially interrupted contact across space, languages were liable to constant mutation. However, those communicating regularly developed forms in tandem and the lack of mutual intelligibility between those at the extremities of the continua was never apparent to speakers at contiguous points along the line. At no single geographical point would there have been noticeable discontinuity. In the sedentary life of pre-modern times, few people would have appreciated the extent of change across a linguistic area; most people would have understood their neighbours and this would have given them some basis for association – to be accepted or rejected according to the power of other variables, such as religion or feudal allegiances. On the other hand, those living along the lines of cleavage between dialect continua would have been very aware of linguistic boundaries and their impermeability. They could not easily associate across the divide until they had found a solution to their communication problems. It is precisely along these fracture lines – between the Slavonic, Germanic, Romance and Celtic dialect continua – that we find numerous examples of how difficult accommodation is between peoples from completely different linguistic systems.

Hobsbawm's repugnance for the linguistic dimension of nationalism is well-founded. In all European nation states which developed the nation and the community of communication *post facto* and which have sought to weld speakers from different phyla into one community, there has been much coercion and some violence as the central authority attempted to impose linguistic unity on the periphery. A spate of militant authors in the 1970s (Hechter, 1975; Lafont, 1971; Larzac, 1971, etc.) criticised linguistic unification as cultural supremacy that necessarily entailed subordination and dependency. In general response to Hobsbawm, one might say that language is always an issue in group formation; it may not be sufficient reason for association, but it is a condition, if not necessarily a pre-condition. If there is no possibility for intra-group communication, this lack presents an enormous stumbling block.

Moving Language

Smith, Greenfeld and Armstrong made the point that people employ the reasons for association that suit them; ignore those that are inconvenient. The irrational and emotional national consciousness of which these authorities speak is fired by the individual's attachment to place and to cohesion promoted by language-borne as well as non-language borne culture. They agree in principle with Renan's and Bauer's claim that language and place do not have to limit allegiance. This seems to me to be a moral stance taken to preclude exclusion on grounds of *jus soli* or language group membership. And laudable in its intention. However, language change may actually be quite difficult. The factors which these authorities see as adoptable and abandonable are different in kind. Some, like religion and culture, may entail a heavy psychological price where there is change, but are ultimately a question of will. Language is, however, a different matter. Language shift may have a psychological dimension, but it is also a question of apprenticeship and effort over time. The cognitive demands may mean that some individuals never manage the change. There are no short cuts to becoming a member of a different community of communication and where a whole group shifts this may well pose difficulties for older speakers and result in a lost generation who are left behind linguistically. The realities of second language acquisition need to be kept in mind on this point.

Language as the Fundamental Organising Principle

Brass' quote perhaps reveals the opposite of his analysis. Not to have a label for one's idiom, does not mean that one does not value it. It may simply reveal that it is so central it needs no name. It simply is. Because people do not think explicitly about language, it is dangerous to assume, as both Brass and Hobsbawm do, that language is not important to them. Whether societal organisation is monolingual, bilingual, plurilingual, the linguistic reality one is born into is accepted unquestioningly. Means of communication only become salient when the *status quo* is challenged and societies are forced by outside agents into linguistic adjustment and change. In such circumstances speakers will reflect, react and know their linguistic difference and allegiance. Primitive societies often labelled their language in a negative way; they could not name what they spoke but they were very aware that there were those who spoke languages they could not understand and they named *them*. The French linguist, Emile Benveniste (1969), notes how names for outsiders in ancient times were often derived from descriptions of their lack of intelligibility. *Barbaroi* is the Greek onomatopoeia for those who babble incoherently, i.e. speakers of other languages. In Russian, the words for dumb, speechless, mute (nemoj) and German, foreigner (nemets) sound similar and popular historical linguistics maintains they come from the same root.

It thus seems both counter-intuitive and against all the available evidence to argue that language is not a key variable in nationalising processes. The general rule is that those who can understand each other associate more willingly than those who do not. Once this requirement is on its way to fulfilment, those who are promoting the group formation can employ all the other elements of nation building to far greater effect. Language may not be sufficient on its own for meaningful association but it is an essential element. In the examples of nation state formation which seem to contradict this assertion, one of the first and urgent tasks for the political elites was to foster the creation of a community of communication. Here the rule is adhered to *post facto*. There are few polities which appear to contravene the rule completely, and they will now be considered.

The Linguistic Realities of Multilingual States

There has been a pragmatic acceptance in all European nation building of the importance of language for national unity. As we have seen in the case studies in Chapter 2, one of the first acts of each new state has been the language planning necessary to promote one variety as the national language. It is, of course, self-evident that the choices are indicative of power relationships. The standard national language is typically based on the idiom of those with political power – as in the adoption of the language of the monarch and the court as the standard for English. The modern state ensures the eventual dominance of the chosen variety in a number of ways: the growth of various forms of media, education and literacy for all, conscription into the melting pot of a national army, contact with a state bureaucracy conducted in the national language, participation in a democratic political system.

However, while some may accept language shift willingly for reasons of economic or political advantage, most will be forced to do so. Language shift in nation state building is often accomplished in a top down way and through coercion. In a similar way to the situations which arise after conquest, colonisation and migration, minority linguistic groups incorporated into nation states are usually required to accommodate to the dominant group, at least in public life.[7] There are few examples which appear to contradict this completely.

Belgium is often cited as an illustration that the multilingual state is possible. It actually demonstrates the very opposite; the state has only been able to contain its internal contradictions and its tendency to disintegration by recognising that it is multinational and by installing a loose federal structure which endorses the desire of its component 'nations' to be separate. There are four separate linguistic communities in Belgium: the Walloon, Flemish and German[8] communities are monolingual and only the Brussels region has any claim to bilingual status. The 1994 Belgian constitution instituted a 'federal state consisting of communities and regions' recognising *de jure* the *de facto* independence of the linguistic groups (Beheydt, 1994). Many of the functions of government have been devolved to the Walloon and Flemish authorities, which have naturally moved apart, since the need to cooperate is less.[9] Rigid linguistic divisions in the army and the education system underpin the argument that this is a state with two nations. Regiments are organised on linguistic lines and bilingualism is only required from a narrow band of superior officers. In the schools any crossing of the divide is made less likely by official insistance that Flemish families educate their children in Dutch medium schools and French in French. Writing of Brussels, Siguan says:

> Observé de l'extérieur, ce phenomène fait apparaître peu justifié qu'une ville officiellement bilingue offre deux réseaux scolaires rigoureusement séparés plutôt que d'opter pour une solution beacoup plus souple et plus opératoire dans le but d'assurer à tous les élèves une compétence égale dans les deux systèmes linguistiques. (Siguan, 1996: 75)

The internal organisation of Belgium appears to be another example of the European desire to achieve the congruence of the political entity and the community of communication; here it has been achieved at the level of the region rather than of the state.

Switzerland with its history of confederation is the other model cited to prove the possibility of truly multilingual political entities in Europe. It has often been cited as an instance of nation building where a common language has not been absolutely necessary. For example, Max Weber argues that:

> (A) common language does not seem to be absolutely necessary to a 'nation'. In official documents, beside 'Swiss people' one also finds the phrase 'Swiss nation'. (Weber, 1948: 172)

But in this Swiss 'nation', the principle of organisation is territorial and each linguistic group has sought the congruence of the political and the culturo-linguistic at cantonal level (Camartin, 1985). The boundaries between linguistic groups are well-delineated and there is little movement of individuals across them.[10] The equality of the three official languages is only held in place by a rigorous adherence to the principle of territoriality and has a tendency to break down when communication is needed between the linguistic groups, for example, at the level of state institutions, where the weight of German both in terms of number of speakers and economic power is felt keenly. In a study, dating from the early 1980s, Camartin noted:

> la tendance rampante à l'unilinguisme dans les documents de travail du Parlement ou de l'administration et les doutes quant à une représentation équitable des fonctionnaires de langue maternelle française et italienne dans les cadres de l'administration fédérale. (Camartin, 1985: 270)

An official report later that decade recognised that:

> La tendance à une utilisation accrue de l'allemand au dépens des langues latines est cependant indéniable. (Département fédéral de l'intérieur suisse, 1989: 96)

So it does not appear that the Swiss have actually solved the problem of achieving equal linguistic rights and unfettered communication within a multilingual state. On the one hand there are clear centrifugal forces, with the three main language groups maintaining greater contact with their fellow speakers in adjacent states than they do across the linguistic frontiers within the country.[11] On the other hand, there is a creeping domination of German in all business carried out at federal/state level. One can argue that many Swiss continue to perceive themselves to be part of the Swiss nation, which is testimony to the weight of common history and the shared ideal which founded their state. It is more difficult to argue that they provide a model for the organisation of a multilingual polity, since their solution has once again been traditional cultural-linguistic/territorial congruence.

Conclusion

Looking at the evidence so far one could say that, far from being a negligible factor, one of the basic organising principles of nationalism is language. Language has been important in two distinct ways: as a means of mobilising a proto-national group, the 'ancestral' language, differentiated from adjacent idioms and elevated to the status of defender and carrier of the authenticity of the group, has been a powerful mobilising agent; as a means of ensuring a community of communication it is a prime requirement of all nationalist projects – whether it predates or post-dates other stages in the process. As a differentiating symbol, a national language can simply remain iconic. Citizens do not necessarily need to master it, as is the case of Irish in Ireland. As a tool of communication it has become central to the way the state functions. Citizens do need to master it, or be excluded from much civic life. In most western European states, linguistic cohesion has largely been achieved, either with or without individual bilingualism, albeit with different methods, with different degrees of coercion and, ultimately, with different degrees of success.

This project of constructing nation states has resided on the belief that people are not trapped within their language and has demanded of many people that they move linguistic group (on the French model) in order to become members of the fictional nation of their nation state. However, underneath the apparent public linguistic unity of the European nation states thus achieved, languages which had been eclipsed in the public domain continued to be employed and have been recently resurfacing. Speakers of 'minority' languages have been demanding recognition of their difference against a background of the fracturing of some former states into smaller entities and the growth of autonomous regional power in others.

At the same time, in a continent where transnational corporations increase in number and power, where the technologies for information exchange are developing rapidly, where a supra-state appears to be evolving, there is also growing pressure to communicate across national boundaries, to be part of a larger community of communication than the national. Under these twin pressures, national language, like the nation state, may prove to be less secure than in the recent past, and this is what we shall now examine.

Notes

1. In *Marxism and the National Question*, Stalin attempted to define the criteria for nationhood. A common language, a common territory, a single economy and a common character were the four essentials.
2. He was writing in the early 1980s.
3. At a different point in his argument Gellner recognises that 'diverse Slavonic, Teutonic and Romance languages are in fact no further apart than are the mere dialects within what are elsewhere seen as unitary languages' (Gellner, 1983: 44).
4. Norwegian has two written standards both of which are recognised as official languages in Norway: Bokmål (Book Language) and Nynorsk (New Norwegian).

5. There are no language censuses at state level in France. These data come from small scale studies.
6. Welsh was the language of the Strathclyde Britons; Gaelic was brought by Celtic settlers from Ireland; Inglis derives from the Anglian speech of the invaders of south-east Scotland; Norn from the Norse of Nordic settlement in the far north. Welsh was replaced and Gaelic displaced by Lallans. Norn died out in the eighteenth century although the English variety spoken in the north retains many features of it (MacKinnon, 1991). The mother tongue of the vast majority of Scots is now English, established there both by decree and by the English-medium education system. Out of more than five million Scots counted in the 1981 and 1991 censuses about 80,000 (under 2% of the population) claimed to have some knowledge of Gaelic, and such figures, relying on self-reporting, will probably tend to be slightly high. Lallans remains, but as a spoken language; literacy is overwhelmingly in English. There is a very small literary output in Lallans.
7. In some circumstances there may be coercion in the private sphere as well. Catalan was forbidden in all domains and functions during the Franco regime (Strubell, 1998).
8. The German-speaking area is very small and comes under the jurisdiction of the French-speaking authorities in some matters.
9. Furthermore, in the few areas where the national government is active, the European Union also has growing power and competes with the state.
10. Attested by language censuses which report stable proportions of mother tongue French and German speakers in French and German cantons. Italian and Romansch show greater tendency to shift (1970 and 1980 language censuses reported in Dessemontet, 1984).
11. This is true in the case of cross border employment (cf. Infobest, 1997 published by communauté des Chambres de Commerce et d'Industrie du Rhin Supérieur (CCI de Colmar et du Centre-Alsace, du Sud Alsace Mulhouse, Aargauische Industrie – und Handelskammer, Handelskammer beider Basel, IHK Hochrhein-Bodensee Konstanz/Schopfheim, IHK Südlicher Oberrhein)) and of audiences for television and radio (Département fédéral de l'intérieur suisse, 1989).

Chapter 4

The weakening of the concept of sovereignty. Globalisation and internationalisation in the legal, political, economic and cultural domains. The growing role of English as the medium of these phenomena

In this chapter I want to examine the progressive globalisation of human affairs in the second half of the twentieth century. It would be foolish, given the events of the last decade, to claim that nationalism and the nation state are set to disappear. Nonetheless, growing political internationalism, an increasing acceptance of intervention in the internal affairs of the state, economic globalisation, continuous technological advance and a popular perception of cultural convergence have denationalised many aspects of national life. The long term effects of this are hard to predict. Significant social change is difficult to analyse from a contemporary perspective, but we may be sure that it will be complex rather than unidirectional.[1]

However, the concept of sovereignty does seem to be losing ground in the legal, ideological, political, defence, economic and cultural domains, as I hope to demonstrate. And if this is the case, power must be relocating elsewhere. One view is that power is leaking both up and down from the state to reconceive the political community in more pluralistic terms. There has been some discussion (Bull, 1977; McGrew, 1992; Held, 1995; Schlesinger, 1992; Wallace, 1990) of the emergence of a new political order, one which would permit overlapping authority structures, similar to practices accepted before the birth of the nation state. Bull imagines this 'new mediaevalism' might emerge:

> (I)f modern states were to come to share their authority over their citizens, and their ability to command their loyalties, on the one hand with regional and world authorities, and on the other with sub-state or sub-national authorities, to such an extent that the concept of sovereignty ceased to be applicable. (Bull, 1977: 254–5)

79

My focus is once again the role that language plays in the construction of these political and social structures and the tendency for this role to be neglected or obscured. In parallel with the relocating of certain aspects of power at the supranational and subnational levels, two new developments in language policy and language use are discernible. Firstly, there is a general belief that English is both the vector and the beneficiary of globalising tendencies. Although this conviction is largely impressionistic and without much rigorous scientific proof, the anecdotal evidence is so consistent and in such volume that it does build to a convincing case. Secondly, there is a renaissance of some of the languages, such as Catalan, Welsh and Corsican, that were eclipsed in the period of high nationalism. Languages which were thought to be disappearing are now resurfacing to play a role in the public domain, even if this role is somewhat circumscribed. In this chapter, I intend to concentrate on one aspect of this process: the relocation of power to the supranational level and globalisation. Limiting myself once again to the European context, I will attempt to evaluate how the phenomenon of globalisation is affecting language use and to assess how language both limits and aids the process.

The Weakening of the Concept of Sovereignty

If the concept of the sovereign nation state has lost some of its appeal,[2] this is perhaps because in the European context it proved a very dangerous form of political organisation. As nationalism drew together the nation within the boundaries of the state, it also fractured the continent. Nations, it seemed, could be easily persuaded that the state was worth dying for. By the mid-twentieth century, Europeans had experienced two wars which though labelled 'World' had their genesis rooted firmly in European rivalries and much of their ferocity linked intimately to European nationalism. In 1945 as the barbaric realities of the Second World War started to become public knowledge, the European nations had to come to terms with the moral bankruptcy into which nationalism had once again led them. This was ultimately true for the victors as well as the vanquished. The populations which had supported the Axis powers were brought face to face with the outcomes of the extreme nationalism of fascism, as the true extent of the persecution of non-Aryan and dissenting groups was revealed; the Allies, even though they occupied the moral high ground through having vanquished the Fascists, still had to reconcile their victory with the horrors of the methods they had inflicted on the civilians as well as the armies of the enemy nations. The total destruction of cities by firebombing and the atom bomb corrupted the relief of victory for many.

This climate of repugnance for the crimes of the war led to the International Tribunal at Nuremberg[3] which held individuals to account before a supra-national court for crimes against *humanity*.[4] The legal framework at Nuremberg marked a highly significant change in the legal direction of the modern state in that it

> laid down, for the first time in history, that when *international rules* that protect basic humanitarian values are in conflict with *state* laws, every individual must transgress the state laws. (Held, 1995: 101)

This new philosophy challenged the principle of military discipline and attacked national sovereignty at one of its key points, the absolute right of the state to command total obedience in what it conceives as the national interest.

International law has continued to affirm the primacy of basic human rights over the sovereignty of the state and to recognise that the rights and duties granted by citizenship can sometimes be superseded by the liberties and obligations of international law in a number of subsequent developments. The UN adopted the International Bill of Human Rights in 1948. In Europe, the European Convention for the Protection of Human Rights and Fundamental Freedoms (1950) provided for the collective enforcement of these principles. In practice this has come to mean, *inter alia*, that citizens may decline to serve in the army of their state and that they may challenge their governments in the European Court of Human Rights, if they are unable to right miscarriages of justice in any other way. The 1992 declaration of the Helsinki Conference on Security and Co-operation in Europe reaffirmed this principle, recognising that:

> (human rights) are matters of direct and legitimate concern to all participating States and do not belong exclusively to the internal affairs of the State concerned. (CSCE, 1992: 2)

David Held summarises the position in the mid 1990s in the following way:

> International law has recognised powers and constraints, and rights and duties, which transcend the claims of nation states[5] and which, while they may not be backed by institutions with coercive powers of enforcement, nonetheless have far-reaching consequences. (Held, 1995: 2)

By the end of the century these institutions appeared to be acquiring means of enforcing resolutions. The phrase 'will of the international community' was used increasingly as a rationale for imposing sanctions on governments who did not respect a basic level of human rights. States started to designate troops for use in international missions.[6] Commentators noted that the mighty still tended to impose order on the less powerful but not necessarily obey the rules themselves.[7] Nonetheless, despite these reservations, in the conflict between recognition of human rights and respect for sovereignty the world appeared to be moving towards agreeing on the primacy of the former.

This attack on the absolute sovereignty of the state has been strengthened by the late twentieth century tendency to bracket legitimacy and the nature of the political power of the state. The European Convention on Human Rights explicitly links legitimacy with democracy; the Council of Europe and the European Union make democracy a condition of membership; the Helsinki Agreement called for the 'strengthening of democratic institutions' (CSCE, 1992: 2). These legal changes bear witness to a widespread desire to bridle the power of the individual state. They may be bringing about a certain weakening of nation-based identities, in that, in certain extreme conditions, the nation state is no longer the ultimate arbiter of the fate of the individual (Boutros-Ghali, 1996).

The latest institution, the UN International Criminal Court created in July 1998,[8] is able to try crimes of genocide and aggression, war crimes and crimes against humanity and takes the process even further. It formalises and extends the ad hoc tribunals set up by the UN to try those accused of war crimes in the Former Yugoslavia and in Rwanda. The International Criminal Court will not need to wait for Tribunals to be set up and the UN should then avoid the accusation that the international community has been selective in singling out certain crimes for Tribunals, while ignoring others.

The International War Crimes Tribunal for the Former Yugoslavia has already convicted a number of Croats, Serbs and Muslims of war crimes in Bosnia-Herzegovina, although the leaders most responsible, such as Radovan Karadzic, have so far evaded capture. In May 1998, the Tribunal's chief prosecutor called for the indictment of the Serbian president, Slobodan Milosevic, and four other leading Serbian for 'crimes against humanity and violations of the laws and customs of war'. She accused the five of individual responsibility for murder, mass deportations of 740,000 Kosovan Albanians and persecution on political, racial and religious grounds. The court instructed all UN countries to seize the men if they attempted to go abroad and to freeze their assets.

Further international courts may also be set up to deal with lesser crimes in a supranational way. Certain politicians[9] have interpreted the Amsterdam Treaty as a call for a federal court to deal with crimes which cross borders, such as drug trafficking, illegal immigration, terrorism and custody of children. Were this to become reality, it would greatly extend the scope of the European judicial space which is at the moment linked closely to the observation of EU directives and regulations.

Another example of the challenge to sovereignty and the inviolability of political leaders came from the UK. The House of Lords' decision to allow the extradition of General Pinochet to Spain to answer accusations of war crimes committed by his subordinates during his presidency of Chile represents a significant advance in the acceptance of the idea that there is an international law over and above the national. The Lords judged that the 1984 Torture Convention, adopted in British Law under the 1988 Criminal Justice Act, overrode any plea that a head of state should be immune from prosecution.

There is, as yet, no real consistency in those pursued by international justice and those who avoid the legal process. As ever, there are political dimensions: influence keeps powerful groups such as the Chinese and the Americans above the law; political expediency permits others, such as Laurent Kabila and Khieu Samphan, to retain immunity. However, Boutros-Ghali, interviewed in 1999, said that he believed the sovereignty principle to be generally on the wane:

> La communauté internationale a accepté des limitations de sou- veraineté très importante sur le plan économique, mais les Etats continuent de s'accrocher à certains attributs de la souveraineté, notamment ceux qui concernent la justice. Le mouvement d'opinion, cependant, est lancé. Et je pense que la mondialisation politique et économique va s'accompagner d'un mouvement similaire de mondial- isation de la justice (Boutros-Ghali, 1999).

Language in International Courts

The new supranational courts guarantee equal treatment and ensure greater human rights regardless of the litigants' country of origin and are, in this sense, an agent for equality between peoples and an advance in human affairs. However, because of the language and cultural knowledge needed to exploit them fully, some people may have easier access to international justice than others. We are not all equal before international law. Most litigants are bound to be distanced from the court proceedings by inevitable language barriers. This level of legal court provokes a situation reminiscent of earlier times in Europe. In the pre-nationalist era, a defendant would not necessarily have understand the language of the court, which would have been either Latin or the language of the ruling class or group.[10] In contrast, appellants or defendants before a court of a nation state usually have some knowledge of the language of the law because it will be the national language and they will have passed through the national education system which uses that language. Today, the supranational courts return us to a situation where a common language for all the actors involved is as unlikely as in the pre-nationalist era. This causes a gulf between the individual and the law and a lack of unambiguous and reliable channels of communication for speakers of different languages who may find themselves forced to cooperate or challenge across linguistic divides.

In the various higher courts of Europe, the plurilingual situation is managed in different ways. The European Court of Justice, located in Luxembourg, ensures the respect of European Community law. The procedural language is chosen from among the eleven official languages of the European Union.[11] In the case of direct appeal the language is chosen by the appellant; in the case of interpretation or contravention of EU law by member states, the language will be the language of the member state:

> (B)ut in practice this language is very often supplemented by the so-called working language of the court. This is the language that the judges use for their internal communication, for the reports of the proceedings, for questions in the session, for the final argument. From the very beginning of the European Court of Justice it was the French language that was usually adopted by the judges as the common medium of deliberation. (Koch, 1991: 155–6)

There are fifteen judges, one from each of the member countries. Their method of working is collegial and they may, in important cases, come together in a plenary session. Despite the EU's commitment to equal rights for all the official languages of the member states, it was perhaps inevitable that such a situation together with the requirement of the law for continuity and ease of reference would produce one major working language.

The European Court of Human Rights was set up under the aegis of the Council of Europe to guarantee basic human rights in Europe. The official languages of the ECHR are French and English, which is the rule throughout the institutions of the Council of Europe. All official documentation is produced in both languages and both versions are equally authentic. The members of the ECHR are elected by the delegates to the Council of Europe; the applicants' competence in French and English is an important factor in their candidacy.[12] Within the legal procedures framed in French and English, appellants and defendants have the right to use their own language and to be provided with interpretation and translations of documents.

The United Nations Courts have different regimes. The International Court of Justice in the Hague has two official languages: French and

English. The new International Criminal Court has provision for the judges to decide the language of the trial in each instance. There is as yet no custom and practice to examine. The experience from the International War Crimes Tribunal for the Former Yugoslavia was that English was used extensively both within the proceedings, in documents provided to the court and in briefings with the media and that defendants spoke a variety of Balkan languages which were translated.

So the practice of the supranational European courts dedicated to the protection of the rights of the individual is plurilingual, in that the litigants and defendants may use their national language and have the proceedings in the court interpreted for them. However, the languages of the underlying process, the languages of deliberation and record, are English and French. This has the advantage of allowing for continuity in the legal process and reduces the ambiguities that are a feature of constantly translated texts. However, we must recognise that the adoption of official languages for international courts doubly distances the ordinary citizen from the process. A defendant or a litigant with poor command of English and French is in the hands of the interpreter as well as the lawyer. Moreover, the role of English and French in international law gives advantage to the speakers of these languages as much as it disadvantages the non-speakers. English and French speakers experience one less hurdle in their access to power and influence: as users of the legal process they have easier access to information and can make their case more fluently; as professionals they are advantaged by being able to work in their first language.

Political Internationalism

The catastrophe of the Second World War with its 'episodes of carnage without parallel' (Hobsbawm, 1995: 52) caused many Europeans, even in the midst of the hostilities, to be psychologically receptive to the concept of political as well as legal internationalism and provoked a profound desire for future pan-European cooperation and a new European order to make war on the continent impossible. A number of the Resistance leaders and activists who contributed to the founding of the Union européenne des Fédéralistes in 1946,[13] had started to develop ideas about European federalism before the end of hostilities. Winston Churchill made two influential speeches calling for European Union (21 March 1943 and 19 September 1946), although, in his interpretation, Europe did not include the UK.

At the global level, the two decades following the war saw the founding of a number of different institutions with the primary aim of locking states into forms of co-operation which would prevent recourse to war as a first solution to dissension. The prognosis was, however, not good, with the failure of the League of Nations in the 1920s and 1930s throwing a shadow. Good intentions were clearly not enough; structures had to be such that states could not flout the international organisation when it suited them to do so. Then, too, the division of the world into the communist bloc and western capitalism meant that in the medium term at least there would be two internationalisms and that these would confront each other. The United Nations, set up in 1945 with the principal aim of preserving world peace through diplomatic means, spanned both the western and communist worlds, but in its early years was crippled by the cleavage between these two blocs. Other agencies – the GATT, the IMF, and the IBRD (World Bank) – focused on economic co-operation for similar ends but were restricted to the western capitalist world.

The move to regional co-operation in late 1940s Europe was also prompted by the extent of the destruction that continent had experienced: the areas which had been battle fields were in ruins, those spared actual fighting suffered from the breakdown of political, civil and economic networks. The necessity was to restore agriculture, rebuild homes, the infrastructure and the industrial base, and the need was on such a grand scale that it meant that many European states could only do this if they could have access to external sources of funding. A substantial part of this was provided by the US in the form of Marshall aid, which constituted enormous financial input into Europe and which the government of the US was unhappy to see diluted by competing national plans. The Americans demanded that the Europeans co-ordinate the administration and deployment of aid and in 1948 the Organisation for European Economic Co-operation[14] was set up to comply with this and to discourage a return to the old nationalist trade solutions to economic crises: protectionism through tariffs and quotas.

This outside pressure was in accord with the continuing strength of support for regional co-operation within the continent in the post-war years, fuelled now by capitalist-communist divisions as well as more traditional fears. There were two tendencies in Western Europe – pragmatists and minimalists on the one hand, ideologues and integrationists on the other. Both sought a political formula that would guarantee no more fratricidal European wars. The integrationists believed that this could only be done through new political structures, since treaties are too easily broken when the ambition of states decides such action to be in their interest. Jean Monnet, a leading member of the French integrationists, envisaged that it would be necessary to build a single political entity, a United States of Europe because:

La coopération entre les nations, si imposante soit-elle, ne résout rien. Ce qu'il faut chercher, c'est une fusion des intérêts des peuples européens, et non pas simplement le maintien des équilibres de ces intérêts. (Monnet, 1955)

France was central to the integrationist group. The experience of three devastating wars which had found France and Germany facing each other as enemies within the space of a century made France desire the containment of her powerful neighbour. Locked into close political and economic union, Germany would no longer pose a threat. Supporters of this vision of Europe called for the creation of federal political structures and a European customs union.

The minimalists exhibited a preference for a milder form of collaboration, with organisations which operated on the principle of intergovernmental collaboration. The most enthusiastic proponents of such arrangements were the UK and the Nordic Countries. This group principally wanted defence co-operation, partially to guard against renewed intra-European hostilities, but also as a response to the global divisions of the Cold War era. Western Europe was to be part of the western bloc. The members of the group were also prepared to collaborate to safeguard human rights. Economic and political union, however, were not on the agenda.

Both these tendencies found concrete and lasting expression – in the European Union, in the Council of Europe and in NATO, all of which have contributed, in different ways and to different degrees, to internationalism on a regional scale. Inevitably they also led to a weakening of the autonomy of the individual European states, to a mutation of identities and to closer contact and co-operation of citizens at a micro-level, with all that implies for language contact and language shift. In the event the language effect in each inter/supra-national organisation was to be different.

NATO employed English and French for its founding treaties and protocols,[15] but, dominated by the United States, has always used English as its working language. Although the principal officials of the NATO international staff and the presidents and chairmen of the Military Committee have come from all the participating nations, the top echelons of military command[16] have always been American, a policy which has meant anglophone dominance in the command structure. The UK was the other country which provided major NATO commanders (Allied Commanders-in-Chief Channel) and so added to the anglophone effect. France's withdrawal of French forces from the integrated military structure during the period 1966–1996,[17] reduced francophone influence and further intensified the dominance of English. When the French returned they had lost the influence necessary to tip the linguistic balance. Finally, the acceptance of English as the language of the committees and the language of manoeuvres has been reinforced by the recent enlargement of NATO.[18] The former Warsaw pact countries have not negotiated from a position of strength and have not questioned the practice of English as a working language.[19]

The Council of Europe was set up in 1949 to foster a modest programme of cultural and educational exchange among the peoples of Europe, to promote democratic government and civil liberties within their states, and to encourage their governments to consult and cooperate. The Council began with ten members, and has now grown to thirty-nine members.[20] French and English are the official languages used for deliberation and record within the Council's institutions. Because Strasbourg has been the host for these institutions (European Court of Human Rights, Council of Europe Parliamentary Assembly), the language in the offices and of the services has tended to be French. Among the delegates to the Assembly and the jurists of the court, however, the tendency is towards English. This has been particularly true since the Council's expansion into Central and Eastern Europe. After the crumbling of the USSR and the Warsaw Pact, the countries of Central and Eastern Europe suppressed Russian as the first foreign language. Its replacement was usually English, perhaps German, rarely French (Radnai, 1994).

The European Union has always been committed to plurilingualism, with all the official languages of the member states used as working languages. The question of language in this polity is one of its most knotty problems and interesting challenges and one to which I will explore in greater detail in Chapter 7. At the moment it is perhaps enough to note the curiosity that, whereas the *intergovernmental* Council of Europe has adopted French and English in order to have official *lingua francas*, the European Union, which is in some respects a *supranational* organisation makes no provision for any common medium.

Global Policing

The changes in the legal principle of sovereignty and the inviolability of state borders were bound to provide the climate for a growing acceptance of what the French term 'droit d'ingérence', the right to intervene in the internal affairs of a sovereign state if the circumstances appear to warrant such intervention. This growth can be demonstrated by the increasing number of UN 'peacekeeping missions' in the period 1948–1995. There were eighteen separate operations in the period up to 1990, six of which were still unresolved in 1990. From the end of the Cold War there were thirty-one UN missions in all.[21] In the last five years the UN has increasingly provided peacekeeping forces. And if we add in the Allied Coalition against Iraq, the Unified Task force in Somalia and NATO action in Kosovo which were under US[22] rather than UN command, the increase in *ingérence* during the 1990s was substantial.

NATO's intervention in Kosovo in the period March–June 1999 is the most clear example to date of the new position. The intervention was presented both by NATO and by many Western commentators as a humanitarian action, to secure the rule of law and respect for human rights within Kosovo. The word 'war' was deliberately avoided (Grundmann *et al.*, forthcoming). The action took place within the frontiers of a sovereign state and the international forces intervened to protect the citizens of a province of that state from actions by its government. The Westphalian order and the idea that international law concerns states alone and cannot be implemented without their consent appear to have become history. A new source of legitimacy stems from the amorphous 'will of the international community'. The consent of states is no longer an absolute requirement and the 'droit d'ingérence' seems strongly rooted.

This trend has two implications for the linguistic argument. The first is that the acceptance of *ingérence* stems from and leads to a further weakening of boundaries around the sovereign nation state. Secondly, increasing use of international forces as either peacekeepers or enforcers of resolutions means that once again it becomes necessary to find a common medium of expression. The linguistic outcome has been, as before, an increased use of English. This was foreseeable because of the military dominance of the US and its central role in many of the missions. However, there is growing evidence of the role of English as a *lingua franca* even where American influence is minimal.

UNPROFOR, the UN Protection Force deployed in ex-Yugoslavia between March 1992 and December 1995,[23] provides a good example of this. At that date it was the largest peacekeeping operation in the history of the UN. Numbers of troops varied from month to month due to rotation, but the composition of the force at 30 November 1994 was typical. Thirty-seven countries were providing troops. Of these, Bangla Desh, Belgium, Canada, Denmark, France, Jordan, Malaysia, Netherlands, Pakistan, Poland, Russian Federation, Spain, Sweden, Turkey, Ukraine and UK each had forces of over 1000 military personnel in the field. There were no US troops. The UNPROFOR commander was French and the three subordinate commanders in Croatia, Bosnia-Herzegovina and Macedonia were Jordanian, British and Norwegian. This nationally and linguistically heterogeneous force reported difficulties in the standardisation of weaponry and munitions, in the interoperability of procedures, systems and customs (Eide & Solli, 1996). However, the language barriers between sections of the Force which might have featured in the list do not seem to have been experienced as immensely problematic. The practice of using English at the highest echelons of command is well established with even those groups most usually opposed to English hegemony (e.g. the French[24]) sometimes employing English as a *lingua franca* in the military and technical domain. It is reported that French was also used as a language of command, but mainly between francophone groups; it played a lesser role as a *lingua franca*. The general impression on language use in this UN mission is that, although the necessity for interpreters and translators remained strong, there was a reasonable competence and preparedness to use English throughout the command structure. The reported use of English as a medium of communication between Ukrainians and Bangla Deshis would appear to support the thesis that it has achieved the non-official status of *lingua franca*.[25]

It would not be surprising that the troops in the KFOR brigades in Kosovo report that in this international force too, English plays the role of *lingua franca*. The fact that this force was at first commanded by an English speaker, Lieutenant General Sir Mike Jackson, could only strengthen the probability.

A single *lingua franca* is not the actual policy of the UN, which has **six** official and working languages: Arabic, Chinese, English, French, Russian and Spanish. However, the primacy of English within the organisation has been evident for some time. A graphic illustration of the true hierarchy of languages in the organisation was provided by Kurt Waldheim's message from the UN to be carried by the 1977 Voyager expedition into outer space. The Secretary-General's message to other galaxies was in English – and only in English!

The Single Capitalist World Economy

A number of authorities see political and legal internationalism and the globalisation of the capitalist system as intimately linked, maintaining that the success of the global capitalist system resides in the hegemony of the United States and that the globalising process is only possible because of the relative security provided by the *Pax Americana* and the international security agencies it dominates (Gilpin, 1986; Kennedy, 1993[26]).

Many scholars[27] in the field of globalisation would see the ultimate success of capitalism in establishing itself as the dominant philosophy as one of the causes, perhaps the major cause, of globalisation:

> The entire globe is operating within the framework of this singular division of labour we are calling the capitalist world economy. (Wallerstein, 1984: 18)

Capitalism had its origins in sixteenth century Europe, growing in importance to play a central role in the formation of nation states and in the phenomenon of colonialism. For a period the competing ideology of marxist socialism presented a serious challenge and a number of theorists predicted the crisis of capitalism and its demise. However, it was to be communism which suffered the crisis and capitalism which proved triumphant. These events have caused the transformation of many aspects of society within a very short time. In the last two decades of the twentieth century, the theories of Gramsci, Lukács and Althusser etc. have been eclipsed and those of J.S. Mill, Talcott Parsons and T.H. Marshall etc. reinstated. The revival of liberalism and the decline of state intervention, occurring first in the US and the UK, have spread across Europe, evident in the neo-liberal policies of the EU and the conversion of the former command economies (Sassen, 1995). Capitalism in its postmarxist, neoliberal form[28] has become the dominant economic system of the world.

In the single capitalist world economy of the end of the twentieth century the power of the nation state has necessarily dwindled:

> The major dynamics at work in the global economy carry the capacity to undo the particular form of the intersection of sovereignty and territory embedded in the modern state and the modern state system. (Sassen, 1995: 5)

Sassen argues that there is a new geography of power which stems from developments in three areas. Firstly, production, trade and finance are organised to a large extent by global financial markets and transnational corporations which ignore state frontiers. The deregulated global financial markets make it possible for money to flow across most state boundaries, and the new technologies make this flow instantaneous. The sums involved in these capital movements are so enormous that the global capital market has the power to constrain the policies of governments, or discipline those who go against the market. Transnational corporations site production wherever the cost of labour and local financial incentives make it most profitable. For example, 50% of the work force of Ford, GM, IBM and Exxon are based outside the US (Sassen, 1994). The 'offshoring' of production has also spread to other domains; now services such as telephone enquiries, clerical work and database processing are also geographically dispersed, placed where it is most cost-effective to do so. The choice of location depends on the 'good behaviour' of states and national work forces. If there are significant tax or wage demands, or restrictions through state legislation, the transnationals simply relocate to other states prepared to organise free trade zones or tax regimes more beneficial to the corporation. There have even been reports that multinationals have pressurised the UK government to join the Euro, because it suits their purposes.[29] Thus, because of the volatile reactive nature of the financial markets with their single aim of maintaining profits and because of the state's need to attract capital investment, governments have reduced control over their economies. Decisions are located at the transnational as opposed to the national level, the social relations of production are no longer confined to national territory and the whole process becomes detached from national interest with international investors' requirements paramount.[30]

In terms of language, TNCs and global financial markets have promoted English as *the* language and *lingua franca* of international capitalism (Pennycook, 1994). This is inevitable where the US dominates. It is more surprising in networks where other countries are increasingly influential, as, for example, the Pacific Rim. Language use is a notoriously difficult thing to quantify and perhaps the surest way of monitoring the position of English in the Pacific Rim economies is to note the time allotted to English language courses and the weight given to English language qualifications in the economic and business courses of their education systems and to note the language skills required of those seeking employment in international business and finance. An examination of business school course descriptions and job advertisements in these countries points to the continuing role of English in the global world economy (Rahman, 1990; Martin, 1990; Nyland, 1990).

The second element which Sassen identifies in the new geography of power is the new legal regime. In the deregulated market, the governance of activities has moved in two new directions: to the international or supranational domain and to the private sector. Firstly, a number of international regimes and global and regional institutions have grown up. The Group of Seven leading capitalist states (G7)[31] is the most powerful forum for global economic regulation (Lewis, 1991). The International Monetary Fund (IMF) and the World Bank ensure continuing funds for world trade and development, and thus for continuing consumption. Regional organisations such as the European Union, NAFTA, ASEAN etc. oversee the establishment of free market conditions in their respective spheres of influence. Secondly, the private sector has become immensely powerful, providing the international commercial arbitration, which is now the main method for resolving transnational commercial disputes, and the credit rating agencies, which are now the gatekeepers for investment funds sought by corporations and government. Sassen sees the new legal regimes as both privatising and denationalising:

> The current relocation of authority has transformed the capacities of governments and can be thought of as an instance of Rosenau's 'governance without government' . . . Some of the old divisions between the national and the global are becoming weaker and, to some extent, have been neutralised. The new transnational regimes could, in principle, have assumed various forms and contents; but, in fact, they are assuming a specific form, one wherein . . . the highly developed countries play a strategic geopolitical role. (Sassen, 1995: 17)

In this process it is clear that Americanisation is also taking place. The highly developed countries who are playing this 'strategic role' in the legal domain are the US and to a lesser degree the UK. The law firms which are most active in conflict resolution are Anglo-American and it is their practices which are being diffused throughout the world (Dezalay & Garth, 1995). The two agencies, Moody's Investors Service and Standard and Poor's Ratings Group, which dominate the global credit rating system are both American. Americanisation of international business law brought about through the growth of the US dominated private sector and reinforced by the international organisations (GATT/WTO, IBRD and IMF etc.), in which American methods and philosophies are seen to prevail has caused the situation in which:

> American business law has become a kind of global *jus commune* incorporated explicitly or implicitly into transnational contracts and beginning to be incorporated into the case law and even the statutes of many other nations. (Shapiro, 1993 quoted in Sassen, 1995: 20)

It would be unlikely that this Americanisation did not also imply an increase in English language use.

Sassen's third component in the new geography of power is the growing importance of electronic space. The new industries of information technology, telecommunications and the audio-visual media ensure a flow of knowledge on a scale undreamed of in earlier epochs. A number of technologies and structures unified the world banking and investment systems. From SWIFT (standardised world interbank and financial transactions) set up in 1973 to real time stock exchange dealing on the Internet, introduced in the 1990s, the financial world has become progressively more integrated. Some commentators (Rosenau, 1980, 1989, 1990; Holsti, 1985) see this as the real instigator of globalisation, allowing information and economic control, and therefore power, to spread from the territorially bounded nation state to a multi-centred world of transnational networks.

The technological communications revolution was both an instigator and the outcome of what has been called the postindustrial society (Bell, 1973). A characteristic of advanced economic systems is their capacity to access information and apply knowledge. Studies of both the US and the USSR show:

> the greater the complexity and productivity of an economy, the greater its informational component and the greater the role played by new knowledge and new applications of knowledge (as compared with the mere addition of such production factors as capital or labor) in the growth of productivity. (Castells, 1993: 16–17)

This has led to a shift in all the advanced capitalist economies from material production to information gathering and processing, both in terms of the proportion of GNP this represents as well as in the percentage of workers engaged in these activities. The quality of information and the skill in acquiring and processing it are now key elements in the economic success of companies and countries. Achieving access to information and doing something useful with it depend essentially on the development of two areas: the revolution in telecommunications and information technology to create the material infrastructure; a highly skilled and educated work force to acquire and process information.

Both these areas have implications for language use. Firstly, the costs of the new technologies are so immense that R&D is very often carried out by consortia, working in transnational teams. The language of cooperation is usually English because of the growing tendency towards English use in the scientific community. Secondly, the exchange and processing of information on the networks depends on the language skills of those encoding and decoding the information. Obviously, these processes must take place in a language of which the users have some knowledge. Traditionally it has been English which dominates the information flows and the interactions. Again this is difficult to quantify because of the variety of channels for information flow and the size and complexity of those flows, but there are discernible trends. Taking the Internet as an example, it is notable that international pressure, political or interest groups wanting to disseminate their point of view are forced to publish in English to gain the widest readership possible[32]; the most powerful search machines use English and English language data bases; the recorded visits to comparable sites (e.g. the news agencies AFP, Reuters, AP) is higher for anglophone than for francophone.[33]

Sassen might also have added a fourth element to the new geography of power. The global nature of many problems (e.g. crime, health, the environment, population growth, poverty etc.) has led to a growth of transnational non-governmental organisations. Transnational NGOs are not new; the World Alliance of Young Men's Christian Associations was founded in 1863, the International Veterinary Congress in 1863. Their number, their importance, their role have, however, mushroomed in the 1990s.[34] Held *et al.* (1999) estimate that in 1996 there were 5472 international NGOs, with new organisations being constantly created. Boutros-Ghali (1996) recognises the important role they now play as a basic form of popular participation and their ability to mobilise the international community to work alongside or in place of national governments to find transnational solutions to global threats.

The growth of NGOs provokes more transnational structures, more international cooperation and consequently more dialogue and contact between speakers from different language backgrounds, with all that implies for language conflict, shift and use. Once again, precise and reliable data on current language practices in this domain are immensely difficult to acquire. However, the impression from small scale research projects is that here too use of English is well-established and increasing.[35]

In summary and in response to the earlier question on whether there has been a relocation of power, we could say that the increasingly transnational structures of the political and economic world – supra-national legal courts, transnational companies, international capital, global communications, transnational pressure groups and networks – mean that the nation states exercise exclusive authority in an increasingly limited number of areas and that there are, *de facto*, two seats of power in the modern world. Of course the two worlds interact continuously: the sovereign states legislate for the transnational world, most typically in association with other nation states; the two worlds exchange information and co-ordinate actions.

Moreover, there are not simply more formal agreements, more structures, more institutions and more conferences to allow this exchange and coordination, there is also constant informal contact between individuals within those structures and institutions, made possible by the new technologies. McGrew argues that this intricate web of interactions together with all the other moves towards transnational relations and structures is leading us towards 'a kind of hyper-pluralist 'transnational identity' (McGrew, 1992: 80).

But all the evidence suggests that this is no hyper-pluralism in language.

English is the language of this global economy, not just in exchanges where one of the partners is English-speaking but also where there is no clear link to the historically English-speaking world. This should not surprise us. There is widespread agreement that 'the spread of English went parallel with the spread of the culture of international business and technological standardization' (Ndebele, 1987: 4). Phillipson (1992) and Phillipson & Skuttnab-Kangas (1994) conclude that this is not just a natural development and that the encouragement of English acquisition and use has been long-standing British and American government policy in the protection and promotion of business interests.[36]

The Globalisation of Culture

Both multinational capitalism and the new technologies play a powerful role in the globalisation of culture. The new forms of accessing information and exchanging opinion allow the circulation of image, sound and word to happen with an immediacy and in quantities not possible in the past. Baudrillard has termed the current situation 'this obscene delirium of communication' (Baudrillard, 1985: 132). Cultural products can cross physical space with ease and at a relatively low cost to the consumer. Perhaps before continuing I should define what I mean by culture, since the word is polysemic in English, and the meanings diverge still further when we examine all the languages which possess the term. In the present context I use culture in a very limited sense to mean tangible creations, mostly produced for our 'passive-entertainment', 'news-receptive' society,[37] which can be clearly traced as they cross frontiers. Their availability and volume make the individual open to innumerable and ever-changing influences. Baudrillard uses the image of the schizophrenic to describe this

> absolute proximity, the total instantaneity of things, the feeling of no defense, no retreat. It is the end of interiority and intimacy, the overexposure and transparence of the world which traverses him without obstacle. He can no longer produce the limits of his own being, can no longer play nor stage himself, can no longer produce himself as mirror. He is now only a pure screen, a switching center for all the networks of influence. (Baudrillard, 1985: 132–3)

In this view, late twentieth century culture is characterised by availability, fragmentation, chaos, ephemerality and discontinuity. These together with the rejection of metatheories and grand narratives concerned with finding pattern or order in the proliferation of cultural styles define the post-modern period. There is no dominant intellectual movement. The eclectic nature of the post-modern vision, described by Baudrillard, Lyotard, Derrida and the other post-modernists, stems from the mushrooming of multiple influences available through the global contacts made possible by technology, from reluctance to be constrained within single fashions or trends and from the individual's readiness to break with the patterns of earlier traditions.

For some commentators, this willingness to break with tradition seems to be intimately linked to the logic of late consumer capitalism. Jameson argues that the continuous demand for new consumer products means in the cultural context that:

> our entire contemporary social system has little by little begun to lose its capacity to retain its own past, has begun to live in a perpetual present and in a perpetual change that obliterates traditions of the kind which all earlier social formations have had in one way or another to preserve. (Jameson, 1985: 125)

This is clearly demonstrable in the media exhaustion of news. Facts and stories from all over the world are consumed on this day, not that, and then consigned to the dustbin of history. We are better informed than in earlier epochs but the sheer scale of the information overwhelms us, washes over us and is ultimately discarded without making the impact commensurate with its importance:

> One is tempted to say the very function of the news media is to relegate such recent historical experiences as rapidly as possible into the past. The informational function of the media would thus be to help us forget, to serve as the very agents and mechanisms for our historical amnesia. (Jameson, 1985: 125)[38]

This is fully in line with the planned obsolescence of late capitalism and the ever more rapid changes in fashion and styles encouraged by an unprecedented penetration of advertising within the context of a mediatised society.

Another new development is that information is no longer 'consumed' nationally. New technologies, such as satellite, make national controls on broadcasting obsolete and, together with the victory of deregulation, signalled the end of state monopolies. Events are experienced collectively across the world, as, for example, in the live broadcasts from Baghdad during the Gulf War, from Bucharest at the fall of Ceausescu, from Sarajevo during the siege, from the burning villages of Kosovo. In the domain of information, state monopoly of the broadcasting channels has been challenged, and power has once again moved to transnational capital.

Incidents are no longer interpreted according to nationalist bias but the transnational perspectives which have replaced it stem from ideologies moulded in the vast media empires of a relatively small number of media moguls, such as Murdoch's News Corporation and Turner's Broadcasting System (which incorporates CNN). Other inventions, such as digital television, increase the number of channels and choice of programmes available to the consumer and so have a fragmenting effect. The era is passing in which the previous night's television programme provided a common subject for casual conversation in the workplace or in the street, in which the common experience of popular television programmes contributed to the formation of a national identity.[39] The Internet, conceived to be non-hierarchical,[40] has a similar fragmenting effect, allowing cheap, free, easy transnational contact.

By definition a systematic evaluation of the cultural flows in this deregulated explosion of information exchange is impossible. However, it is a reasonable assessment to claim that the transnationalisation of media is intimately bound to the spread of English, and to cite some examples. To illustrate how the satellite networks are dominated by English we might use the Pacific Rim as an example once again and demonstrate how present English is on its regional channels. Murdoch's and Turner's empires have penetrated the market and English can be heard on Star TV[41] and CNN. English is also massively present on European satellite channels, although it faces some competition from francophone, germanophone and Dutch-medium consortia, who have joined together to provide the broader base necessary to survive deregulation and compete successfully against the Anglo-Saxons. Even the Norwegians, Danes and Swedes ignore their slight language variations in order to be able to produce economies of scale and cooperate in Scandinavian TV3.

On the new privatised channels made possible by digitilisation US programmes dominate because of their low cost. Production costs are amortised by sales in the US and so they can be offered at very attractive rates to other markets. They find favour with private companies concerned to make profits. In the countries which favour subtitling over dubbing this exposes the viewers to an immense amount of spoken English. The EU attempted in 1989 to stem this trend through a Directive requiring that 50% of all national television provision be European in origin.[42]

The Internet is difficult to censor and mostly escapes state surveillance. It contributes to civil society, allowing exchanges of opinion and information between private citizens – always with the proviso that these are the wealthy and well-educated who can afford the equipment and have the language skills necessary. On the Internet dialogues take place in any language common to the participants; that this is often English results from the dominance of English as the first foreign language in many education systems.[43] The Internet also escapes the full logic of market forces. Gates' Microsoft is constantly threatened by anarchic non-profit-making consortiums. It is proving difficult to make a profit from the Internet, except in terms of providing the hardware needed. Much information can be accessed without payment, leading to problems for authors' rights but securing a great advantage for users, in a world where access to information is increasingly the new wealth. By the same tokens, the Internet is also a medium for anti-social and anti-state activity, a channel for propaganda, rumour and pornography.

Thus cultural products are, in this reading, wide spread, short-lived and very often in English. Optimists speak of cultural convergence and theorists of a contemporary preference for flows over unities, the nomadic over the sedentary, mobile arrangements over systems (Harvey, 1989). However, we would be naive if we did not recognise that the cultural flows are in their great majority from the United States to other parts of the world. What has been termed 'cultural convergence' (Saatchi & Saatchi, quoted in Robins, 1991) is in fact mostly Americanisation, as the examples (Dallas and Mickey Mouse) which Robins gives to demonstrate this convergence clearly illustrate. In Robins' analysis the new global cultural industries are creating a 'universal cultural space' because there is a recognition of

> the advantages of scale, and in this sphere too, it is giving rise to an explosion of mergers, acquisitions and strategic alliances. The most dynamic actors are rapidly restructuring to ensure strategic control of a range of cultural products across world markets. (Robins, 1991: 30)

The global market with 'its compression of time and space horizons', with its 'decentred space', with its 'permeable frontiers and boundaries' is none the less still a market in which the cultural flows are dominated by the images, the artefacts, the values of western modernity. The global cultural giants may aspire to be 'stateless, headless, decentred corporations' (Robins, 1991: 30). They are, nonetheless, all Western and mostly Anglo-Saxon. The rest of the world gets Hollywood films, American television sit-coms, Anglo-Saxon pop music, CNN news, the uniform of jeans and trainers. The cultural flow in the other direction is the repackaging of the non-threatening exotic for the international consumer:

> Everywhere there is Chinese food, pitta bread, country and western music, pizza and jazz. (Levitt quoted in Robins, 1991: 31)

Language plays a key if submerged role in this global market place. Not all culture derives from language. For non-linguistic culture – food, fashion, music, design, architecture, painting, sport and sculpture – it is only the desire to borrow and share which limits whether exchange occurs or not. But much culture is framed by language and as soon as it is language dependent, borrowing becomes much more difficult. To cross language frontiers we must have recourse to translators and interpreters or choose only culture produced in a language of which we have some knowledge.

Even in Europe where there is more resistance to Coca-Cola imperialism[44] than in many other parts of the world, these linguistic constraints still tend to lead to the consumption of more cultural 'products' from the English-speaking world than from any other single source. Firstly, the volume of translation from English to the other major European languages is far greater than that translated into English from them (Barret-Ducrocq, 1992) and, secondly, the language most commonly learnt as a modern foreign language in secondary schools in Europe is English (Calvet, 1993; Eurydice, 1998). The net effect of both these practices is thus to inject both more English language and more English language borne culture into the lives of many non-English-speaking Europeans.

Certain aspects of the enormous success of English language borne culture may perhaps be traced, ironically, to the cultural and linguistic heterogeneity of the United States in the early part of this century. For example, the film-making industry in its relentless search for markets very soon developed a style which could appeal across the cultural and linguistic divides in its own population. There is a simple, broad brush, lowest common denominator, action-dominated approach in many of the films produced in Hollywood which makes them accessible in a way that the majority of European films, with their prioritising of dialogue or monologue are not (Wright, 1997a, *Observer*, 22 June 1997). Success has bred success: Hollywood's access to funding ensures its technical edge and lavish production style; its control of the distribution networks guarantees that it continues to dominate the world market. We could thus argue that, although the US may have lost some industrial production in the late 1980s (for example, to the tiger economies of the Pacific rim), it will not so easily cease to be the originator of the cultural products which are language borne. Although the consumer can buy a television or computer from any provenance, the consumption of the audio-visual product, of information, of communication is more complex and demands that both producer and consumer know how to cross the language constraints within which it is created and bound. English, institutionalised in most education systems and closely linked to modern capitalism, has the advantage.

Post-modern theories about culture and language actually have little to say about language difference and how this affects cultural 'production' and 'consumption'. For example, Derrida's deconstructionism recognises that writers create texts remembering all the texts that they themselves have read. No new text can stand alone; it will have interwoven into it all the meanings from the words and the texts in the mind of the writer. Similarly, the reader will bring to the reading of the text all the words and texts from his past experience:

> This intertextual weaving has a life of its own. Whatever we write conveys meanings we do not or could not possibly intend and our words cannot say what we mean. It is vain to try and master a text because the perpetual interweaving of texts and meaning is beyond our control. Language works through us. Recognising that, the deconstructionist impulse is to look inside one text for another, dissolve one text into another, or build one text into another. (Thompson, 1992: 263)

If we understand text to mean all language borne culture then it becomes clear that films, plays, novels, journalism, poetry, songs will all be experienced intertextually. However, this intertextuality is limited by our position within defined communities of communication. If we are mono-lingual English-speakers the texts that we bring to our understanding are likely to be texts of English provenance only, since English language products dominate the audio-visual media and since the publishing industry commissions more translations from English into other languages rather than from other languages into English. If we are a speaker of a language of a smaller speech community the way we experience intertex-tuality stems both from the texts which originate from our own tradition and from translated texts, possibly, even probably, of English language provenance. If we come from a language group from which little has been translated (e.g. Finnish, Estonian etc.) then our intertextual readings will be peculiar to our group. Derrida recognises that there will be heterogeneity and that no meaning can be univocal or stable. However, the understanding of post-modernism is that there is flow and choice, that the cultural producers furnish the raw material for consumers to accept, reject, recombine, manipulate, build upon. My argument is that this free flowing situation is constrained by language. Monolingual English language speakers are limited by the texts available to them, which may be multicultural because of the pluricentric nature of English, but which are unlikely to be of multilingual provenance because of the translation imbalance. The choices for monolingual non-English language speakers are constrained by the commercial choices made on translation, dubbing and subtitling, with trade flows showing that they are more likely to receive a text of English language provenance than of any other outside their own national production. Only the cosmopolitan multilingual intellectual has the competences, the contacts and the opportunities to start to buck this trend and to truly accept the 'pluralism and authenticity of other voices' (Thompson, 1992). For a significant majority of the others, the constraints of the market push them towards the consumption of the English language text, either in its original form or translated.

Conclusion

On this evidence, globalisation seems to constitute anglicisation. Transnational corporations, international organisations, peacekeeping forces all exhibit a tendency to use English as an official or *de facto lingua franca*. Where cultural convergence means a sharing of non-linguistic culture, there is an imbalance, a flow from the first world to the third, a preponderance of US productions, with less movement in the reverse direction. Where culture is language borne, the imbalance is even greater. Films, videos, pop songs, television programmes, advertising are exported in enormous quantities from the US to the rest of the world. The reverse flow exists but does not achieve anywhere near the same volume. Dubbed films and programmes together with pop songs and advertising give enormous numbers of speakers of other languages some familiarity with the look and sound of English.

Globalisation also signifies a process where the monopoly of economic and political power has shifted from the nation state to a number of different arena. There is a multiplying and a fracturing of authorities, evidencing two completely different trends. In one case power is being exercised by international organisations with decisions superseding those made at national level; in the other, power is being exercised by transnational capital with decisions escaping the control of the nation state.

Of course, states, enterprises and individuals are pushed to globalise by powerful interest groups, but this is not always against their will. There are powerful pull factors at work as well and globalisation may also represent openness of social and economic access, the breakdown of unwanted parochial restrictions and an increase in personal freedom.

In the way that globalisation demands that individuals disregard former allegiances, but offers them in exchange new opportunities and freedoms, it replicates some aspects of the early period of nation state formation. This is particularly true in the area of language. As was shown in Chapter 2, some nation-states acquired territory and fixed boundaries before beginning the process of welding the heterogeneous groups within those boundaries into a homogenous linguistic and cultural whole through a variety of policies and strategies. Between these two phases there was a substantial lapse of time. In that intervening period, ambitious individuals and groups from the dominated minority groups often made the autonomous decision to acquire the language and the culture of the dominant group. The decision was made purely to aid social mobility and acquire access to power elites and the dominant group. It was not imposed. France was a good example of this. As we have seen there was no requirement before 1789 that the subjects of the French king should speak French in any other context but the court of law. Nonetheless, many non-French speakers chose to acquire French because it was the language of social promotion, conferred economic advantage, gave access to political power and allowed geographical mobility. Even before the centralised policies and coercion of the era of high nationalism ensured language shift towards French, individuals had taken the decision that it benefited them personally to do so.

Returning from the global to the European context which is the focus of this book, can we draw a parallel and see any of this process being reproduced in the increasing numbers of Europeans who have acquired English in an instrumental way? When we examine their motivations, they appear very similar to the reasons why non-French speaking French decided that they would benefit from acquiring French: access to power networks and elites, social and geographical mobility and, most importantly, economic advantage. There are, of course, at the same time many differences in these two contexts, not least in the commitment to cultural and linguistic diversity which has accompanied European integration, and which is a complete reversal of nationalist strategies to achieve cultural and linguistic conformity.

Notes

1. Sassen makes this point when she suggests that 'Economic globalization denationalizes national economies; in contrast, immigration is renationalizing politics (Sassen, 1995: 59).
2. The question immediately arises: appeal to whom? Clearly on a continent which gave the world the term 'balkanisation', and in a decade which has witnessed the resurgence of the desire for political and ethnic/cultural congruence in both the former USSR and ex-Yugoslavia, there is still strong adherence to nationalism among political actors. In the research community, a school of political science refutes the idea that the nation state is weaker now than in the past, arguing that globalisation actually depends on the power of the state. This seems to fly in the face of some of the evidence. The question is discussed by Held *et al.* (1999).
3. There was a parallel Tribunal in Tokyo.

4. Although of course it was the crimes of the defeated, Auschwitz and Dachau, rather than the crimes of the victors, Dresden and Hiroshima, which were to be punished.

5. Following Held, I shall sometimes use the term 'nation state' in this chapter as a way of differentiating the modern European state from other kinds of polity and in particular to make the distinction 'national/global'. I recognise that this usage would be termed misuse by some scholars of nationalism, but it helps clarify the issue here.

6. In June 1999 the British government agreed to designate a brigade of 6,000 to 8,000 men, to be kept in readiness for UN missions (BBC *Today* programme, 25 June 1999).

7. Held (1999: 6) quotes Carr (1981) 'International order and "international solidarity" will always be slogans of those who feel strong enough to impose them on others' and finds that little has changed since the prewar era about which Carr was writing.

8. The Rome agreement was supported by 120 countries; 7 were against; 21 abstained. The International Criminal Court will be based in the Hague like the International Court of Justice. Only states may apply to and appear before the ICJ, which was set up in 1946. It deals with disputes between states, including those concerning hostage taking, frontiers, asylum, maritime rights etc.

9. This has been much discussed by the French political elite. Elisabeth Guigou, in particular, has made herself a champion of this matter.

10. France provides just one example of how the language of the individual subjects of a state is not always the language of the law: French was made the sole language of the law and the court in 1539. However, in the language census carried out in the first years of the Republic, it seemed that only three million out of the 26 million who were now French citizens were fluent French speakers (Ager, 1990). This situation is replicated in many other places and times.

11. In 1997 there were eleven official languages which could be employed, plus Irish.

12. See for example ECHR Document 7616, 12 July 1996 which presents the candidacy of Romanian jurists to the Consultative Assembly.

13. Amongst them Altiero Spinelli. For a detailed discussion of post-war European Federalism, see Lipgens (1982).

14. This later became the Organisation for Economic Cooperation and Development, with a wider brief.

15. The Treaty signed on 4 April 1947 was in both French and English, and both texts were equally authentic. This remained the case for all further protocols and agreements until the Protocol on the termination of the occupation regime in the Federal Republic of Germany which also appeared in German (October 1954).

16. The Supreme Allied Commanders Europe (SACEUR), the Supreme Allied Commanders Atlantic (SACLANT).

17. France's return in 1996 was only partial and stopped short of full participation (Jane's Defence Weekly, 4/7/1997).

18. In March 1999 there were 19 members of NATO. Poland, the Czech Republic and Hungary joined in 1999. It is an integral element of NATO enlargement that Polish, Hungarian and Czech officers learn English.

19. Interviews with NATO staff officers, June 1997.

20. In March 1999 the Council of Europe was composed of 39 members, 1 observer and 3 guests.
21. See Whittaker (1995) for a full discussion of UN missions up to that date.
22. The UN authorised all 'necessary means' to uphold its resolutions to restore peace and security in Kuwait and the Gulf area. After the Allied victory the UN provided the forces to monitor the cease-fire (28 February 1991 onwards). In the case of Somalia, the UN welcomed the US offer to lead a multi-state force to protect the humanitarian organisations (Dec 1992–May 1993).
23. After the Dayton Agreement and the signing of the Paris Peace Treaty in December 1995, NATO took over the role of peacekeeper, providing IFOR, the force which was charged with implementing the treaty.
24. The example given by the British army interpreters who provided the information for this section was General Philippe Morillon who was able to use English and prepared to do so when necessary.
25. Information provided in interviews with NATO interpreters, Ruislip UK, Summer 1997, and with UN desk officers New York, December 1997.
26. The US is the only country with 'a truly global reach, with fleets and air bases and ground forces in every strategically important part of the world, plus the capacity to reinforce those positions in an emergency' (Kennedy, 1993: 291–2).
27. See for example T. Hopkins and I. Wallerstein (1982) *World Systems Analysis*, Beverley Hills and London, Sage; R. Reich (1991) *The Work of Nations*, New York, Knopf; K. Ohmae (1990) *The Borderless World: Power and Strategy in an Interlinked Economy*, New York, Harper Business; L. Preston and P. Windsor (1992) *The Rules of the Game in the Global Economy*, Boston, Kluwer; B. Jones, *Globalisation and Interdependence in the International Political Economy*, London, Pinter; T. Spybey (1996) *Globalization and World Society*, Cambridge, CUP; P. Hirst and P. Quentin (1996) *Globalization in Question: the International Economy and the Possibilities*, MA, Blackwell.
28. There is a body of opinion which feels that postmarxist liberalism is a different beast from the classical liberal variety: 'The present climate of privatization and liberal revival does not signify a wholesale abandonment of the idea of public sector' (Hotton & Turner, 1989: 5).
29. Toyota threatened to change investment plans in the UK if the country did not join EMU. Since the UK attracted 40% of mid 1990s foreign investment by Japanese companies the threat was taken seriously. Japan's preference for the UK stemmed from a constellation of reasons: the language, the flexible labour market, low tariff barriers and public grants among others. The desire to deal in a single currency was seen as strong enough to overtake these other attractions (*Guardian*, 30 January 1997). So far outside pressure has not outweighed internal suspicion.
30. There is some disagreement in this area. One school of thought sees transnationals as organisations unto themselves, having neutral, market dominated relations with all other organisations (Barnet & Müller, 1974, Barnet, 1994). Another school of thought argues that transnationals are not really rootless. Their R&D and corporate control are usually located in the home-base country (Carnoy, 1993). Yet another school makes the case that the physical capital of TNCs is neutral but that the human capital is nationally rooted (Reich, 1991).
31. G8 when Russia is included.
32. For example, the websites of various factions in the Kashmiri conflict (J and K

People's League; World Kashmir Freedom Movement; All State Kashmiri Pandit Conference), the LTTE (Liberation Tigers of Tamil Eelam) and the PLO (Palestinian Liberation Organisation) are in English. Similarly international NGOs involved in monitoring them report predominantly in English (e.g. ICRC, Angry Planet, Amnesty International, Human Rights Watch, Reporters Without Frontiers), although Peace Brigades International uses both English and Norwegian. Euskal Orrialdea uses Basque, French and Spanish in addition to English. The difference between the European and Asian groups may be the different audiences targeted as well as the need to use an alphabet compatible with ASCII for communication on the web.

33. The Internet was dominated by English during the early years of its history, because it was developed by American academics and military in the 1960s and 1970s and was used first in anglophone countries for commercial and research purposes. The francophone community, in particular, have made great efforts to redress this imbalance. The Quebec based Centre International pour le Dévéloppement des Inforoutes en Français coordinates francophone efforts, several institutions are concerned with the development of appropriate French terminology and the governments in the richer part of Francophonie have given generous funding to make sure that French is present on the Web. The Rapport Théry (1994) and the urgent discussion in France on the need to promote francophonie on the Internet (Guillou, 1995) are nonetheless an indication that the French-speaking world recognises the hegemony of English in this medium and still feels threatened by it.

34. For a discussion of the history of NGOs and recent developments see Ritchie (1996).

35. Data from research projects at Aston University. Telephone enquiries to NGOs (Tomkins, 1997), language of NGO sites on WWW (Kibby, 1996).

36. This aim is very clear in, for example, Winston Churchill's speech at the University of Harvard, 6 September 1943.

37. Serge Latouche contrasts this 'world-wide meta-society' dominated by a 'mechanism of exchanges' with other definitions of the word where culture is the 'totality of representations and symbols by which man gives meaning to his life' or by which groups 'organise 'the problem of their social existence' (Latouche, 1996: 39).

38. This interpretation has numerous supporters. Edward Said argues that 'public awareness is saturated with media analysis and stupendous coverage . . . Thus experience is emasculated (Said, 1994: 390). Theodor Adorno categorises war reporting as 'the total obliteration of the war by information, propaganda and commentaries . . . Men are reduced to walk-on parts in a monster documentary film (Adorno, 1974: 55).

39. Benedict Anderson (1983) argues that the novel and the newspaper contribute to the process of imagining the nation. Television programmes have a similar effect.

40. The Internet was conceived by the United States Army as a means of communication in the event of nuclear attack. By design there was no central control which could be put out of action; the networks are freestanding and therefore cannot be easily policed.

41. Star TV was Asia's largest satellite TV broadcaster when Murdoch acquired it. Before 1992 TV in India was a state monopoly. The Bharatiya Janata party made

a pre-election pledge to protect Indian languages and culture in the newly deregulated industry. Star broadcasts out of India and uses some Hindi as well as English. The Hindi medium programmes have been far fewer than the government wished (*Financial Times*, 27 March 1998 and 2 September 1998).

42. For a full discussion of recent developments in European media, legislation and language see Wright (1997a).

43. For data showing the increasing dominance of English as the first foreign language in European education systems see Chapter 9.

44. In France the so-called Toubon law, the argument that GATT should make an exception for culture, the introduction of radio quotas for foreign language songs reflect profound fears that French language and culture is under threat from the 'Anglo-Saxons', particularly the Americans.

Chapter 5

The growth of the European Community. Theories of integration. The role of language

It is within these two contexts, a very strong tradition of nation states and economic, political and cultural globalisation, that European integration has taken place. And one can argue convincingly that the origins of the European Union stem from attempts to counter both. The first motivation for integration was to limit the sovereignty of the nation state, in particular its capacity to make war on its neighbours. Another, later but equally strong impetus was to build a regional economic entity which could compete with the United States and the Pacific Rim in the new global economic order and to block what was felt to be American cultural imperialism.

This dual aim, to achieve some form of European political unity and yet to conserve the traditional particularity and diversity of Europe in the light of the threat of unifying globalisation, is riddled with difficulties and tension. The contradictions stem in part from the unlikely commonality of aims in the idealist camp and the hard headed business community, and the unusual alliances within the European movement. The aims of such disparate defenders and champions sometimes seem irreconcilable and nowhere more so than in the area of languages and communication.

In this chapter I shall give a short history of European integration from the European Coal and Steel Community, through the period of the European Economic Community and the European Community to the present European Union,[1] charting the dynamics of the political and economic actors. The European adventure is arguably one of the last great modernist projects. Conceived by the ruling elites to fulfil these conflicting ambitions it has developed in a top down way, always pushed forward by the vision of those at the centre.

No More War

In 1951 the Europeanists in the French government suggested that German and French steel and coal production be linked in an official way. The plan was to ensure that industries essential to manufacturing armaments be irreversibly locked into joint development, so that belligerent action between partners in such co-operation would be impossible. The invitation to join the Coal and Steel Community was open to other European countries, and France and Germany were joined by the Benelux countries and Italy. The Treaty of Paris, signed in April 1951, set up a Community, which was, significantly, to be directed by a supranational body in the form of a High Authority, a bold departure from the tradition of intergovernmental organisation which had characterised any previous European co-operation. The constituent members were prepared to agree to this measure of integration because they all had much to gain in exchange for a limited loss of sovereignty: Germany and Italy sought political rehabilitation and acceptance by the other European nations; the Benelux countries had the economic motive of links with the stronger economies of France and Germany, France wished to contain a re-emerging German state within a political structure that it would dominate.

The Europeanists strengthened their position during the 1950s and advanced plans for greater cooperation in defence, political and economic matters. In the first two areas there was little success: the European Defence Community was rejected in 1954; little progress was made towards achieving the proposed European Political Community. In economic matters, however, the Treaty of Rome, signed in March 1957, showed that the arguments for European collaboration had found an audience. This agreement stemmed from the same complex motives as the ECSC: a continuing desire to contain the aggressive nationalisms which had led to war; a wish to avoid the egotistical national solutions to economic problems which had fanned the Depression (or at least to operate such solutions at supra-national level); the hope for increased prosperity from a larger market. The same six countries – Belgium, France, Germany, Italy, Luxembourg and the Netherlands – were signatories to the Treaty. A key aim was the creation of a framework for co-operation in the development of nuclear power for peaceful purposes (EURATOM) which, like the Coal and Steel Community, would create transnational links in industries with military potential and significance. EURATOM was to have the monopoly of nuclear material and to build and control nuclear institutions.[2]

The treaty also instigated a common market among the six partners (EEC). The aims of the Common Market were primarily economic (to achieve sustained growth and economic prosperity in the six countries) and to a lesser degree social (to promote social equity throughout the six states). The long-term aim was to achieve free movement of labour, capital, goods and services. A customs union was to be set up and a common policy on agriculture to be implemented. Such co-operation for mutual benefit, were it to be successful, would make secession difficult for individual Member States. The most ambitious Europeanists hoped that the constituent Member States would become irrevocably locked into the process and that the effect of the integration of individual sectors of the economy would aggregate, stimulate further cooperation and ultimately prove irreversible. Two of the institutional structures put in place to govern these ventures were once again supranational: the Commission and the Court of Justice were to be appointed by the nation states but once in office they would both be deemed to be independent of national influence.

When the EEC came into force in 1958, the six Member States of the Common Market gave themselves twelve years to achieve the objectives of the Treaty of Rome. At the beginning much was realised. By 1968 import duties and quotas had been abolished and common duties for non-members agreed. Under French pressure, the Common Agricultural Policy had been set up to guarantee prices for Community farmers and to protect them from imports from non-member countries.[3] However, progress towards a more integrated community was not uniformly smooth: during the 1970s and early 1980s non-tariff barriers to free trade remained firmly in place and in some instances even strengthened: different regulations, standards and norms hindered the free movement of goods; border controls and other bureaucratic procedures added to costs; public procurement remained resolutely national. Three sets of circumstances in particular blocked further Europeanisation. Firstly, the confederal vision of Europe eclipsed the federal when the French president, General de Gaulle, blocked the Commission's bid to acquire greater power, including the right to raise revenue directly (1965) and vetoed the plan to introduce qualified majority voting into the Council (1966). Secondly, the economic crises of the early 1970s caused by OPEC policies on oil prices and supply led to each Member State behaving in a protectionist and defensive way to combat domestic inflation and protect markets. Lastly, the enlargement of the Community to include the UK, Denmark and Ireland brought into the Community two countries (UK[4] and Denmark) who felt constrained to join for economic reasons but who displayed a marked lack of enthusiasm for any kind of political integration (Dinan, 1994; Middlemas, 1995).

Throughout the late 1970s and early 1980s the feeling was that the original impetus had faded and that the ideal was diluted. The term 'Eurosclerosis' was coined to describe the impasse (Dinan, 1994). Greenland's decision to secede in 1982 seemed wholly understandable. Europeanists pushed for new impetus. Initiatives to 'widen' and 'deepen' the Community were to set it back on the twin track of securing political stability in Europe and greater prosperity through closer economic ties. The widening occurred as Greece, Spain[5] and Portugal shed their dictatorships and applied for membership of the Community. Their recently established democratic systems made them eligible for membership and it was hoped that this membership would help strengthen and guarantee their democracy systems.[6] Greece joined on 1 January 1981, Spain and Portugal on 1 June 1986. The Community was here fulfilling a role as continental political stabiliser, pulling states into structures within which maverick behaviour would be more difficult.[7] The prime motivation for the three states' applications remained economic; they wanted the same benefits that the Community appeared to be delivering to their northern neighbours and for investment flow to help build their infrastructures and industrial bases.

The introduction of the European Monetary System in 1979 to establish relative stability among the Member States' currencies was the first attempt to reinvigorate the integration process. However, any further attempts to 'deepen' in the economic sphere were hobbled by the 'British Budgetary Question', which brought Community business to a virtual halt for several years in the early 1980s while disputes raged over contributions and CAP expenditure. Only with their resolution in 1984 could the Community relaunch strategies to achieve the political and economic integration that had been its early ambition. In the mid-1980s the economic, political and international circumstances seemed to be propitious (Dinan, 1994). In particular, new leaders with the aspiration to achieve such union came to power in France and Germany. Helmut Kohl, who became Chancellor in 1982, and François Mitterrand, who won the presidential elections in 1981, were both influential in furthering the integrationist cause. Mitterrand came to his European commitment slowly and certainly not before 1983.[8] From then onwards, he became the prime advocate of monetary union and a supporter of political rapprochement.[9] Kohl was the principal defender of political union (Forster & Wallace, 1996). The Franco-German motor of European integration was reborn.[10] In the institutions of the Community itself, there were charismatic personalities. Jacques Delors, a committed integrationist, was a particularly able and energetic president of the Commission from 1985 to 1994.

In the commercial and industrial world, powerful lobbies[11] argued energetically for further progress towards economic integration, in particular the achievement of the single market. In the European business community there was a general belief that the scope of national policy in the states of Europe was no longer adequate for global competition and that policies needed to be decided and implemented at the pan-European level in order to compete with the US and Japan (Halliburton & Hünaberg, 1993).

A Commission white paper set out the reforms that would be needed to create a real single market in Europe. It contained 300 concrete measures (later reduced to 286) to remove all the remaining physical barriers (for example, border controls), all the remaining technical barriers (for example, lack of common standards) and all the remaining fiscal barriers (for example, differences in value added tax) to a true common market. And all this was to be achieved within a strict timetable. The white paper was accepted and signed as the Single European Act (SEA) in 1986, and after ratification became binding on the Member States on 1 July 1987.

The Dooge Report and the Intergovernmental Conferences (IGCs) which had prepared the SEA had recognised that Member States were now co-operating in areas that were clearly political rather than economic. The SEA formalised some of these powers, including a number which the Community had assumed informally in the areas of social cohesion, research and technological development and environmental controls. It set out a framework for developing the common approaches to foreign policy which had been an aspect of Community co-operation since 1974 when the heads of state of the nine had agreed to meet three time a year and to include this area in their deliberations. In fact since 1975 and the Lomé convention, a treaty of co-operation between the EEC and forty-six African, Caribbean and Pacific countries, the Community had been conducting diplomacy on the pattern of a sovereign state with particular success in group to group relations: by the end of the 1980s the Community had links with ASEAN, the Arab league, EFTA, the Contadora group, the ACP countries, the Council of Europe and CMEA.[12] Such collective diplomacy appeared to many to be a new departure; these are civil power relationships, since no group has military capacity in itself (Edwards & Regelsberger, 1990).[13] In the area of trade there has also been increased common foreign policy. Here there is less need for political will for co-operation since it is dictated by the organisation of a single market, which has meant that it has seemed suitable for the Community to replace individual Member States as the responsible body for negotiating with third parties. It is already working as a single economic entity in this context (Weatherill & Beaumont, 1993). The Community is thus represented as a body at GATT/WTO, UNCTAD and OECD negotiations.

The final reform in this phase of European development was the decision to increase the powers of the European Parliament, as the democratic corollary to the increased legislative powers accorded to the Community to achieve the Single Market. The Common Assembly dated from the Treaty of Rome but had merely been a consultative body whose members had been appointed not elected. In 1979 this had been changed and there were the first elections by universal direct suffrage, but the power of the parliament continued to be limited to a mere advisory, consultative function. In 1987, the SEA shifted some of the power in the Community away from the Council of Ministers and towards the Commission and the Parliament. In particular, Parliament gained the right to amend or reject legislation through the procedures termed codecision and co-operation,[14] to approve all major international agreements including the acceptance of new members of the Community through the assent procedure, and to approve the choice of Commissioners and Commission President. This was felt to be a first step towards righting the democratic deficit of which detractors accused the Community (Delors, 1989).

In the next episode of the move towards integration, political events outside the confines of the Community were to have an immense impact on its development. The collapse of communism[15] led in a very sort space of time to the reunification of Germany (1990) and to the admission of former East Germany into the Community. This new, more populous, geographically larger Germany raised spectres, particularly in France.[16] Containing the German giant seemed sufficient reason for further moves towards integration which would anchor its eastern neighbour into a more meaningful political union (Forster & Wallace, 1996). The end of the communist empire also removed a military threat on the eastern border of the Community but left in its place an instability which was menacing. The Community saw the need to support the former Comecon countries' struggle to implement market reforms and build democratic structures, as much to protect their own security and avoid waves of economic refugees as for altruistic motives. The Europe agreements that came fully into effect in 1994 were designed to this end, and had both a political and an economic dimension. Economically, they gave Poland, Hungary, the Czech and Slovak Republics, Bulgaria and Romania limited access to the common market. The Community would provide aid through the Phare pro-gramme[17] and loans via the European Investment Bank for economic reconstruction. Politically, they demonstrated that the Central European states had committed themselves to pluralistic democracy and to the market economy, which would make them eligible, ultimately, for full membership of the Community.

The end of the Cold War also permitted the accession of Sweden, Finland and Austria who joined the Union on 1 January 1995. Their various traditions of neutrality and their geographical positions on the borders between western and eastern Europe had held them back from earlier participation in the European movement. When the geo-political landscape altered, they applied for and gained membership.

The consequences of this actual and potential enlargement of the Community cannot be foreseen. On the one hand, increasing the membership has been applauded by certain less committed Member States (the UK in particular) in the belief that a union of 20+ states can only be a trading bloc and will thwart integrationist ambitions (Dinan, 1994). On the other hand, there is a widely held view that an enlarged Community organised intergovernmentally would be inoperable and that the present confederal arrangement would have to give way to a more federal model. The federalists are very optimistic; in this camp enlargement implies stronger institutions, much greater integration, in order to avoid complete paralysis.

Other contemporary events also had the effect of pushing the Community into assuming a clearer political identity. The war in the Gulf and the conflict in Bosnia both seemed to demand some concerted action from the governments of the Member States. The Community was unable to organise a common response in either case. In the Yugoslavian crisis, a war at the actual border of Community territory, it was left to the UN and subsequently to NATO to intervene and provide peacekeeping forces. This lack of ability to co-ordinate a response to a crisis so evidently 'European' fuelled the feeling that the Community was an economic force but a political nonentity. Many commentators and analysts attacked the European Community for its 'chaotic and disagreeable lack of policy for Bosnia' (Coffey, 1995: 112).

The Treaty on Economic Union, which was negotiated in the winter of 1991–1992 and which came into force in November 1993, may be seen as the Member States' attempt to transform the Community from an entity based on economic integration and political cooperation into a union of a political nature, including a common foreign and security policy (Delors, 1992a). The TEU aimed to give the Community some political teeth. The Treaty demonstrates clearly how increasing economic co-operation necessarily provokes political co-operation and, further, that there is a momentum in the process which is difficult to brake: abolishing trade barriers makes it more likely that there will be a convergence of economic principles; abolishing internal frontiers causes a need for common policies on drugs and co-operation between police forces; sharing common external frontiers demands agreement on matters of asylum and immigration. The TEU took integration beyond a single market to new areas: some of these were still of an economic nature, such as European Monetary Union with a planned single currency before the end of the century; others increased political co-operation, such as the Common Foreign and Security Policy (CFSP) and co-operation on Home and Judicial Affairs; the Social Chapter introduced the concept of common rights and conditions for Europeans in the workplace. The new European Union rested on three 'pillars', The first was the economic pillar, which preexisted the TEU. The governance of this pillar is the supranational regime set up in previous treaties and acts. In the second (Common Foreign and Security Policy) and third (Home and Judicial Affairs) pillars, decision and policy making belong to the Member States' governments and the Council of Ministers rather than the Commission

The negotiations at Maastricht heralded a massive leap forward in the process of European integration, which provoked reactions within the populations and the governments of the nation states. The backlash to monetary union was the fiercest. The UK insisted from the start on the right to opt out. The fears for loss of sovereignty that a common currency entails was a major cause of the Danish refusal to ratify the treaty in their first referendum and for the very narrow margin of approval given by the French (Middlemas, 1995). The pain of fulfilling the economic criteria on inflation rates and indebtedness was acute and there were strikes and demonstrations in many Member States against the austerity necessary to comply with the requirements for the common currency. At several points, it appeared unlikely that all the Member States would fulfil the criteria for admission within the timetable and a 'two speed' Europe might emerge. Nonetheless, the political will to forge ahead remained strong among the political elites of the countries with a traditionally strong commitment to European union. The integrationists had learnt from the reactions to Maastricht and prepared the various populations for monetary union; by 1996 vigorous campaigns were already under way in France, Belgium, Germany and the Netherlands (*The European,* 19 July 1996). The Commission had also realised the need to win the hearts and minds of the political actors at national level and had taken steps to involve the national parliaments (European Commission, 1995a, 1996d).

The countries which were to be part of Economic Monetary Union in the first wave were announced at the Brussels summit of May 1998. Only Sweden, Britain and Denmark decided not to participate at this stage. Greece was excluded for failing to meet the economic criteria. In the same time frame the European Central Bank was set up and its first governor, Wim Duisenberg, appointed. In January 1999 the Euro was introduced in eleven Member States. It was to coexist for a period as a virtual currency alongside national currencies until the introduction of notes and coins. When this happens, Europeanists hope that the concrete existence of a single currency may take on a symbolic function and give some impetus to integration (Tournier, 1999). The anti-European backlash which accompanied Maastricht seemed to have dissipated. Even in the UK, the majority seemed to have accepted Europeanisation. The problem which replaced it was widespread apathy, exhibited very clearly in the lack of interest paid the negotiations and signing of the Treaty of Amsterdam in 1997 and in the low turnout for the European elections in June 1999.[18]

The other significant decisions taken at Maastricht were procedures to strengthen the powers of the European Parliament and the introduction of the concept of subsidiarity. Both were presented as developments to improve the democratic legitimacy of the European Union. Subsidiarity was defined as the need to keep decision making close to those most concerned. Political power should devolve to the level of government best placed to make decisions on a particular area and action at European level should only take place if it cannot be achieved by the Member States acting alone and should leave scope for flexibility in national implementation (TEU, Article 3b, 1992)

Both those who wanted to limit European integration and those who wanted to further the process supported the idea, interpreting it in wildly differing ways. The idea was adopted enthusiastically by those who wished to retain the 'Europe des patries',[19] because it seemed to provide a forceful argument against relinquishing anything more than minimal powers to supranational institutions.[20] However, an expressed commitment to 'the principle that decisions should be taken by public authorities at a level as close as possible to the citizen' (TEU, Article A, 1992) was taken and used against the nation state by regions and local authorities champing at the bit of nation state centralism,[21] as well as by integrationists in the European institutions.[22] The second group saw it as a way of diluting the power of national governments by giving ammunition to regions who wished for more autonomy vis-à-vis the nation state.

The links between regions within the EU framework were formalised within a Committee of the Regions, provided for by the TEU and established in March 1994. This Committee represents hundreds of regional and local authorities and its sub-national networks of co-operation have introduced another dimension into European integration.

The role of the Intergovernmental Conference (IGC) which led to the Amsterdam Treaty, signed in June 1997, was to tackle the unfinished business of Maastricht. Even as the TEU was being drafted, it was recognised that there would need to be a review of how it was working, given the importance, not only of the new situation facing Europe, but also of the new areas of cooperation which it introduced. The primary purpose of the revision was to prepare the Community for enlargement. Ten former communist countries from Eastern and Central Europe, as well as Turkey, Malta and Cyprus, had applied for membership of the EU.[23] This virtual unification of the whole continent could not be contemplated without setting in hand changes to the institutional structure designed for the original six. The reassessment of the role of the institutions of the European Union in an enlarged community was, therefore, a prime aim.

The Amsterdam Treaty revision was also a response to two other concerns: a perception that some of the Maastricht provisions had not proved effective in practice, and the need to bridge the perceived gap between governments and their peoples (Edwards & Pijpers, 1997). In the first category, the IGC targeted the two new pillars of co-operation, Common Foreign and Security Policy and Justice and Home Affairs, which have remained strictly intergovernmental and where the Commission and Parliament cannot instigate legislation or propel initiatives forward. In the second category, the IGC addressed the issues of the democratic deficit,[24] unemployment, European citizenship and rights in all Member States, transparency in decision making and subsidiarity.

The Amsterdam Treaty did not attract enormous media attention because, consisting of revisions to the Treaty of Rome and the TEU, it contained nothing radically new. However, an examination of the detail of the text shows that these revisions all strengthen the steady progression towards European integration. The single market was reinforced, as the protection of nationalised industries was made more difficult. European citizenship was defined as separate but complementary to national citizenship. The Treaty inaugurated a debate on the harmonisation of work legislation and conditions. It recognised the role the Community plays in regulating health matters. It planned greater powers for the Parliament and wider competencies for the Commission. The definition of subsidiarity was reworked to make it clear that the concept only applied to domains for which the Commission did not have full authority. The primacy of community law over national law was reaffirmed. There was to be more qualified majority voting and more transparency in the decision making of the Council. The Treaty stated that the Community would guarantee human rights and non-discrimination in respect of sex, ethnic origin, religion, handicaps, age or sexual orientation. It brokered an agreement to decide the status of asylum seekers within the EU. It agreed the defence of external frontiers. It suggested the need for a European military capacity to respond to crises in Europe and beyond.

In the text, this seems like a distinct step from confederalism to federalism. In the real world there may be less progress, which is what happened with the TEU. Two events in the Spring of 1999 suggest that aspects of the Treaty are hopes for the future rather than elements of policy which will be rapidly enacted. The accusations of budgetary irregularities and mismanagement of funds which led the Commissioners to resign en masse (March 1999) may put a brake on plans to extend the powers of the Commission, certainly until the affair is resolved. The military intervention in Kosovo to stop the Serbian government's persecution of ethnic Albanians, carried out by NATO forces under American leadership (March–June 1999), was a strong reminder that the security and defence ambitions of the European Union are not yet reality.

Theories of Integration

Three points clearly emerge from the facts so far: firstly it is evident that some kind of integration has taken place and an entity which could be termed a supra-state is evolving; secondly, this entity has not developed as far as the federalists hoped but is much further evolved than the minimalists ever envisaged; thirdly, the power of this supra-state is limited since the authority of the intergovernmental Council of Ministers still outweighs that of the supra-national Commission and European Court of Justice. So the nation states have retained ultimate power. However, the future is unclear. From the earliest days of the European project there have been three schools of thought on its possible futures. The neo-realists maintain that Europe will remain essentially an association directed by intergovernmental mechanisms. They argue that the nation states will not relinquish sovereignty in any substantial way and that the federalists and neo-functionalists who refuse to recognise this are deluded. The neo-functionalists speculate that the incremental weight of multiple small initiatives towards integration will cause the Community to evolve from a common market into a true political union. The concept of 'spillover' suggests that integration in one area (economic), will produce integration in another (political). The third group, the federalists, reject unplanned and incremental integration because of the democratic deficit which accompanies it. Within the Community they have fought for transparency and accountability. From the 1940s onwards they have argued[25] for significant powers for a European parliament. In this, they pose an overt threat to the sovereignty of the nation state and while citizens in some of the Member States would be prepared to consider aspects of federal organisation (e.g. Italy, Greece, France, Ireland, Belgium), others reject the idea in its entirety (e.g. Sweden, Denmark, Austria).[26]

At the present time it seems as if full federalism is the least likely of these options: the French and Danish citizens who registered their disquiet at the lack of accountability and democracy in the EU at the time of Maastricht did not see democratic federal structures as the solution – rather a retreat into national sovereignty. Danish citizens remain very wary (Laursen, 1996). The French position sometimes appears schizophrenic; committed Europeanists at times, they are also concerned to preserve sovereignty.[27] The Danish and French hesitations are replicated in the other Member States. So planned federalism does not at the moment appear likely. Neo-realism also appears to have been overtaken by the speed of events. The theory seems less tenable in a situation where qualified majority voting in the Council has become the rule for many issues, where ultimate legal power in many areas has passed to the European Court of Justice and where codecision and cooperation procedures have increased the power of the Parliament. Neo-functionalism appeared defunct during the 1970s and the early 1980s when the impetus to integration stalled. However, it seems a fair description of developments since the SEA which suggest that the Member States have now interlocked themselves so closely that retreat from Europe would be almost impossible (Hirst, 1995). The posturing of high politics may still posit the possibility of states leaving the Union; the reality of 'low' politics shows that retreating from Europe would cause immense difficulties. This was illustrated in the British case during the beef crisis of 1996. As the British blocked the business of the Community in order to obtain rulings in their favour, Jacques Santer, the president of the Commission called on them to accept Community decisions or be prepared for calls to resign membership. This was reported in the British press in the very same issues which carried stories on how Britain was now sharing embassy accommodation with other Member States (*Observer*, 9 June 1996). Such interdependencies seem likely to ensure that no state can easily withdraw from the Community, even if, on their own, they do not ensure further integration through spillover.[28]

This short summary of European integration illustrates how fast the nation states have relinquished elements of their sovereignty and how far the creation of a kind of supra-state has advanced. In the economic, political and juridical spheres, the EU has many of the attributes of a single polity. European interdependence is manifest in one European economic space, one European political unit representing the region in a number of world arena and one European law taking precedence over national in many instances. However, the EU does not replicate the nation state in all domains and in particular there has been no suggestion that there should be the linguistic and cultural homogeneity that was encouraged within or imposed on the nation state. Indeed EU policy is the very reverse, seeking as it does to promote cultural diversity and linguistic pluralism. The different traditions are explicitly valued and the vitality of the kaleido-scopic European cultural heritage is overtly supported – particularly in order to provide a bulwark against the cultural hegemony of the United States.

This commitment to plurilingualism is not unproblematic. The nation states promoted linguistic uniformity for a number of reasons felt to be self evident. Political, economic and legal co-operation cannot happen without communication between actors from different groups, whether linguistic or other. Feelings of solidarity and identification rely heavily on the discourses which are developed within a community of communication. Yet, curiously, in much of the writing on European integration the question of language is simply not raised. And if the language question does feature, there is usually an unquestioning acceptance of the official commitment to plurilingualism.[29] The brief history of the Community which I have given above follows the classic pattern of such accounts[30] in that, at no point, is the plurilingual nature of the entity even mentioned. Nor is the matter much discussed in the literature which deals with theories of integration. There seems to be a conspiracy of silence on the matter, although it is clearly highly significant in such a plurilingual setting where problems of communication impact on every stage of the progress. One wonders what the concept of *integration* can actually mean in a polity where there is no common medium, no *lingua franca*, to provide even the most basic community of communication. What are the implications for *co-operation* in the political, economic, defence and legal spheres where the actors may not be able to communicate? Can the *democratic deficit* which is perceived ever be ameliorated without solving the communication problem?

Why is language not mentioned? Is it because in some situations plurilingualism really poses no problem? This may be so in limited areas. In a free trade area where the main contact is trade and where it is only goods which move definitively only a small class of people are concerned with language difference. Two groups are necessarily affected: firstly the members of the diplomatic and political class who negotiate the trade accords and who will be drawn from elites educated to have the language skills necessary for their role; secondly, all those who might be considered to be merchant class, involved with the buying, selling and transporting of goods across national boundaries and who, traditionally and inevitably, need to accommodate language difference. These latter must either acquire the limited language skills necessary for the task themselves or employ language professionals to do it for them. In both cases the numbers affected are small and the occasions for contact across language barriers restricted. But in the situation of greater economic contact created by the European

Community, where an ever increasing degree of co-operation and contact is envisaged (aspects of the production process shared between different national groups; research organised in a transnational way; a proportion of students acquiring part of their education in another Member State; etc.) the need to consider plurilingualism and the constraints and patterns it imposes became much more pressing. When the Single European Act introduced the free movement of people, services, capital and goods, the language variable took on a greater, more complex and more significant role. In particular, the movement of labour and the selling of services across national borders which are also linguistic borders depend heavily on the linguistic capabilities of individuals and their success in solving the communication problems that must arise.

Perhaps the question of language is omitted from the debate because it is too sensitive a question to be aired in the present phase of integration. As we have seen in earlier chapters, the nations of the constituent Member States have been socialised into a national linguistic environment. The national language has immense symbolic power for the vast majority of Europeans as well as providing the homogenous national community of communication. Fishman's view that:

> (L)anguage is the recorder of paternity, the expresser of patrimony and the carrier of phenomenology. Any vehicle carrying such a freight must come to be viewed as equally precious, as part of the freight, indeed as precious in and of itself. (Fishman, 1977: 25)

is a widely held view in a continent where linguistic nationalism still has resonance and the ideal of the monolingual nation state still holds sway. This is the background the peoples of Europe would bring to any frank discussion of the difficulties for integration caused by Europe's plurilingualism. Any proposal of effective policies to aid communication between the citizens of its constituent parts, such as the adoption of a *lingua franca*, would surely cause a ferocious nationalist backlash, similar to but much greater than the reactions to the proposed single currency.[31] Thus discussion would be possibly counter productive for integration and this would account for integrationists' reluctance to address the problem of plurilingualism honestly. They may feel, given the intra-European discord any attempt to plan for a community of communication would cause, that it is better to let the issue resolve itself in an unplanned way. This does not explain, however, why the language question is absent from the anti-Europeanists' battery of reasons why the Community cannot work. There are several lines of attack that they could use: political, cultural and economic. They could argue that without a means of communication among themselves the citizens of the Community will not be able to use the limited democratic powers that they possess in any effective way and that a 'democratic deficit' is inherent in such a plurilingual structure. They could argue that there is a very real possibility that extensive co-operation in the economic sphere will lead to extensive language contact and inevitably, according to the patterns observed in the past, to some language shift for the smaller language communities, with all that implies for loss of cultural identity.[32] They could argue that linguistic difference is an enormous cost in such a plurilingual entity and that the costs in accommodating multilingual packaging, market research, product promotion and advertising detract from the much vaunted economies of scale of the SEM. These arguments are not often heard.

If we do fill this gap in the debate and ask the questions prompted by the plurilingual nature of the entity, what should these questions be? The first might be 'Can the EU make any progress towards becoming a democratic polity without solving its communication problems?' The second might be 'Is it inevitable that there will be profound linguistic consequences if the economic, political, defence, social and legal ties that the European Union has brought about between Member States continue to deepen and strengthen?'

If we decide that there are only minimal linguistic effects in this process, how then can we define a multilingual polity with no *lingua franca*? How would it actually function? For this would indeed be a new political animal. The multilingual empires of the past and the multilingual democracies outside Europe would be different from such an entity in a number of ways. A multilingual democratic European polity would be moving against the trend and different from the democratic experience of Europeans to date.

Notes

1. The European Economic Community (EEC), set up by the Treaty of Rome in 1957, was later merged with the European Coal and Steel Community (ECSC) and the European Atomic Energy Committee (Euratom) in 1967 and called the European Community (EC). This organisation then became one of the pillars of the European Union (EU) set up by the Treaty on European Union (TEU) which was signed in 1991 and came into force in 1993. For consistency I shall refer to the European Community for events pre-1993, since this appellation can be seen as an umbrella term.
2. However, there was an ambiguity. National states would not give up their right to own and promote their own nuclear industry if they wanted to and the links with the military applications of nuclear power were fudged. The US offer of cheap enriched uranium to the consortium ensured that the idea would become reality. It also meant that the US would retain close links with a group that

would remain dependent on the US as long as it did not build its own separation plant.

3. The CAP was a condition of French participation in Europe (De Gaulle, 1971) and was negotiated at the Treaty of Rome 1957.

4. The UK had applied for membership under Macmillan's premiership but had been rejected, primarily because of de Gaulle's opposition (1963). He feared, probably correctly, UK opposition to the Common Agricultural Policy, and reduced Community autonomy, if UK participation permitted greater American influence.

5. Spain had applied for membership in 1962 but had been rejected because the Franco regime was undemocratic (Tsakaloyannis, 1997). Even after the end of the Franco era, the Spanish application was held up because of French and Italian fears of competition from cheap Spanish agricultural produce (Bainbridge & Teasdale, 1995).

6. 'Like Portugal, Spain was attracted to Community membership as a means of re-entering the European political and economic mainstream after more than a generation of near-total isolation' (Bainbridge & Teasdale, 1995: 421–2).

7. Expressed in Genscher's speech to the Bundestag:

   Greece, only recently returned to the democratic fold will march in future with the community of European nations. (quoted in Dinan, 1994: 102)

8. Up to 1983 Mitterrand pursued a policy of national independence and state intervention. This proved economically disastrous and Mitterrand underwent a pragmatic conversion to the free market, for which the Community would provide the framework.

9. In his *Lettre à tous les Français* 1988, Mitterrand said unambiguously 'Les Etats-Unis de l'Europe; j'y crois'.

10. This is the opinion of a large number of political and academic commentators (e.g. Lafont, 1993). Nectoux (1996), for example, says:

    In the mid-1980s, the revived Euro-enthusiasm of France and Germany supported by countries such as Italy and Spain, was crucial in relaunching an integration process which had been largely stalled since the 1966 Luxembourg compromise. (Nectoux, 1996: 31)

11. For example, the European Round Table, a group of industrialists from very high profile European multinationals – Gyllenhammer (Volvo), Agnelli (Fiat), Dekker (Philips), Harvey-Jones (ICI), Maucher (Nestlé) and others.

12. ASEAN – Association of South-East Asian Nations; EFTA – European Free Trade Area; Contadora (South America) linked with Rio group and Group of Eight; ACP – African, Caribbean and Pacific group; CMEA – Council for Mutual Economic Assistance, i.e. Soviet Union and allies.

13. However, a desire for national advantage is still likely to overcome the requirements of the group whenever there is conflict of interest. The Commission and the European parliament are more enthusiastic than the Council on moving to collective diplomacy and eventual common foreign policy (Denman, 1997).

14. After the TEU was ratified, Parliament had the right to negotiate and to veto certain legislative proposals if no agreement can be reached with the Council Ministers (Codecision), to be consulted twice on legislation and to propose amendments (Co-operation). The Council of Ministers can only overturn such amendments by a unanimous decision (European Parliament, UK Office, 1997).

15. In 1989 in Central and Eastern Europe and in 1991 in the USSR.
16. For indications of the French mood, see for example Michel Colomès in *Le Point*, 22 février 1992, No 1014, p. 19, Joseph Rovan in *Le Figaro*, 3 août 1993, 'Imaginer une autre Europe'.
17. This was 1 billion ECUs in 1993, 2/3rds of which was provided by the EU, 1/3rd other western democracies. The scheme in its entirety is administered by the EU.
18. The turnout percentage fell in all Member States compared to 1994. For figures see Chapter 6.
19. The phrase was first used widely by de Gaulle and reflects French policies of the 1960s.
20. For example, John Major and Valéry Giscard d'Estaing understood subsidiarity to mean retention or restoration of power by/to national governments (European Parliament, 1990). The British Conservative Party manifesto for the 1994 European elections expressed a resolve to extend the application of subsidiarity to more and more areas of EU policy-making. See Conservative Party (1994). Major and the Conservatives had taken Article 3b of the TEU at face value and saw subsidiarity as merely a way of regulating power-sharing between national governments and European institutions.
21. For a discussion of how national associations of local authorities campaigned for the establishment of a legal basis for the principle of subsidiarity see Taylor (1995). In the regionalist/autonomist movements, the demand to respect the subsidiarity principle has proved a powerful strategy, used to some effect (e.g. Alex Salmond and the Scottish Nationalists, in the campaign leading to the referendum on Scottish devolution).
22. Si nous voulons enraciner notre projet, lui conférer plus de transparence et d'efficacité, il nous faut notamment laisser toutes leurs potentialités aux régions, où la démocratie est en quelque sorte à la portée de la main: l'application d'un principe de subsidiarité bien compris peut le permettre (Delors, 1992b).
23. A number of applications to join the Community were considered in the mid-1990s, in particular from Cyprus, Turkey and Malta. The applications in the round after that were the 'Visegrad' four – the Czech Republic, the Slovak Republic, Poland and Hungary. The cost of these four countries' accession which was likely to account for as much as 60% of the total EU budget made it likely that enlargement to the east would be slow. Lobbying for the Baltic countries' inclusion started in the late 1990s. Jacques Santer's speech *Agenda 2000* given to the European Parliament 16 July 1997 confirmed that the first round of accession negotiations would be with Hungary, Poland, Estonia, the Czech Republic and Slovenia. Slovakia was relegated to the second phase along with Romania, Bulgaria, Lithuania and Latvia because of concerns about human rights for minorities and democracy. The accession of Cyprus and Turkey trails because of the ongoing and unresolved conflicts between the Greeks and the Turks.
24. For further discussion of the EU's democratic deficit see Chapter 6.
25. The early federalists were mostly grouped within the Union européenne des Fédéralistes, founded in 1946. They included many Resistance leaders and activists, such as Altiero Spinelli, who had started to develop a position on European federalism during the Second World War. For a detailed discussion of the early federalist movement see Lipgens (1982).

26. A survey of 65,000 citizens in the fifteen Member States in Spring 1996 found that a majority of the Belgians, the Irish, the French, the Greeks and the Italians were in favour of an elected European government to replace the Commission and Council, the Netherlands, the UK, Finland, Luxembourg and Portugal were divided on the issue. The Austrians, the Swedes and the Danes were firmly against (INRA/Eurobarometer, 1996).
27. France's refusal to renounce the Luxembourg Compromise is some evidence for this (cf. Stone, 1993).
28. A full treatment of this question is given in Schmitter (1994).
29. Politicians and political scientists who do not have English as a mother tongue are more likely to discuss language and linguistic pluralism (e.g. Rocard, 1987). This is particularly true of the French, who display a very strong antipathy to 'le tout anglais' (for a French view of this see Calvet, 1993). The commitment to pluralism is particularly strong in France and Greece (European Language Council, 1997).
30. See for example the works of Walter Lipgens, William Wallace, Stanley Hoffmann, Keith Middlemas, Peter Coffey, Alan Milward, Juliet Lodge, John Pinder and Desmond Dinan. There is substantial language blindness in the context of this subject in the case of most of the writers who might be seen as in the Anglo-Saxon tradition.
31. This can be anticipated in the energetic anti-English lobby that has already marshalled support. See Chapter 10.
32. This danger is perceived in the context of globalisation and the incursions of American English; it is not normally considered in the context of the Community.

Chapter 6

Theories of democracy: participatory and liberal representative democracy. The essential role of language in democracy. The democratic deficit in the EU and the need to develop new practices for a multilingual polity

This chapter examines the role of the community of communication in a democratic polity, and explores how far the plurilingualism of the EU restrains its political actors, bureaucrats and peoples from following the mainstream traditions of European democracy.

What does democracy mean to Europeans? We generally recognise that it is part of a European heritage. Its genesis in Athens at the end of the sixth century BC is noted in every school curriculum; the British parliamentary tradition is acknowledged as the oldest model of a certain kind of representative democracy[1]; the French Declaration of the Rights of Man is recognised as a founding document for the concepts of sovereignty of the people and equality of citizens, and the democratic innovations on the eastern seaboard of America in the late eighteenth century were instituted by a diaspora that was also part of this European heritage.

At the end of the twentieth century, Europeans are generally agreed that democracy is a positive thing, inviting approval and bestowing legitimacy. We are currently witnessing an immense surge in the popularity of the idea; since the end of totalitarianism in its right wing form in Spain, Portugal and Greece and in its communist form in Eastern Europe, multiparty democracy is, or at least is claimed as, the mode of government of most of the nation states of Europe. This differentiates the region from those surrounding; in the Arab world, in Eastern Asia, in Sub-Saharan Africa, the idea of democracy is a much less potent force (Bromley, 1993; Potter, 1993, Hawthorn, 1993).

But what Europeans actually understand by democracy is not a single concept; it is and has always been an umbrella term for a variety of political arrangements and movements. The Athenian tradition of democracy is accepted as the origin of the idea but its offspring are very different both from it and from each other. One historic split appears between the Anglo-American concept of democracy and the kind developed on the continent following the French model. Another dichotomy exists between capitalist and socialist democracy. Those committed to grassroots democracy in radical pressure groups or alternative movements would reject the very idea that the liberal representative version is democratic in any more than a token way. Interpretations are very diverse, traditions very disparate and there is a confusing tendency to employ 'democracy' as a 'hurrah' word, 'a propagandist device indicating approval of whatever is the practice or policy or institution to which it is applied' (Lively, 1975: 1). However, despite the devaluation and imprecision the term has suffered, the potency of the idea survives and, as I shall discuss below, there are some elements common to all its varieties.

Since democracy can be categorised as a concept with a long European pedigree and as a form of political arrangement with almost universal acceptance in Europe, it is curious that the new form of polity which is being developed in the area, the European Union, is actually so deficient in many of the defining variables of a democratic state. This seems particularly ironic since commitment to democratic procedures is a condition of membership.[2] The EU is accused of a 'democratic deficit' both by those who wish to draw back from further integration and those who wish to progress towards a kind of federation. Opponents and supporters alike recognise a lack of democracy in the institutions of the EU themselves (Weale, 1995), a lack of legitimation of the polity by the citizens (Bellamy et al., 1995; Bankowski & Scott, 1996) and a stalling of the political will to overcome the deficit (Castiglione, 1995; Habermas, 1992). The EU's departure from the general democratic trend is to some extent because it is a young polity, still to find its final shape, and to some extent, because it is novel and without precedent. It is not a state in the old nation state sense of the term and the kind of state which it is becoming is not at all clear (Weiler, 1997; Habermas, 1997; Grimm, 1997). So our first difficulty when enquiring whether the EU is democratic is caused by the question a democratic 'what?'. We are attaching an adjective to an entity which is not a fully evolved polity and, indeed, may never be. Can we call the EU a state? At best we can say that the EU is a supra-national polity in formation.

The second difficulty concerns the present form of the institutions of the EU, where the classic democratic ideals of the separation of executive and legislative powers and the transparency of government appear to be transgressed (Castiglione, 1995; Duverger, 1991; Bellamy, 1996). Both the Commission and the Council can be seen as the executive.[3] It is principally the lack of accountability of the Commission, its tendency to enlarge its remit without recourse to any elected body and the lack of transparency endemic in both Council and Commission which causes discontent. There has been a great deal of pressure for change in the role and comparative weight of the institutions, and for more authority to be given to Parliament. The Maastricht and Amsterdam treaties both extended parliamentary power to an extent,[4] although the EP still remains the junior and least influential member of the EU institutions.[5]

The third source of discontent stems from the fact that the EU is organised according to criteria which Lively (1975) describes as 'weak' democracy. In his typology of democratic arrangements, the situation in which rulers are chosen by representatives of the ruled is minimalist democracy, only one category away from benevolent dictatorship. This is broadly the regime which pertains in the Commission and the Council, with both being nominated by national governments.[6] It could be argued that since members of the Commission or the Council are the delegates or appointees of elected governments this presents no grave infraction of democratic practice. However, the fact that neither can be removed by a European electorate runs against normal democratic tradition. The European electorate can elect and remove the members of the European parliament, but this body still has relatively little input into or influence over the legislative activity in the EU, even after the Maastricht and Amsterdam reforms. In this situation the sovereignty of the people means little and the ways to make the rulers accountable to the ruled are not evident (Duverger, 1991; Castiglione, 1995).

What democratic control do European citizens possess? Voting out the European Parliament changes nothing because it has little power. Voting out national parliaments would have a secondary effect on the EU, but the European voters could not coordinate their action on this, and, at the present time, are unlikely to censure national governments for such a purpose. For populations able to remove their own governments when they are dissatisfied with them, this lack of control is experienced as undemocratic. Of course, the EU is still evolving and it may yet become a more democratic polity. It has already taken seriously accusations of its own 'democratic deficit' and has grown into a more democratic institution in each phase of its existence. Direct elections, more powers for the Parliament, citizenship and greater transparency have all been responses to calls for greater democracy.

There is, however, another hurdle to be overcome before the EU can be fully democratic, and this might prove the most intractable. The expectation of those who have experienced the nation state model of representative democracy is that the voters should be reasonably homogenous and *able to communicate with each other.* The fifteen nation states which at present constitute the EU bring to it a firmly rooted tradition of nation-wide debate at times of referenda and elections. In some countries these roots are deeper than in others, but it is the tradition to which they all now subscribe. This model does not easily transpose to the EU. There is no European *demos* as such, conceiving itself as a unity, recognising interdependence between social groups, promoting a unitary civil society and developing a forum for debate (Habermas, 1992). Achieving consensus through consultation and exchange of opinion is not an option for the peoples of the EU. In the view of some commentators this is its fundamental weakness, for where there is no negotiated consensus for laws, they may be challenged (Bankowski & Scott, 1996). The link between the EU's multilingualism and its democratic deficit is not often referred to explicitly, but a very strong argument can be made that lack of direct channels of communication are a major factor in the perception that such exists.

Among all the reasons for the EU's democratic deficit, it is this hurdle, caused by the lack of a community of communication which is least likely to be addressed in the near future. The reasons for the silence on the subject are unclear, but stem perhaps from the way that identity and national pride are bound closely to language. The nation state tradition which imposed linguistic and cultural homogeneity, making democratic debate possible in national forums, becomes one of the main blocks to this development at supranational level. National languages have acquired a symbolic function as badge of membership of national communities, with the result that, in the *Europe des patries* tradition, equal treatment of and respect for each of the national languages is sacrosanct. So although democracy appears to require some degree of homogeneity, any steps in this direction would be in clear opposition to the resolve to preserve linguistic and cultural diversity within the Union. This concern has been present since the institution of the Community and is expressed in the founding treaty and many subsequent texts.[7] The linguistic and cultural diversity of Europe is well rooted and there is no possibility that a single language would ever be imposed top-down by political elites in a European super polity in the way that single national languages were prescribed in nineteenth century nation building.

A European community of communication could be created less radically by requiring that Europeans acquire a *lingua franca* in addition to their mother tongue. While slightly more feasible, this still remains in the realms of fantasy. Although bilingualism would be nothing new for speakers from autochthonous and allochthonous minorities, for the majority it would be a radical departure from the monolingual public life which has been a feature of the nation state. Then too, the disagreement and discord that would arise should Europeans have to choose one language as a *lingua franca* can be easily imagined. The choice of one nation's language to be the official *lingua franca* for the whole would certainly bruise national sensibilities. A *lingua franca*, particularly if it were to be English, would be perceived as a threat, carrying with it the distinct possibility of undermining other languages and cultures. Anglicisation might worry many Europeans as much – if not more – than the democratic deficit caused by the lack of a European community of communication.[8]

The Democratic Heritage

The central point in this argument hinges on whether or not democracy can function within a community which does not possess the means to discuss and debate as a group. If we review the spectrum of democratic possibilities that the Europeans have inherited and examine the role of the community of communication in each of them, we shall be in a better position to judge whether it is plausible to see communication as a key if not *the* key issue in building a democratic Europe. If, as I hope to demonstrate, debate and consultation are among the defining variables that all varieties of democracy share, then the linguistically diverse EU is faced with a daunting task if we wish it to become democratic in any of the accepted senses of the term.

The first of the possibilities is the tradition of direct democracy, a kind of popular power in which citizens engage in self-government and in which politics is discursive, educational and needful of active citizenship. This was the kind of participatory system practised in Athens between 508 BC and 320 BC. In this period, government was assured by an assembly of all male adult citizens who met about forty times a year to discuss and vote on all matters of state. Even war, its strategy and its military leaders were the concern of the assembly.[9] The judicial system was organised in the same participatory way, citizens being chosen by lot to be judge and jury in the courts. After debate, they voted on the guilt of the accused and the punishment appropriate to the crime. The franchise[10] was strictly restricted to adult, male, Athenian citizens. Women, slaves, subject-allies and metics were excluded and so perhaps no more than 40,000 out of a population of 250,000–300,000 took part. If this was majority rule, it was the majority of a very partial constituency. It was also, by definition, a constituency which used one single language.

This was extremely important because the ability to use language expertly to persuade others of one's case was paramount. No advantage accrued from statecraft built up over years of experience in a certain post;

no influence derived from an individual's position in a hierarchy. All political authority depended on the individual citizen's ability to develop and sustain an argument, to support it with evidence, to analyse and to advocate (Lloyd, 1992). The pivotal role of debate[11] in such a system led to the development of rhetoric as a skill and the techniques of argument were subjects of study and theoretical elaboration.[12] All contemporary witnesses concur on this, whether they approved or disapproved of democracy. In the *Politics,* Aristotle argued that aristocracy, etymologically 'government by the best', was preferable to the civil strife that might result from rule by a mob swayed by 'worthless demagogues' using their powers of rhetoric for their own purposes (Aristotle, 1988). Thucydides' authorial asides show his contempt for the decisions of the *demos* which could be arbitrary, whimsical and manipulated by the orators (Thucydides, 1997). Plato proposed that only a restricted circle of intellectual aristocrats, 'the thinking part of the community', have sole title to government (Stobart, 1911). As in all democratic arrangements there was a tension between what was beneficial to the polity as a whole and what was advantageous for the various factions. In the opinion of these authors, the ideal that the assembly, through debate, would secure the common good was an ideal not often attained.

Other authorities, however, portrayed the benefits of the system. Euripides' Theseus countered the accusation that orators sway the populace with the response that no man with good ideas is barred through poverty or lowly position from bringing these ideas before the public. Protagoras argued that free and compulsory state education would ensure the competence of citizens in their task and counter the risks of demagogy (cited in Rodewald, 1975: 83). All this exchange of opinion between its supporters and opponents is testimony to the role debate played in Athenian democracy. The discussion on whether participatory democracy is desirable or not to be found in the work of Aristophanes, Thucydides, Plato, Herodotus, Euripides and Aristotle would only have been possible in a society which encouraged debate, and, although Socrates died for his dissension, his death was an exception in a system which generally encouraged exchange of opinion.

There is some agreement that the Athenian system functioned with little bureaucracy, fostered a sense of public duty and a tradition of civic virtue, and secured the citizen's commitment to prioritise the requirements of the community (Farrar, 1992). So we might ask why it was eclipsed. Since the Athenian period, participatory democracy has resurfaced in Europe only intermittently and only for brief periods. There was a short renaissance in the city states of medieval Italy and southern France, where the consul system challenged the idea that government must be 'a God-given form of lordship' (Skinner, 1992) and in the Swiss cantons, where yearly assemblies of citizens continue to take place to this day. A form of democracy existed among some Germanic tribes, as in the example of the Icelandic *Althing*, and also in the co-operative industrial and agricultural movements of the early industrial revolution. Hannah Arendt (1962) argues that the early days of revolution were typically periods of intense debate where participation approximated to the democratic practices of Athens.[13] Thereafter, history has shown that direct democracy failed to become a permanent feature of political arrangements, as she illustrates with examples from the American and Russian revolutions. Apart from these few examples, there is little to find in the way of full-blown participatory democracy.

The failure of direct democracy derives to some extent from its need for 'face to face' societies, small communities which can meet and debate. Direct democracy in a larger polity has always seemed unworkable. However, recent developments in electronic media have caused a number of theorists to reconsider the feasibility of direct democracy (McLean, 1989; Budge, 1993). They offer a convincing argument that extensive consultation of the people is well within society's present technological capacities. Television, the press and the *Internet* can provide information, telephones permit participation in phone-in discussions and opinion gathering for polls. The spread of personal computers networked and linked to the *Internet* makes such participation and consultation even easier. Powerful computing facilities allow for the fast interpretation and dissemination of results. Communication, consultation and debate become feasible between the power elites and the voters, and among voters. In theory, certain features of participatory democracy, such as the monitoring of delegates (leading to the recall of those who fail to represent the views of their electors), the right of the ordinary citizen to initiate legislation and the possibility of allowing everyone access to decision-making through referenda[14] could be organised in a virtual forum.

However, the difficulty of finding a way of organising debate and consultation was not the prime reason for the demise of participatory democracy. Political elites have always feared that power in the hands of the masses would cause the state to degenerate into anarchy and violence. This fear has been a permanent feature of the argument against democracy in both ancient[15] and modern times.[16] The debate was, like democracy itself, abandoned by the Romans whose own short-lived democratic experiment ended in rule which Rodewald (1975) categorises as paternalistic and/or authoritarian. After the fall of the Roman empire, the small kingdoms which emerged during the early medieval period were mostly ruled by monarchs who were Christian or became so. The development of the concept of the divine right of kings to rule removed the need for the people to participate in government. The moral certainties of Christianity did away with the necessity for consultation and debate. God's law was not negotiable and Christianity demanded that people abide by the interpretation provided by the church. Democracy was in little evidence for fifteen centuries.

When the philosophers and political theorists of the 17th and 18th centuries began to question the concept of the divine right of kings, the debate about who should govern returned as a subject of enquiry. Fear of majority rule became a major preoccupation once again and few were ready to accept democracy in its full Athenian sense. Jean-Jacques Rousseau drew a distinction between *la volonté de la majorité* which would be aggregated egotisms and the rather mystical *volonté générale* in which the people come together to desire the common good (Rousseau, 1954).[17] Edmund Burke feared that the crowd was foolish and could not be trusted to rule (Burke, 1790). Even James Madison wrote that:

> democracies have even been found incompatible with personal security, or the rights of property; and have in general been as short in their lives as they have been violent in their deaths. (quoted in Birch, 1993: 45)

The French and American revolutions took the debate on democracy from theory to reality. An actual laboratory was available to test out the theories. For those who feared popular rule, the years of Terror during the French Revolution (1792–1794) gave evidence of the violence and anarchy that mob rule could inflict on society. But where some saw the glare of hell, others saw only light (Hart, 1982). For many, the American Bill of Rights and the French Declaration of the Rights of Man were so self-evidently true, so clearly derived from 'natural law' that democracy must be the 'natural' and, therefore, in the long run the inevitable form of government (Bryce, 1921).

If the democracy debate has lasted through the nineteenth century to the present day with no lasting consensus on a single definition nor a single way of implementing the idea, this derives from a central dilemma in the concept. There is an apparent incompatibility of liberty and equality, both of which appear necessary adjuncts to democracy. For the political theorists of the eighteenth century, the pressing need appeared to be to mount a defence against the power of the sovereign state, to find a way of countering despotism and exploitative ruling cliques. Democracy would be the means of spreading political power among the people and thus reining in the ascendance of narrow elites. Benjamin Constant noted the difference between the liberty of the ancients, which was participatory democracy, and the liberty of the moderns which had become personal liberty, guaranteed by the institutions of the state, rather than a role in government (Constant, 1988).

For some economic and social theorists of the nineteenth century, however, democracy was meaningless unless accompanied with measures to promote social justice and economic equality. For those wanting liberty, the intervention necessary for redistribution of wealth was anathema; for those wanting equality, unrestricted freedom nourished poverty and injustice. This basic dichotomy gave rise to the various democratic traditions.[18]

In Britain, there is a strong tradition of defence of personal liberty in the face of state intervention. From Locke arguing for limits to the power of the state (1978 1690), through Bentham and James Mill making a moderate utilitarian case for democracy, and Macaulay placing his faith in constitutional monarchy's power to guarantee individual liberties (1967, 1848) to J. S. Mill calling for a private realm immune from interference by the state (1996), British theorists have shown a preoccupation with individual liberty. Male suffrage was extended in the nineteenth century and finally accorded to the adult population in its entirety in 1918. British support for this was principally a desire for the political equality of citizens as a framework for the elaboration of institutions to promote freedom of choice and security against oppression (Held, 1993). In subscribing to the concept of popular sovereignty, the British did not believe that they were also supporting participatory democracy. In their version of democracy, it was for the citizens to elect and remove their governments but for the government to act in the interim. Clarification of issues and debates would take place at election time; thereafter representatives would act according to their interpretations of the best interests of those they represented. And for the British, democratic powers were primarily political powers. Those who called for societal and economic equality to accompany the political liberties were few[19] and relatively unsuccessful until the welfare state of 1945.

The experience of the US was profoundly different from the UK since it was less classbound, less shackled by precedent, and the revolutionary moment encouraged and made possible wide-scale change. Nonetheless, the Americans remained, like the English, far more attracted to ensuring liberty through democracy than to achieving social and economic equality via democratic political procedures. American democracy came to be a commitment to popular sovereignty,[20] the encouragement of competition between sectional interest and pressure groups and the division of powers between institutions (Birch, 1993). The Founding Fathers' belief in popular sovereignty was expressed in a system of frequent elections which ensured that politicians remain respectful of the electorate. The tradition of pluralism made it a culture which accepted that groups would work for their own interest but that this was acceptable as long as the practice was open not clandestine.[21] The separation of the legislature, the executive and the judiciary divided power. The ideal was the weak state which would allow the citizen the maximum liberty and security to concentrate on the real interests of life, which were private and economic rather than political. The American interpretation of democracy made it a set of rules for the delegation of power rather than the experience of participation (Fontana, 1992). In the long term the US state renounced any commitment to the economic egalitarianism which had been a feature of the early republic.[22]

The European concept of democracy stems more from the French tradition than the American, although both fed off each other. French democracy is clearly shaped and legitimated by the philosophical theories of Rousseau who propounded a collective ideal and the concept of civic virtue. Unlike American democracy with its belief that representatives of competing groups should come together to discuss and agree a consensus, the French tradition made representatives independent of the sectional interests which had elected them and the makers of *national* laws for the *national* good. The people would experience democracy by participating in sovereignty. Touraine explains this in the following way:

> The idea of a voluntary social bond is synonymous with the idea of citizenship, assuming that the acceptance of a bond is voluntary only if it can be freely renewed or broken; but a collective identification with a leader or a nation means the loss of individual will in favor of merging with a higher collective experience, against which there is no possible recourse. (Touraine, 1997: 79)

In the French version of democracy it was for the assembly and the government to 'embody' the will of the nation. The political representative was not to be a delegate, nor mandated to a programme, nor to be instructed by interest groups. The very existence of interest groups runs counter to this vision (Rousseau, 1954: 38). This model tends to the requirement that the people be a homogenous group capable of achieving the consensus necessary to exercise their sovereignty. This led to a strong tradition of civic education and a conscious inculcation of the 'republican spirit'. This was the template accepted and used in the constitutions of many European states.[23] France's last constitution (1958) with its move to presidential rule and the increased use of referenda can be seen as part of this tradition;

democracy continues to be a collective ideal rather than individualistic and adversarial. And at the end of the twentieth century, the legacy of the *Contrat social* remains influential: the relative power of the 'souveraineté du peuple, omnicompétence du politique, toute puissance de l'Etat' is still an issue (Julliard, 1985); a weak communitarian tendency continues to be the distinguishing feature of one of the founding EU member states.[24]

The third version of democracy in the European tradition is the one party democracy practised in the communist bloc. The marxist tradition recognised that the struggle for political equality represented 'a major step forward in the history of human emancipation' (Held, 1995), but held that true democracy could only come when social and economic equality were achieved. Multiparty systems and competition between interest groups cannot guarantee such equality because the dice are always loaded in favour of those with economic power. According to Marx the capitalist economy will inevitably produce systematic economic inequality and therefore restrict political freedoms. The solution was to be the replacement of the liberal democratic state by a 'commune structure', in which each small community would elect representatives to go forward to larger arena, which in turn would elect representatives to go to the national parliament (Marx & Engels, 1848). Marx confidently expected that such arrangements could reproduce the democracy that had disappeared 'into the blue haze of heaven with Christianity' (Marx, 1844 quoted Held, 1995: 14). There would be no party system; the choice would be between individuals. However, in the event, in all the 'peoples' democracies' the Communist party had total control of the state, the army, the media, the bureaucracy and every other political institution, and the choices available were devoid of all meaning. However, this was not the main cause of this system's demise. One party democracy managed to survive as long as it delivered the security and economic and social order it had promised. It crumbled when it could no longer do this.

And as a final note to this overview, we should remember that European liberal representative democracy has been under attack for much of the period of its development; fascism and communism were powerful competitors. The victory of this form of democracy in Western Europe was assured when the Allies won the Second World War, but fascism and communism provided robust competition until the 1970s and 1980s. Nor should we forget that universal suffrage is a comparatively recent commitment for many European countries; the franchise for women has only recently been achieved in all states.[25] In others, the record is still less than exemplary in the case of immigrants: not all people born on European soil automatically have citizens' rights.[26] It would be prudent to remember these shallow roots and troubled history when considering the apparent victory of liberal democracy as the accepted form of government in all the nation states of Europe.

Such is the background against which the EU is evolving. Since the one party system has been eclipsed and is no longer relevant in Europe, the influences to which the EU is subject are those of the western half of the continent. There is a choice: from the Anglo-Saxon world comes the liberal representative tradition, characterised by a two party adversarial system, first past the post voting procedures, a recognition that there is an interplay between interest groups and, recently, the commitment to extreme free market economics. The 'continental' tradition, on the other hand, offers a model of weak communitarianism, a commitment to multi-party, proportional representation with its resultant, not always stable, coalitions, and a greater tendency to state intervention and support. This leads to different political manoeuvring. In the first category, both parties tend to move towards the middle ground in order to ensure a majority and electoral success. In the second, it is in the parties' interest to retain their specificity to maintain their voters' support. In the first, the electorate can judge the government they elect on its record of implementing its electoral promises; in the second, the difficulties of coalition may provide an alibi for those manifestos not accomplished. In addition, the degree of centralisation of power and the amount of devolution within federal arrangements also varies widely. The many differences of these various traditions along with the other distinctive national features that European democracies have developed makes European democracy a mosaic and far from meaning the same thing to all of us.

Language and Liberal Democracy

Held provides a definition which can encompass the diversity of this mosaic, categorising democracy as:

> a cluster of rules and institutions permitting the broadest participation of the majority of citizens in the selection of representatives who alone can make political decisions (that is decisions affecting the whole community). (Held, 1993: 20)

This cluster includes free and fair elections for government, universal suffrage in which every citizen's vote is equal, the freedom to oppose the government, to stand for office and to associate to promote sectional interests. This is a very language dependent process. Each element hinges on the possibility that those to be represented and those who stand for office can communicate both within the groups from which they come and between them. There is inevitably a lot of talk in representative democracy, both to set it up and to maintain it. A community of communication is as essential to this form of democracy as it was to participatory. Debate may not be so general, take place so regularly nor be so demanding of participants' time but it must take place at two key points: in the association to promote and represent group interests and in the process of persuasion before elections and referenda.

One might imagine that if ideal representative democracy were realisable, the relatively homogenous group with few communication difficulties represented by the modern European nation state would be the polity best suited to it. Moreover, the concepts of nation state and representative democracy reinforce each other. The tendency of the nation state to strive for the congruence of cultural nation and political state is fuelled by the idea of a sovereign people and contributes to it. The ideal of one nation, one state, one language brought into being the cohesive community of communication necessary for the practice of democracy.[27]

In a model liberal democracy there would be free and simple access to accurate and uncensored information; an electorate skilled enough to evaluate evidence and decide upon issues; a public forum where facts and opinion could be exchanged; the frank admission of sectional interests and a social norm which frowned on apathy. These five elements would reinforce each other. Participation in an ongoing debate would make the people more skilled. Greater sophistication would make the people request pertinent information. Openness about interest would lead to greater understanding of bias, and awareness and avoidance of manipulation. The centrality of these political activities to daily life would draw in the vast majority. The ability to influence and set the agenda would not be the sole privilege of narrow power elites. Now, although most political elites in most European nation states would pay lip service to each of these elements, they remain ideals and reality is situated at some distance. However, we come far closer to achieving these goals within the communities of communication provided by the nation states than we do in the plurilingual circles of the EU. To compare the democratic deficits experienced in the nation states of Europe and the EU, we could examine how each deals with these elements.

Accurate Information and a Skilled Electorate

Freedom of the press is a cornerstone of representative democracy and always among the first demands of any democratic pressure group in an authoritarian state. Tocqueville (1946) reported that the democratic process in the young democracy of the United States was served by the number of newspapers it possessed and the ease with which they could be set up. Financed by advertisements and guaranteed protection by the law, they could be free of the influence of powerful economic and political interests. They were so numerous that all shades of opinion could find expression, yet none dominate. At the times when the press spoke with one voice on a subject it was reflecting a ground swell of public opinion and could then be a very powerful instrument for putting issues on the political agenda.

However, when powerful economic and political sectional interests control press, radio and television[28] and set the agenda, the forming of public opinion is manipulated from above. The media can no longer provide the communication circuit necessary for the untrammelled and informed debate which is the only means for representative government to access the sovereignty of the people (Habermas, 1984), and loses its function of limiting and controlling established power. Such developments have led members of the critical theory school to dismiss the claim that the public communicative sphere continues to provide an arena for evaluation of government by rational-critical debate (Horkheimer & Adorno, 1972).[29] For them, its role is now simply to provide the means for social integration and political manipulation.

In *The Theory of Communicative Action* (1981, 1984) Habermas argues that the process of communication is at its optimum when organised and 'controlled' at a local level, by the individual rather than by organisations. As soon as the communicative processes are owned and directed by organisations, they will be blocked whenever there is a conflict of interests. His solution to the problem posed by the concentration of media power in the hands of a few media moguls is to turn to the structures of civil society which retain grass root control. He argues that such associations can fulfill the functions met in the earlier days of liberal democracy by a free press which permitted the debate necessary for democratic functioning and that it is in this arena that the citizen can make himself heard.[30] If Habermas is correct, the channels of civil society allow a variety of sources of information to be accessed and circulated at local level, and local issues to be discussed in public forums with less manipulation than in the national arena.

At supra-national level the cause for the lack of a representative press is not just the stranglehold of press barons and media moguls but the lack of an audience. The plurilingualism of the EU naturally splits the readership into national groups. The few experiments which have tried to tap into a postulated European audience and create a European forum have had first to overcome the communication problem. So far they have had little success in providing specifically European channels of communication.

The European focusing on European politics and business, was marketed internationally during the 1990s. Unsurprisingly, since it was an English-medium paper, its popularity was greatest in anglophone countries and over fifty percent of the readership was accounted for by the UK, the US, Canada and the rest of the world. Less than fifty percent of the readership came from continental Europe and a significant proportion of this was from Central and Eastern European countries who used it to access international business news as markets in the old communist countries began to liberalise (*The European* fact sheet, 13 August 1996). The paper's monolingual approach, its support of free market economics, its UK ties and its virulent anti-Commission stance made it unlikely that it could ever be a forum which would unite the various national audiences in the EU. And, in the event, it failed to gain a substantial market share in Europe. Readership was small and confined to a narrow business class. In 1997 it was relaunched as a tabloid in a bid to boost circulation. In December 1998 it was closed.

Two further Europe-wide media ventures were started in France. Euronews, a television news channel based in Lyon, broadcasting the same content and images with a voice over in five different languages, became available throughout Europe for those who could pick up the satellite signals. It was not commercially successful. Among a number of other failings, the depersonalised format was criticised. Euronews was in financial difficulties in late 1997 and is now owned by a consortium of European public broadcasters (51%) and ITN (49%). ITN has operational control of the channel which since the takeover has extended coverage to 90 million homes in 43 countries in Europe, Africa and America. In Summer 1999, cable access became available in Russia and a five language Internet news service was inaugurated (Euronews press release, summer 1999). The globalisation of what was originally a news channel within EU boundaries has meant a change of focus in the news coverage. At the time of writing the other four languages were still available, but audience numbers for the English medium service were showing by far the most growth.

L'Européen is a weekly magazine, launched in March 1998 with the backing of *Le Monde* and Barclays. It is in French and in many respects resembles a national French weekly in the focus of its news stories and the slant of its editorials. It does, however, cover European news very thoroughly and promotes European integration in its features and competitions. Circulation is largely in the francophone areas of Europe. It is not a European paper so much as a *pro-European* French paper. None of these initiatives solved the problem of addressing the European public as an entity.

The other source of information about European affairs which is not filtered through national media is the EU's own information agencies. The various publics receive exactly the same information from the Commission and from the European Parliament, translated into each of the official languages and available in information centres throughout the various countries, by post or on the Internet. Most of it is free and easily available to those who bother to access it. It is of course unashamedly top-down information, which fulfills a PR function for the EU and is not conceived to stimulate critical debate. One of the reactions to the accusation that the EU has a democratic deficit has been to make access to documents easier. Jacques Santer promised greater transparency as did Tony Blair in speeches given before the UK presidency of the EU.31 Perturbed that European citizens had not fully appreciated the benefits of the Union, the political elites planned to explain to them how and why policies were being developed. What is still lacking, however, is a healthy, undeferential source of comment on political activity at EU level which is available to all EU citizens regardless of language group.

National Media on Europe

European citizens rely on their national media for information and comment about policies and politics at supra-national level. A wide variety of agenda affects the way policies are presented to the European public by the national governments and through the national media. The distortion can be positive or negative, as events, policies and personalities are mediated through the national political perspective and edited to fit the national agenda. As Riffault says:

> The image of the (EU) institutions as such depends heavily on the extent to which their activities are monitored by the media, which in some countries are more likely to make an issue of a crisis in Brussels, Luxembourg or Strasbourg than to report on the painstaking day-to-day progresses in those institutions. (Riffault, 1991: 35)

This was evident at the time of Maastricht. There was little public or national parliamentary interest in the negotiations in the more pro-European countries, and, surprisingly, minimal debate even in France and Denmark in the run-up to the referenda. The UK, where the press was largely anti-European, was the exception (Dinan, 1994). But the debate in Britain was hardly illuminating; the anti-European British press was largely fighting the last war and not confronting the actual issues of the TEU.

The British press often provides an extreme example of how information about the Community may be filtered and interpreted through a nationalist perspective. At times the British public has been manipulated by nationalist interests to take an anti-Community stance. The alarmist headlines of the tabloids, for example *The Daily Mail's* wail 'Is Chancellor Cabbage set to swallow Britain?' (*The Daily Mail*, 29 March 96), are unsophisticated and may be demonstrably inaccurate in their facts and analyses, but the readers' letters in the tabloids suggest that a proportion, if not a majority, of their readers has been persuaded to agree with this point of view. The serious British press has also tended to adopt nationalist perspectives and an anti-European tone. The Murdoch owned *Times*, for example, has displayed a consistently anti-European stance, which has manifested itself both in outright attacks on EU policy as well in constant, minor and often gratuitous attacks on European institutions and personalities. Even newspapers which are mainly pro-Europe take an aggressively anti-European line whenever the bureaucracy of Europe is at issue.[32] When a national press acts like this, taking an overwhelmingly anti-EU line, there is little that the pro-European lobby can do to counter it. Adequate channels and forums for by-passing and short-circuiting the national media do not yet exist.

Class Bias

Acquiring information about events at supra-national level is thus as problematic, perhaps more problematic, than doing so at national level. There are, of course, some groups who can access a wider variety of sources to inform themselves. Educated citizens who are multilingual and multiliterate will have access to information and analyses from outside the immediate community of communication. The ability to gather information from a wider base than the immediate community will be of most use to those from the very smallest language groups, permitting them access to a wider base of relevant information. For those from larger communities multilingualism permits the gathering of the views of the 'other' in a more comprehensive way.[33] The educated citizen is also more likely to possess the critical abilities to deconstruct the spin put on information and to discern hidden agenda. And finally, those with the economic means to access alternative networks to inform themselves, are also in a privileged position to disseminate their own views and knowledge (Budge, 1993). New media technologies allow the retrieval and dissemination of news outside the traditional forums, permitting those who can participate a means of supplementing the diet provided by the media empires. In fact, it could be argued that the Internet replicates to some extent the unfettered press that Tocqueville saw as such an advantage for early US democracy.

To summarise one would could suggest that those with the education, the motivation and the means to access the information necessary to form their own opinions can probably do so even within the managed information systems of late capitalism. Those who have neither the ability, the desire nor access to wider sources will be more easily manipulated. This is hardly new. Presumably the orators in the agora found certain groups more difficult to sway than others. The traditional criticism of democracy has always been twofold: that the people cannot be consulted because of the logistical impossibility of doing so; that the people do not have the education and experience to make decisions and are open to manipulation. Now, the technology is available to overcome the logistical difficulties. To worry that citizens will be controlled by media in the hands of the power elites is to fail to take into account the increasingly high levels of education of most European populations,[34] which make psychological manipulation through crude propaganda less likely.

As we might expect, the gulf between those well able to inform themselves and evaluate that information critically and those who are hampered in doing so widens when the political debate moves from the national to the supranational level. Those without the economic means or linguistic/educational background to access a variety of channels of information are destined to take the national media line on European matters. Here a reasonably legitimate preoccupation with national interest intermeshes with the hyped jingoism which may sell papers within the nation state to provide a very unbalanced and partial view of what is happening at supranational level. Strong transnational media would not have to pander self-consciously to a national audience, could reflect what other parts of the Union were thinking and could build a European consensus of opinion. This is not happening on a large scale for a variety of reasons, not least of course, the language barrier.

Debate

A politically educated citizenry in possession of the information necessary for governance then needs the forums and channels in which to discuss the issues and make its feelings known to the establishment. Public debate is essential. It is not so regular as in participatory democracy but it must take place at election time and within the associations which promote sectional interests.

Public debate in the first years of the American democracy impressed

Tocqueville who gives a vivid description of the energetic discussions he witnessed:

> No sooner do you set foot upon American soil than you are stunned by a kind of tumult; a confused clamour is heard on every side; and a thousand simultaneous voices demand the satisfaction of their social wants. Everything is in motion around you; here, the people of one quarter of a town are met to decide upon the building of a church; there, the election of a representative is going on; a little farther the delegates of a district are posting to the town in order to consult upon some local improvements; or in another place the labourers of a village quit their ploughs to deliberate upon the project of a road or a public school. (Tocqueville, trans. Steele, 1946: 176/177)

Debate continues to play a vital role. Political discussion helps make other forms of participation meaningful; voting without debate is meaningless. All citizenship theorists emphasise the importance of talk; Lindsay, Dewey and Ross see discussion among ordinary citizens as the essential of democracy (Thompson, 1970). In the election process or at times of referenda we take part in what becomes in effect a nation wide conversation.[35] We may be cynical[36] about the veracity of the claims of political parties and the partisan way in which political actors present themselves and their programmes to the electorate, but we also use the opportunity of these occasions to voice our opinions on policies and challenge political positions. It is less than a consultation process but more than information passed from the centre to the periphery. Phone-in discussions, television studio debates, letters to newspapers, opinion polls and question time in public meetings permit the electorate to participate. Each of these forums may be managed, the agenda may be controlled but where sections of the population are intent on making their voice heard, they can usually do so. Public debate and the influence of opinion leaders within small groups may serve as 'insulators against the manipulative potential of the media' (Thompson, 1970: 91).

This possibility for people to make their voice heard suggests that Habermas and the critical theorists have permitted themselves too strong a reaction to the media. Events show that not all communication between the establishment and the public mediated through the press, TV and radio is relentlessly top down. The media continue to catch the public mood and portray it to the power elites in the way that Tocqueville noted.[37] This gives a channel to public moods which might not be expressed in a formal way, such as the formation or membership of the associations of civil society (political parties, trade unions, pressure groups and campaigning organisations). And where the media fail to give voice to public mood, where public concerns are not put clearly on the political agenda, and where there is no evident striving for a solution, there may be recourse to direct action with demonstrations and/or riots.[38] This is, in itself, a powerful reason to monitor the public mood.

Of course, for all citizens to exercise political autonomy and play a role in the framing and enactment of legitimate law would demand equality of condition and expertise (Habermas, 1992). This is self-evidently not so and the right of access to processes of opinion and will formation is once again more exploitable for those with the critical and linguistic capacities and economic means mentioned earlier, the citizens whose capacities and means allow them to state, defend and disseminate their point of view through associations and political parties. The process is wholly dependent on communication and those who have neither the linguistic/cultural abilities nor the economic/technical means to influence it, cannot easily be part of the democratic process. The ability to put and defend an argument, the eloquence to win hearts and minds are the essential skills where power stems from the power of persuasion and not the power of force.

A European Public Sphere?

The European public sphere does not exist in the same way that national public spheres exist because of the lack of a forum and the common medium which would make it possible. For most people, discussion of European issues takes place at national level. Only the political elites, working on a pan-European level, have a trans-national view. For the mass of people the European debate will be filtered through considerations of national interest and perspective. National politicians and national journalists will be the gatekeepers of information. The general public will not be able to access the opinions held in other member states unless the gatekeepers decide to make them public, or, to recap the earlier argument, they come from educated and economically advantaged classes, with access to other channels of information. What the gatekeepers pass to the people depends both on what they consider to be in the national interest (information is likely to be filtered and interpreted) and on what their own language skills allow them to access.

This shapes the debates which take place. The discussion on European Monetary Union illustrates this clearly. In the period before its introduction most European citizens did not know the stance of their fellow citizens in other member states on this issue. They only had glimpses of opinions from the other communities of communication. The flow of information was uneven, with more exchange between some classes and peoples than between others. The European business and economic communities were in contact and an in-depth discussion took place in the specialist media that cater for this sector. This was true, even for the British press, which otherwise had a very national focus on the issue.[39] The extent to which the debate had progressesd to being transnational within this group was reflected in the opinion submitted to the Amsterdam summit by 331 European economists. Certain pairs of countries took note of opinion within each other's population. In particular, the French and German readers of the serious French and German press could learn the views of high profile figures from the other state and gauge how opinion was forming outside their borders. The cross frontier debate between Tietmeyer and Bourdieu[40] attracted a lot of interest.

Elsewhere, however, the transnational dimension was often bypassed. In the British and Scandinavian press the editorial pages of the serious press focused largely on issues of sovereignty and identity. In Britain, the yellow press took its usual xenophobic line with *Sun* headlines such as 'You don't want Euro Bankers to run Britain'. In general, the European media's focus was overly national for an issue which is transnational. The trade union activity of Autumn 1996 in response to the economic pain of meeting convergence criteria was widely reported in a piecemeal way as a series of 'foreign' strikes.[41] Even the Internet appeared to be failing in this area with structured debates on the euro apparently attracting little interest (*The Observer*, 23 February 1997). There has been silence where there should have been rigorous scrutiny. After all, the EU has already established the precedent that the richer parts of the European Union will fund the poorer, the more affluent sections of European member states the less affluent (e.g. in the Common Agricultural Policy, in the Social Fund and in the financing of Regional Policy and Cohesion[42]). In such a context of general responsibility the debate about monetary union is not just about national advantage and disadvantage, but about its effects throughout the EU. This perspective was largely missing from the debate on the Euro.

This is likely to change. National public spheres developed in response to challenges posed by contentious issues (Grundmann, 1999) and it is conceivable that the public sphere at supra-national level may develop in a similar way. Issues which can only be dealt with transnationally (e.g. EMU, the environment) may in the long term synchronise and harmonise national agenda and bring about the emergence of a European public sphere (Mény et al., 1996). However, the plurilingual nature of the sphere will still mean that the flows of debate and information will either be top down, from centre to periphery with people receiving what is translated for them, or will circulate among an elite which has the level of foreign language skills and contacts which permit it to transcend the normal channels.

Transparency

To the distortions caused by debating nationally and with national preoccupations issues which are trans- or supranational are added the obstructions caused by the lack of transparency in the institutions of the EU. For example, as is normal in the Council of Ministers, the Treaty of Maastricht was negotiated in secret, with the effect that even in those countries whose populations were allowed referenda on the treaty, the deliberations were partial. There was no soliciting of public opinion at an early stage; the various populations permitted to do so[43] were only asked to accept or reject the final aggregated package, not to contribute to the debate (Dinan, 1994; Lane & Ersson, 1996). Transparency was discussed at the European Council meeting in Edinburgh in 1992 and since then some concessions have been made to public worries and criticism about unnecessary secrecy. As these concessions are implemented it has become clear that there is more lip service to accountability than real openness. All important negotiations, votes and trade-offs still take place in secret (Hayes-Renshaw, 1996).

Weale suggests that it is not difficult to see why the level of public participation and discussion in EU politics has been so low. On the one hand the EU has always been a technocratic vision of how to achieve European integration with a top-down approach; on the other, the national politicians in the Council act mostly 'to maintain political capital and control within their own national systems' (Weale, 1995: 82). Even where there has been progress in the deliberative process, in the growth in importance and substance of the IGCs, for example, this debate has still remained within the political class and has not filtered down to citizens in general (Edwards & Pijpers, 1997). It seemed that the ratification difficulties of the TEU caused the European political class to be more aware of the need to take the citizens with them and so opened up dialogue. I would argue that this has not resulted in any greater debate, simply in more PR. The democratic deficit is being addressed through greater information, which is only one aspect of the problem. Whatever the truth of this, the desire of bureaucrats at European level to keep the citizens out of the process and the desire of politicians at national level to retain the importance of the national focus inevitably combine with the fractured language situation. European democratic debate is inherently difficult and the obstacles are not being overcome.

Interest Groups and the General Interest

The danger of democracy has been seen to be the 'tyranny of the majority' voting in its narrow self-interest. The conflict between self-interest and the general interest is necessarily mediated through debate. The ideal result, consensus, comes from understanding the point of view of the other with only the force of the better argument being counted. In reality this is likely to be a combatative process and the deliberations which lead to this desirable end will include bargains, threats, warnings, compromises (Elster, 1998). Eloquent and skillful use of language, veiling threats, selling beliefs, framing compromises, is at the heart of the process.

Associations and parties must communicate in two forums. Within the group it is necessary to hold the meetings and the conferences where the members and activists discuss policy. Such a forum may be managed so that the ruling elite (or even single leader) can pass its decisions on policy to those who will promote them (for example, in canvassing the general electorate) or the debate may be a true exchange, with opinions sought and given and policy developed from consensus.[44] This form of debate is very often in the ancient face to face tradition of democracy, taking place in party conferences, protest meetings, rallies etc. Thereafter, the group needs to convince the greater public, or at least enough to form a majority that their policies are for the general good. For this purpose, communication largely moves once again to the forum provided by the media, along with the various channels that the new media and technologies of the second half of the twentieth century have made possible: personalised mail shots, telephone as well as door step canvassing, interactive Internet sites, with the new technologies making it feasible to customise information in the appropriate language for the recipient.

The organisation of sectional interests and the building of political parties is once again a very language dependent process, being part open debate and forming of a political project, part elaboration of a discourse about and around the group which will make it attractive and electable and which may ameliorate the group's image or soften certain aspects of its purpose. When sectional interest groups are not a natural majority this process must be managed so that the group gains the acceptability and applicability necessary for it to triumph in a wider arena. Braud's (1980) analysis of the linguistic formulae adopted to obscure the principal preoccupations of French political parties reveals how discourse must be elaborated to make minority interest groups appeal to the majority. Only those who can mask their narrow interest base gain widespread support at national elections.[45]

Choice of language and title can be used in the opposite sense, to limit appeal. This is unlikely to happen where a minority interest group is trying to attract a wider electorate but is highly likely in referenda on devolution or autonomy, where the sectional interest group seeks to limit membership. The Scots Forward campaign before the 1997 referendum on Scottish devolution used both Gaelic and Lallans for some of its publicity. For the strict purpose of communication, this is of course unnecessary since there are no monolingual Lallans or Gaelic speakers left in Scotland. The strategies and policies decreed by the government in London at the height of its efforts to construct the British nation have seen to that. Written Lallans was used in the referendum campaign in the spirit of 'secret language' and 'insiders' club', with a symbolic rather than a communicative function. Since it is mostly a spoken rather than a written language, the early effect was one of amusement. However, within the few months of the campaign it acquired increased status, shown perhaps most clearly in the number of Chambers Scots-English dictionaries sold in the period (*Guardian*, 2 September 1997). Gaelic also had a rising profile between devolution and the opening of the Scottish parliament in Summer 1999. In the election campaign it was used symbolically, both by the nationalists, who traditionally do so, and by Labour as well. In the business of the Scottish parliament it has become an official language alongside English. When language is used in this way, there may well be political advantage for those politicians able to capitalise on their membership of linguistic groups – and disadvantage for those who cannot.

Associations will form among those who have similar political agenda and who stand to gain from a pooling of power and influence, always with the proviso that the various elements who could profit from such association can communicate easily. The community of communication provides a 'virtual' agora, a forum for the exchange of ideas. Where this is not so, association either does not take place or is immensely more problematic. The history of Belgian syndicalism exemplifies this, split as it is between two linguistic traditions (Jacobs, 1973; Kendall, 1975).

Europe-wide parties have not yet secured enough success to suggest this is not problematic. The integrationists have placed much hope in their role as agents of unification. This is stated quite unambiguously in Article 138A of the Maastricht Treaty:

> Political parties at the European level are important as a factor of integration within the Union. They contribute to the formation of a European consciousness and to the expression of the political will of the citizens of the Union.

But MEPs still remain closely linked to the national parties who select them and organise their campaigns (Andersen & Eliassen, 1996). The groupings in parliament are simply alliances of national parties, only collegiate not binding and have often been remade.[46] There are no European parties as such nor even common manifestos. The close relationship of European political life with the national has ramifications: a period in the European parliament is often used as way into a career in national politics or as a refuge following rejection at national elections; European elections have always been used by voters to express satisfaction or dissatisfaction with national governments much more than to pass comment on European developments. This was true when Lafont wrote of the early elections:

> Mornes, les citoyens européens le (le parlement) réeliront deux fois sur des critères de familles politiques organisés nationalement, sans avoir jamais à juger d'un programme européen, ni des pouvoirs des députés qu'ils choisissent. (Lafont, 1993: 188)

It remained true in the 1994 and 1999 elections.

Within the parliament, the national parties group under supernational umbrellas: these were the EPP, the PES, the ELDR and the EFG in the 1994–1999 parliament. They overcame their inbuilt communication difficulties to hold yearly congresses to co-ordinate their policies and actions. However, as the representatives of interest groups, the political groupings, while crucial to the workings of the European parliament, have not been very influential in any other arena (Salmon, 1996: 22). It has not necessarily been the party machines which had control of power in the EU:

> Lobbies, interest groups, consortia, cartels and professional associations are all in a systematic relation to the European Union's structures. (Gaffney, 1996: 21)

It was these groups which often provided the expertise in matters such as economic and monetary union which demanded highly specialist knowledge (Mény *et al.*, 1996).

In this area of lobbying and interest group, the EU remains highly complex and opaque. And this opacity of interest contributes to the lack of open government along with policies made in national trade-offs, agreed behind closed doors, discussed in the closed circuits of information constructed by language difference and insufficiently monitored by a weak parliament. In the Parliament, there is a keen awareness of this weakness, as the following statement by Mr José María Gil-Robles, its president, on the entry into force of the Amsterdam Treaty on 1 May 1999 makes clear:

> The negotiations on the Amsterdam Treaty have shown us that the reforms must not just be conducted through diplomatic procedures but must make provision for more active involvement by the Commission, the European Parliament and national parliaments.

The EU has developed rapidly in a number of domains. It is difficult to predict where this will happen next, but the tradition of national interest groups 'fixing' behind the scenes and business lobbying the Commission may become a more transparent process, given that the Parliament is beginning to flex its muscles.

Apathy

The last criterion for the ideal liberal representative democracy discussed above was the centrality of political activities to the citizens' daily life and their interest in and commitment to the process. In both the national political process and the European, apathy can also be shown to have a language dimension.

The extent of participation of citizens in national elections can be evaluated along two continua. On one continuum the voter can be situated according to criteria of apathy/interest, rejection of/commitment to the electoral process. At one end will be the voters who either feel their vote makes no difference or who are totally uninterested. Both categories are likely to decline to vote. They are unlikely to attempt to inform themselves. At the other end of this continuum will be the part of the electorate which constitutes the politically active, the politically committed. The other axis measures the capacity of the individual to take part in the pre-electoral or pre-referendum debate. At one extreme is the voter from a territorial or immigrant minority who may not master the majority language well enough to follow the debate in its complexity; the voter whose lack of literacy does not allow access to all the channels and forums in which the debate takes place; the voter whose education did not progress to a level which permits analysis of the message and the implications of the message. Both inter- and intra-language difficulties affect the process. At the other end of the spectrum is the fluent, literate, educated and interested voter who can access all levels of the debate and evaluate more easily the viability of the electoral promises offered in the manifestos.

No desire to take part in
the electoral process

Unable to inform oneself in order to take part in the electoral process	Will not vote	Will not vote	Able to inform oneself in order to take part in the electoral process
	Will not vote	Will vote	

Desire to take part in
the electoral process

In three of the four quadrants voters may decline to vote from lack of interest or lack of knowledge, or both. This is already true in national elections where a reasonably homogenous electorate, informed by national media and parties in the national language, engages in a national debate, monitored and encouraged by national opinion polls, before voting. It is even more likely in elections for the European parliament where those who feel unconcerned or uninformed become even larger percentiles of the electorate. The turnout figures for the European elections reflect this.

1984	61%
1989	58.5%
1994	56.8%
1999	49.9%

(source: Eurostat, 1994; European Parliament
website 15 June 1999)

These figures mask great disparities. In Belgium, Greece and Luxembourg voting is compulsory; in Italy there is strong social pressure to do so. Figures from these countries boost the mean percentages and balance the countries with low turnout. In 1994, the turnout figures of 36.4% in the UK, 36% in the Netherlands and 35.5% in Portugal (Eurostat, 1994) made commentators question the legitimacy of the Parliament (Economist 18 June 1994). In 1999 the turnout had dropped even lower: 24% in the UK, 29.9 % in the Netherlands, 30.1% in Finland and 38.8% in Sweden (Portugal climbed slightly to 40.4%). Commentators debated whether this was indicative of apathy or a deeper malaise.

Dryzek (1990) regrets that the ideal speech situation cannot exist in the real world. A democratic polity in which the different actors in a debate have equivalent degrees of communicative competence, are all equally free from domination and self-deception, all fully committed, all well-informed and all willing to work together in an unlimited and unconstrained way to reach consensus is always an unattainable ideal. In the EU it appears even less attainable than in the nation state.

The EU and the Democratic Deficit

This chapter started with the accusation that the EU is 'deficient in many of the defining variables of a democratic state' and for each element of the ideal democratic polity there were hindrances to implementation at EU level, over and above those experienced in the nation state.

This state of affairs in the Union has arisen in part because the constitution making processes in the Union have been underplayed (Castiglione, 1995; Weiler, 1996) and there has been a general lack of awareness and debate as the European Community has grown into a *de facto* polity. This is particularly true of the Commission, which has become an unelected centre of power in the Weberian sense.[47] The Commission has expanded opportunistically into new areas, e.g. social matters, environmental concerns (Weale, 1995), which were originally outside its remit. Popular reaction has been to rail at the lack of democratic accountability and at the absence of transparency and purposely to misunderstand the legislation emanating from the Commission even where it is clearly contributing to the general good.[48] Reactions have been strong in Britain, where a very strong, centralised bureaucracy is often caricatured as a French, continental tradition to be rejected (Jennings, 1995) and in France where an untrammelled market is sometimes presented as a liberal incursion from a harsher Anglo-Saxon tradition (Walzer, 1997).

If there is more than a little truth in categorising the EU as a technocratic and undemocratic bureaucracy, what could be done to rectify this? Weale and Castiglione both suggest that the EU needs a constitutional moment, a convention on the model of the historical event in Philadelphia in 1787, so that there can be open debate on the appropriate location for decision making (supra-national, national or sub-national) rather than that this should happen by default.[49]

Obviously the need to reconcile entrenched and conflicting interests would be the prime difficulty in any constitutional deliberative process. However, the multilingual and multicultural nature of the EU would also provide an immense hurdle, and which, on the evidence of the European integration process so far, might not be recognised and tackled explicitly.

The variety of linguistic traditions brings together people who might use the same word etymologically but who will bestow slightly different meanings on it. Budge gives the example of 'switches from English to German or Greek, for example (which) have a considerable potential for altering the import of political words and the level of abstraction of the discussion' (Budge, 1993: 137). The different understandings of the concept 'federalism' stemming from the different political experiences and social settings of the Member States provide an example of how this can happen in practice.[50] Language divisions reinforce differences in political culture in a Union which brings together the British, whose political tradition has never embraced constituent assemblies and the Germans whose recent history includes strong citizens' movements but whose experience of successful democracy is relatively short, and which splits into the tradition of constitutionalism with its preoccupation in limiting the powers of government and the state's authority and statism which seeks the common good in a more interventionist way. In a constitutional moment, the different traditions are likely simply to replay themselves within the different communities of communication. Castiglione's hope that constitution making would be an appropriate apprenticeship for democracy at EU level must remain utopian until we solve the question of a forum. Language difference would fracture popular consultation, making it a national debate rather than European and on the evidence of past European elections and referenda, discussion would be diverted from supra-national considerations to national affairs.[51]

In this matter of realising supranational democracy we are faced, albeit in a different way, with the same magnitude of problem that accompanied the move from small scale participatory democracy in the city state to representative democracy in the larger polity. To cope with that expansion a different way of managing participation had to be developed. I believe that something similar will have to happen in order for there to be a democratic forum in the European Union. There are no models for this. The United States has an electorate of much the same size and a federal structure, but US presidential elections take place after a nation-wide debate in one single language. India is a multilingual polity with a large population which is also a democracy but also fails to provide a model for the EU situation since Hindi and/or English are available for use as official *lingua franca* alongside the state languages.

Budge (1993) forecast that there could be a return to a form of participatory democracy through the development of the new media and information technologies. There is perhaps a very minor possibility that machine translation allied to the Internet and interactive methods could provide the framework for the third conception of democracy. The technology of machine translation remains, however, a long way from the sophistication necessary to be of any use in such a function. And even were the inherent problems to be solved, the different connotations in the various European languages noted above would still prove a stumbling block. Before machine translation can come to grips with finding equivalence we need the kind of metalinguistic pan-European debate on our political self-organisation that we find impossible because of our difficulties in communication.[52]

Some political theorists who have recognised that regional and global interconnectedness contests the traditional siting of democracy in the nation state and that the 'very process of governance can escape the reach of the nation state' (Held, 1993) call for democratic arrangements that will take this into account. Held's solution is a cosmopolitan model of democracy with enhanced political powers for the UN, greater legal power for the international courts and the establishment of an international military force (Held, 1993: 46). Held does not discuss which languages the political, legal and military powers of his cosmopolitan model would use, but, as we have seen, globalisation usually implies anglicisation. Held's omission of any consideration of the linguistic means by which suprana-tional democracy could happen suggests a tacit assumption that if cosmopolitan democracy comes to pass, it will do so in English. This is a very anglocentric view and would not pass without contestation. The spread of English is certainly not a solution that would gain unanimous support as a way of creating a democratic forum in the EU.

Held's key point for this present argument is that constituency and representation have different meanings in the late twentieth century. He notes the inconsistencies and tensions that result from a political situation where political power mainly resides with the nation state but where economic power is mostly transnational. I would add that the fundamental difficulty in resolving this asymmetry stems from the different media in the two domains. Economic power is mediated through money and can cross cultural and linguistic divides without provoking major social change. Where political power is democratic, it is mediated discursively through language and is constrained by linguistic barriers whose destruction would demand immense social and individual effort.

In all of this one basic truth emerges: in the democratic process, language is power, as true for the monolingual situation as for the plurilingual. In the monolingual situation, those with mastery of the language, able to put their arguments persuasively, will be advantaged; those with less mastery are disadvantaged perhaps by the fact that accent and usage mark them as outsiders of a cohesive group and certainly by the fact that lack of linguistic competence prevents them putting their arguments persuasively. In the plurilingual situation, the language issue becomes even more pivotal. In a relatively conflict free situation, pluralism means advantage for those with competent linguistic access to all the groups concerned, who can build bridges and coalitions, and customise their message. In a conflict bound situation, language is both a marker of difference and a limit to developing contacts. It is symbolically and practically a stumbling block to resolving difference and developing consensus. It may be a banality to say that democratic processes take place more easily in a community of communication than across language cleavages. However, since these linguistic banalities seem to be often overlooked or ignored, it may be well worth labouring the point.

This apparent necessity for a community of communication in a democracy brings us to a paradox. Equality and liberty have always proved difficult to reconcile in democratic theory and practice. Nowhere is this more evident that in the question of language. Equality is served by the eradication of linguistic difference and the construction of a community of communication that allows all to participate in the democratic life of the state. At the same time, the right to use one's language is a fundamental libery which a democracy must respect.

Notes
1. From 1688 onwards British political power resided in parliament rather than the monarchy (e.g. parliament decided taxation; there was freedom of the press and of association). See Held (1993) for further discussion.
2. Reaffirmed by Jacques Santer in his Agenda 2000 speech given to the European Parliament 16 July 1997 and in the Treaty of Amsterdam, Article 6 and Article 49.
3. Before the European Parliament's powers were widened to include codecision and coprocedures, the responsibilities of the EU institutions were presented in the following way: the Commission proposes, the Parliament, discusses, the Council decides and the Commission executes.
4. The Treaty of Rome gave the EP the right of censure. The Treaty of Maastricht gave the EP the right to approve the president of the Commission and the commissioners, and to take a greater role in legislating under the procedures of codecision and cooperation. The Treaty of Amsterdam extended the EP's competence within codecision and cooperation to new domains, and gave it the right to be consulted on issues in Pillar Three. For further information on how the role of the European Parliament has developed in the area of coprocedures and codecisions see Lodge (1996) and Tournier (1999).
5. It was widely believed that the Parliament would never use its powers of censure since these could only be used in a very blunt way to attack the whole edifice of the Commission. In Spring 1999, however, threats that it would do so

over questions of fraud and mismanagement caused the whole Commission to resign.

6. In this analysis EU political arrangements do not even meet Joseph Schumpeter's minimalist definition of democracy. Schumpeter redefined democracy as 'the freedom to choose a governmental team' (Touraine, 1997: 83). Lively (1975) finds this is not a sufficient condition for democracy.

7. Linguistic pluralism is safeguarded in Articles 217 and 248 of the Treaty establishing the EEC, in Articles 190 and 225 of the Treaty establishing the European Atomic Energy Community and in the various acts of accession. Both the preamble and Article 126 of the Treaty on European Union signed at Maastricht in 1992 guarantee respect for cultural diversity.

8. Reported, for example, in the work of French and German scholars, politicians and organisations: cf. Calvet (1993), Hagège (1987), Mackiewicz (1997), CERCLE (1996) and Chirac (1997).

9. No ruling elite could arise since the assembly's business was prepared by a council of five hundred citizens chosen by lot with a revolving leader and no citizen was permitted to serve on that council for more than two years throughout his whole life.

10. Those who were enfranchised were not always enthusiastic participants. Scholars suggest that the day to day working of the democratic project seems to have suffered from public apathy and that it was probably to boost attendance that citizens received pay for their participation at certain periods (Hornblower, 1992).

11. The adversarial nature of debate in the assembly and the courts may also have had a profound effect on the development of philosophy and science, in which abstraction, reason and persuasion are equally necessary (Lloyd, 1992).

12. The surviving work of professional speech writers such as Lysias, Isaeus and Demosthenes reveals the high intellectual standard expected of the average jury member. The speeches appealed to logic and to follow them demanded an extensive knowledge of the law (Stobart, 1911).

13. Tocqueville bears witness to this: 'In the parish of New England the law of representation was not adopted, but the affairs of the community were discussed, as at Athens, in the market-place, by a general assembly of the citizens' (Tocqueville, 1946: 38).

14. Bealey (1988) gives these three as the most likely elements of participatory democracy to survive in the modern world.

15. Plato argued that it is not in the best interests of most men to decide their own fate and that the philosopher king must be trusted to rule in the best interests of all. Aristotle rejected full participatory democracy, supporting instead an arrangement of monarchy, aristocracy and democracy in which the three loci of power would provide checks and balances.

16. In Britain, the exchanges of Thomas Paine and Edmund Burke give the arguments for and against majority rule. How to prevent the 'tyranny of the majority' was a preoccupation of Tocqueville, Calhoun and Fenimore Cooper in the American debate. For further discussion of the question see Roper (1989) and Smith (1990).

17. How this was to be achieved has always been problematic and the idea lends itself to totalitarian and quasi-totalitarian interpretations. See Julliard (1985).

18. Lively (1975) points out that the tendency to contrast democracy and totalitarianism is logically flawed. Totalitarianism indicates the amount of control, democracy who controls. This shorthand is used to contrast the one party state with the multiparty system.

19. Thomas Paine in *Rights of Man* is one of them. In this call for social equality he presents costed plans for free education, old age pensions, welfare benefits and children's allowance. He is, however, an outsider who spent much time in the US and France and who had difficulty getting his ideas accepted in his own country.

20. Lincoln's celebrated definition of democracy as 'government of the people, by the people, for the people'.

21. The call for this came from all sectors of society. William Findley, a weaver in Pennsylvania, rejecting the claims of the classical tradition of disinterested public leadership claimed that 'the promotion of private interests in politics was legitimate as long as it remained open and above board and was not disguised by specious claims of genteel disinterestedness' (quoted in Wood, 1992: 103).

22. Tocqueville remarked on the remarkable conformity and economic levelling that he witnessed in the US.

23. Belgium (1831), Italy (1848), Prussia (1850), Sweden (1866), Austria (1867), Germany (1871), Switzerland (1874), the Netherlands (1887), Denmark (1915), Italy (1948) and West Germany (1949). See Held (1993) for further discussion.

24. This weak form of communitarianism can be best described in Touraine's terms:

    The whole of French political life until now has been dominated by a conception of democracy that subordinates political actors to the needs of society-nation-people, its collective consciousness and its rational interests. (Touraine, 1997: 81)

25. Swiss women acquired the vote in 1971.

26. As late as 1996 it was possible to write the following lines:

    In Germany today, one in three children under the age of ten and one in five young people under the age of eighteen are 'foreigners', i.e. they do not hold German citizenship (although many were born in the country). (Kolinsky, 1996: 75)

    By 1999 the law had changed to allow a limited *jus soli*. Parents of children born on German territory have to fulfil residency and other criteria for their child to be eligible for German citizenship.

27. This synergy is illustrated most graphically by the French whose political elites planned for linguistic unification to permit political participation (see Chapter 2). The case of Switzerland which is often cited as an example of multilingual democracy actually contributes further proof of the need for congruence between linguistic communities and political groupings where these are democratic. In Switzerland democracy is 'experienced' at local level more strongly than at national level and many debates and much decision making take place at monolingual, cantonal level.

28. This has always been an issue but power has become even more concentrated. Bagdikian (1983) predicted that between five and ten corporate giants would come to control most of the world's important newspapers, magazines, book publishing houses, broadcasting stations, film making companies, recording studios and video production. The dominance of Microsoft, Disney, Murdoch,

Berlusconi, Pearson and Turner in the 1990s shows how accurate this prediction turned out to be.

29. One may agree with the critical theorists that the media are essentially a tool of the power elites, without necessarily feeling that they are thus completely useless in their role as informants. The sectional interests controlling the media will, to borrow a phrase, only fool some of the people some of the time. Those who have learnt to manipulate are read both by those who have learnt to deconstruct manipulation and by those who may be susceptible to manipulation. It might be more accurate to say that there are gross differences between the critical capacity of different readers to deal with the presentation of information.

30. This does, however, seem to beg the question that association in the public sphere can also be hi-jacked by sectional interests and that pressure groups and the media interact in complex and ultimately inextricable ways.

31. Jacques Santer in speech, *Agenda 2000*, given to the European Parliament 16 July 1997. Tony Blair in addresses to Council of Ministers at Nordwijk, Netherlands (reported, *Guardian*, 23 May 1997) and in Malmo, Sweden (reported, *Guardian*, 7 June 97).

32. See, for example, Hillmore (1998).

33. There are, of course, limits to this. We should be aware that news gathering and dissemination tend either to be parochial or to rely heavily on the big agencies (Reuters, AP, UPI, AFP). The first case means that moving outside our linguistic community may not bring us the insights of the outsider into our affairs but simply the domestic affairs of the neighbour; the second case simply means that we read, in a different language, information from the same source, since it is likely that subjects prioritised by the agencies will appear in various national presses and that what was neglected in one forum will be neglected in all. The North Korean famine of Summer 1997 is an example. The FAO warned that as many as 27 million people were at risk. This had very little coverage throughout the national press in Western Europe. This asymmetry in what is presented as newsworthy has been criticised in the MacBride Commission Report which complained that the agencies' choice disseminated information top down and from centre to periphery.

34. Measured for example by the percentage of young people who progress to some form of higher education.

35. For a discussion of the form and extent of the national debates which took place before the referenda on Welsh and Scottish devolution see Smith and Wright (1999).

36. There are numerous examples of extreme cynicism about the democratic process. Braud (1980) provides an example from the French tradition of criticism of liberal democracy. For him, 'élections disputées' are simply 'quelques coudées d'avance sur les régimes à goulags du Nouveau ou de l'Ancien Monde . . . Le suffrage universel . . . muselle l'expression des conflits réels (Braud, 1980: introduction).

37. Forcing a subject onto the agenda can happen in two ways. In phone-in programmes, letter pages, etc. the agenda is set by the political/media elites and contribution from the greater public is managed by media 'gatekeepers' who filter out opinions which are not desired, through the choice of participants. Unwanted opinions that do get through are extinguished by blocking

certain participants from further discussions. There are, however, occasions when strength of public feeling can force an issue onto the agenda. Arguably, the death and funeral of the Princess of Wales in September 1997 provided one example of this (Yentob, 1997). The debate carried out in the media about the role and expected behaviour of the monarchy seems to have been a reflection of spontaneous public condemnation. Another example from the same year was the revolt against sleaze which led in part to the defeat of the Conservatives in the British General Election. In both cases press coverage may have been a reflection of public reaction or it may have been media manipulation of opinion. The direction of influence is not always clear cut, particularly in the Diana example, and may, indeed have been circular. For further discussion see Smith and Wright (in preparation).

38. The 1981 riots in the UK can be interpreted as a spontaneous grass roots reaction against the perceived marginalisation of one sector of society in the harsh climate of market economics.

39. In Britain *The Financial Times*, the financial sections of the broadsheets, *The Money Programme*, etc. dealt with the economic aspects of EMU within a larger frame than the national.

40. 'Le président de la Bundesbank parie sur l'euro en 1999', Hans Tietmeyer interviewed in *Le Monde* 22 December 1996. 'Warnung vor dem Modell Tietmeyer', Pierre Bourdieu in *Die Zeit*, 1 November 1996.

41. The French strikes of the winter 1995–1996 were an early manifestation of the disquiet felt about the austerity programmes caused by the needs of convergence; they were described in *Le Monde Dossiers et Documents 1997* as strikes against globalisation! As feelings of anxiety about the economy and national sovereignty grew, Spanish civil servants demonstrated in protest to cuts, the Italians reacted nervously to Romano Prodi's deficit slashing budget and the Austrians gave increasing support to Jörg Haider's far-right anti-Europe party. During the winter of 1996–1997 sectors of the German workforce added their voice, demonstrating against the cuts in social welfare that the government was imposing. However, the media tended to report these events as national rather than as phenomena caused by common continental-wide forces. See Wright (1997a) for an analysis of national focus in *Le Figaro*, *La Repubblica* and *The Telegraph*, October 1996.

42. European Union policy states explicitly that 'there is a need to compensate for major inequalities in the capacity of the regions to generate income and in the ability of different social groups to compete effectively in the labour market (Commission, 1996: 115).

43. Danish, Irish and French.

44. This has been the mode of operation in the European Green Party. They refused to have a leader, believing that the democratic development of consensus can only happen without. This may well be true, but leaderless, the party was less effective, in terms of being elected and keeping their agenda before the public.

45. One example, the Poujadists, had little electoral success when they called themselves the *Union de Défense des Commerçants et Artisans*. They were, however, much more successful when they turned into the *Union et Fraternité française* (Braud, 1980: 43). They are not alone in the judicious choice of auspicious titles; parties such as the *Rassemblement pour la République*, the *Union*

pour la Démocratie française, the *Union des démocrates pour la République* have taken great care to mask sectional allegiance and appeal to the whole French nation.

46. In 1994, there were four party federations in the EU: the PES, the party of European Socialists; the EPP, the European Peoples' Party (the Federation of Christian Democratic parties); the ELDR, the Federation of European Liberal, Democrat and Reform parties; the EFG, the European Federation of Green Parties. The regionalists, the conservatives, the communists and the radical right were considering alignments. For further discussion of that era see Hix (1996). By the 1999 elections there were the following federations: PSE, Group of the Party of European Socialists; PPE, Group of the European People's Party; ELDR, Group of the European Liberal, Democrat and Reform Party; UPE, Group Union For Europe; GUE/NGL, Confederal Group of the European United Left/Nordic Green Left; V, The Green Group in the European Parliament; ARE, Group of the European Radical Alliance; I-EDN, Group of Independents for a Europe of Nations.

47. One school of political science sees the justification of the Commission deriving from its efficiency, its ability to deliver policy which meets the needs of the European peoples, the welfare gains and the increased prosperity that it has been able to deliver. 'Its (the Commission's) legitimacy was to follow from its expertise and knowledge' (Laursen, 1996: 120).

48. The Commission has even been driven to issue refutations of some of the myths that have grown up to illustrate its supposed mania for interference and control. A Commission web site http://www.cec.org.uk/myths/index.htm devotes several pages to refuting and correcting common myths and misunderstandings about the European Union.

49. See also Grimm (1997), Habermas (1997) and Weiler (1997).

50. For further examples see discussion of 'the European house/home' in Chilton (1996). Some concepts and terms e.g. 'left/right', seem to have a common meaning throughout Europe (Andersen & Eliassen, 1996).

51. Edwards & Pijpers (1997) demonstrate this in the case of the ratification process after Maastricht; Dinan (1994) reports that this was always so. The result of Pompidou's 1972 referendum on widening the Community resided on national considerations.

52. Work in this area has started. The EU funds a number of programmes to develop multi-lingual terminology and machine translation (e.g. Systran, Eurotra and Eurodictum).

Chapter 7

Managing plurilingualism[1] in the institutions of the EU

The decision to respect the plurilingual nature of the European Union in its institutions has been without precedent. No other international body recognises and works with so many languages. In this chapter I shall look at the legal regime adopted to deal with the plurilingualism of the EU and the political necessity for such a solution. Then I shall examine the administrative and political problems posed by the plurilingual nature of governance in the EU and consider why the policy of absolute equality among all the official languages of all the Member States has often broken down in practice. Finally, I shall consider the contradictions inherent in plurilingualism based only on the official languages of the Member States and the difficulties in continued commitment to equality as more countries accede.

The basic text concerning the use of language in the institutions of the EU is Article 217 of the EEC which made the language regime of the Community the affair of the Council 'acting unanimously'. Under this article, the Council adopted Regulation No. 1 on 15 April 1958 which made the official national languages of the Member States the official languages of the EEC. This resulted in four official languages (French, Dutch, German and Italian) and was a departure from the practice of the European Coal and Steel Community which had used French for its treaty as well as for most of its internal deliberations and administration.[2]

The preamble to the Regulation establishes criteria for determining whether a language will be adopted as a treaty language and thus as an official language of the Community:

> Whereas each of the four languages in which the Treaty is drafted is recognised as an official language in one or more of the Member States of the Community.

This has subsequently provided the legal basis on which the language regime has altered with successive enlargements of the Community. At the end of 1999, after the arrival of Finland, Sweden and Austria in 1995 and before further enlargement, the number of official languages stood at eleven: Dutch, German, French, Italian, English, Danish, Greek, Spanish, Portuguese, Finnish and Swedish. The Irish government did not insist on applying the principle of Regulation No 1 to the letter with the result that only Treaty and legal documents are translated into Irish. Nor did Luxembourg when Luxembourgish became an additional official language in that country in 1984.

In 1958, Regulation No 1 was a clear and non-contentious formulation of which languages could and could not be considered as official languages of the Community, since the six countries involved recognised only their principle national language(s) as an official language.[3] The situation became more ambiguous when the UK (where Welsh has an official status for some purposes) and when Spain (where Catalan, Basque and Galician are officially recognised) joined. The Autonomy of Catalonia, in particular, has argued strongly for the inclusion of Catalan as an official language of the Community, making the case that there are more speakers of Catalan than of Danish. In this they have received some support from the European Parliament who called for the use of Catalan in disseminating public information about the Community, for the translation into Catalan of the Community's Treaties and basic documents, for the inclusion of Catalan in the Lingua and Erasmus programmes, and for use of Catalan in all Community dealings with Autonomy of Catalonia and the Balearic Islands. This parliamentary Resolution (11 December 1990) (OJ NOC 19/42, 28 January 1991) was rejected by the Council and Commission, but the battle is still being fought.

Article 1 of Regulation No 1 refers to both working and official languages as if there might be a distinction but then declares them to be identical. However, Article 6 allows the institutions of the Community 'to stipulate in their rules of procedure which of the languages are to be used in specific cases'.

The European Parliament confirms in its Rules of Procedure that it commits itself to providing documentation and interpreting in all languages and foregoes any leeway it may have for simplification or restriction of its linguistic regime. Rule 15 (1) states uncompromisingly that all documents of Parliament 'shall be drawn up in all the official languages' and Rule 15 (2) decrees that speeches delivered in one of the official languages shall be simultaneously interpreted into the other official languages. However, a distinction is made between plenary sessions and work in committee where the strict multilingual rule may be waived.

In contrast 'it has become the custom in the Council and the Commission . . . to hold discussions in one of the *major* working languages, i.e.

English or French' (Political Affairs Committee, 1982: para 8) and to translate documents into all official languages only at certain points in the process. In the preparation of a Directive, for example, only the Green or White Paper prepared for public consultation as well as the final version of the Directive to be put before the European Parliament and the Council, together with any amendments to be incorporated, will be in all eleven languages. Input from Member States, independent studies, public speeches explaining the policy, draft stages of the legislation, records of advisory committe debates and speech notes for Commission members defending the proposal will simply be in the language of the person carrying out the work with translation as necessary into 'one, two or three vehicular languages' (Heynold, 1995). These vehicular languages are, in essence, French, English and sometimes German. Finally, the publication of the Directive as law in the Official Journal and all the press releases announcing this will be in all the official languages.

Simplifying the Language Regime: The Debate

On several occasions there have been attempts both from members of Parliament and Council to introduce a simpler language regime. Up to the point of writing this has always been rejected. Between 1979 and 1982 a number of individual MEPs and parliamentary committees studied the language question, prompted by the actual accession of Greece and the expected accessions of Spain and Portugal. These enlargements increased the number of pairs of languages for translation and interpreting[4] from thirty to seventy-two. The accession of Greece alone caused a 12.5% increase in language staff at the Commission.

In 1994, just before the accession of Finland, Austria and Sweden, the minister of European Affairs in France, Alain Lamassoure, signalled that France would use its six month presidency (January–June 1995) to tackle the linguistic sclerosis and would try to limit the number of working languages in the institutions of the EU to five.

Neither of these initiatives succeeded in changing the regime of exact equality for all national languages laid down in the 1958 treaty. The 1979–1982 initiative provoked a reasoned debate which eventually came to the conclusion that democracy and the rule of law were best served by multilingualism. The French initiative of late 1994–1995 was robustly attacked, both within the European Parliament[5] and outside. The Greeks were particularly incensed. In Greece, the press mounted a fierce campaign to protect their 'persecuted' language and the writer, Pavlos Matessis, called for a movement prepared to take the French government to the European Court of Justice if it did not drop the proposal.

The two sides of the argument in the 1979–1982 debate (presented in the Nyborg Report, 1982) were each concerned to promote democratic principles. They differed on how this should be done. Those who argued the case for a simpler language regime came from the Political Affairs Committee. Their resolution recognised that:

> (A) united Europe can and must be the expression and guarantee of the qualitative cultural diversity of its members and the assured maintenance of this diversity.

but at the same time that:

> (A) Europe built in this way must be politically 'articulate', that is it must, above all, be capable of representing its interest both internally and externally as clearly as possible, i.e. in a linguistically comprehensible manner. This is obviously not possible in a Tower of Babel. (paragraph 5, Opinion of the Political Affairs Committee, adopted 26 February 1982)

The committee suggested French and English as working languages with Spanish, if and when Spain joined the Community. Their reasoning was that these were each major languages within Europe and of use in communication with the wider world. Interestingly, the person who drafted the proposal was Otto von Habsburg, well known for his personal multilingualism. He suggested that:

> parliament should urge the Ministries of Education or government bodies responsible for Cultural Affairs in the Member States to confine their syllabuses for all levels of language teaching primarily to two or three languages to provide the next generation with the necessary means for communication within the Community and in an international context (paragraph 10, Opinion of the Political Affairs Committee).

Another committee which gave evidence, the Education, Information and Sport Committee, was equally concerned to promote democratic practice in the Community but came to different conclusions. They warned against making some MEPs second class citizens:

> If basic democratic principles are to be observed, each member must have, potentially, the same opportunities to speak, to persuade, to be reported in the media, and so on. Despite the linguistic prowess of

some, these principles would be severely breached were any groups of members . . . to be obliged to speak in a language other than his own. (Education, Information and Sport Committee, 1980: 9)

Among the various ways of simplifying the language situation this committee favoured the suggestion in Renée van Hoof's[6] 1978 report:

Experience proves every day that it is much easier to understand a foreign language than to speak it in a perfectly convincing manner. Might it not be possible, therefore, to use 'asymmetric' language arrangements: to enable everyone to speak in his own language, but with interpretation only into the most widely understood languages? (Van Hoof, 1978)

This particular solution had already been debated and rejected in the European Parliament in 1976 (11 February 1976) and was not to find general favour in 1982 either.

The Education, Information and Sport committee expressed optimism about the development of machine translation and hoped that it might at a future date prove one means of assuring translation and interpreting in the Community. However, they recognised the inadequacies in the technology in its state of development in 1982.

The subsequent debate in the European Parliament and the Resolution which was agreed rejected these calls for smaller numbers of working languages or asymmetrical regimes and reaffirmed the rule that there was to be absolute equality between all Community languages, whether used actively or passively, in writing or orally, at all meetings of Parliament and its bodies. The Nyborg Report explained the arguments supporting this decision, among which the following are the strongest and those which were to resurface in all subsequent debates on Community multilingualism.

The first point concerned the status of Community legislation. As this takes precedence over national law and is applicable without further debate at national level in all member countries, the Nyborg committee reasoned that it must be available at both draft and final stage in all the official languages of the Community. Were this not to be the case, it would preclude national debate on legislation at an early stage and, at the stage of implementation, simply pass the cost of translation from the Community to the national authorities. The second point concerned the right of all nationals of member States to stand as MEPs:

Every citizen, regardless of his or her linguistic abilities, must be able to stand for the European Parliament and be elected if he or she obtains sufficient votes. (Nyborg, 1982: 11)

Any departure from this would have resulted in an educational restriction, which in real terms would probably have been the same as a class restriction, particularly for older members educated at a time when foreign language classes were not available in all sectors of the various education systems. It would have represented a considerable break with democratic principles.

Finally the Nyborg Report drew attention to the many countries which manage with multilingual regimes. With hindsight, the inclusion of Yugoslavia, the USSR, Romania, Czechoslovakia, Israel and Sri Lanka as examples of how governance can be effected in more than one language were not happy choices. Even other examples, such as Belgium and Canada, tend rather to demonstrate the centrifugal forces inherent in language difference.

When the question returned to the agenda in 1994, Lamassoure's proposal to reduce the number of working languages to five simply produced a reaffirmation of Parliament's 'commitment to the equality of the official languages and working languages of all the countries of the Union' (OJC 43/91, 20 February 1995) and a refusal to consider any measures to simplify the linguistic regime for budgetary advantage or administrative simplicity. The French presidency let the matter drop from its six month programme.

The defence of linguistic and cultural diversity implicit in the commitment to plurilingualism in the Community and, particularly, in the European Parliament should not be pigeon-holed as a facet of the intergovernmental, 'Europe of the Nations' tendency. Support for linguistic pluralism extends far beyond this group and has general acceptance as an antidote to creeping uniformity. The need to protect the different legacies of Europe was felt so strongly that it was enshrined in the preamble to the TEU, which expresses the desire for solidarity and an European identity within a framework of respect for differences of history, culture and tradition. However, in a situation where inevitable loss of some nation state sovereignty resulted from the further progress to integration achieved through Maastricht, it would be likely that some parallel development might occur on the linguistic front. This seems to be what is happening in the institutions of the EU. As their work expands, it appears that respect for the plurilingual regime occurs only at certain fixed points.

The Slide to French and English and the North-South Split

All the research in the 1990s reports increasing use of French and English in the institutions of the EU. Schlossmacher's (1994) study of 119 MEPs and 373 high level officials from various EU institutions found that French and

English were used far more than all the other languages of the Member States, and this held for written and spoken communication both within the Parliament and within the Commission and other institutions, and both in the situation where the languages were being used in conversations with native speakers and in exchanges where they were being employed as *lingua francas* by non-native speakers. Administrators and officials claimed greater French use within the EU institutions and in communication with EU Member States but more English use when dealing with contacts outside the EU. This was true of both written and spoken communication. However, Schlossmacher concludes from his research that EU officials are usually competent in both French and English, and, if French is used more within the main institutions, this stems largely from decades of tradition and their geographical siting in francophone areas.

If MEPs reported greater opportunity than the bureaucrats to use their mother tongue, this was only in the formal sessions of the European Parliament, with its provision of translation and interpretation. For much of the time they reported using a *lingua franca*, and this tended to be English. Schlossmacher suggests the difference in choice of *lingua franca* between officials and elected members stems from the foreign language requirement demanded from applicants to the institutions compared to the absence of such a requirement for MEPs. The latters' greater use of English reflects the foreign languages offered in the education systems of the Member States. Without the expressed requirement for French, the default *lingua franca* apparently has a tendency to be English.[7]

When all communication among MEPs and officials was evaluated, Schlossmacher concluded that the language regime of the institutions was bilingual and that MEPs could not rely on their mother tongue alone if it were not French or English:

> Man Französisch oder Englisch verwenden müsse, wenn man schneller ans Ziel seiner Wünsche kommen wolle. (Schlossmacher, 1994: 111)

He found a majority of both MEPs and officials in favour of a restricted number of working languages, even though the idea had just been rejected officially in Parliament at that time. This indicates a certain mismatch between actual practice and declared policy; clearly MEPs are lending verbal support to plurilingualism but accepting pragmatically that it is not working. Schlossmacher's study predates the accession of Sweden, Austria and Finland which has probably intensified some of the trends noted. Firstly, the linguistic regime became even more complex with the addition of another two languages to the interpreting and translation matrix, bringing the number of pairs of languages between which there must be mediation to 110.[8] Secondly, the accession of Sweden and Finland may have strengthened the position of English as the preferred *lingua franca*, given its place in their education systems.[9] Finally, with the accession of Austria the position of German as the language with the largest number of mother tongue speakers in the EU is reinforced.

Schlossmacher's findings have been replicated in other studies. A more recent survey among young trainees at the Commission (Quell, 1997) reports that English and French continue to dominate as the working languages; there is some reported use of German but much less than French or English; the use of the other languages of the EU is, according to this report, negligible and falling. This can be noted, for example, in calls for tender. In theory, the Commission is obliged to issue these tenders to all Member States in all official languages. In practice, the French and English version have often been published first and the principle of multilingualism violated by the requirement that applications be submitted in English and French. This has provoked questions in the European Parliament (Quell, 1997: 75; Labrie, 1993: 126) and anger among language groups who feel disadvantaged.

This is in accordance with findings from my own 1996 survey of MEPs' language networks, which also revealed significant shortfall between the ideal of plurilingual policies and the bilingual/monolingual reality. Respondents confirmed that it was only in the formal plenary sessions of the European parliament that strict adherence to plurilingualism was observed. At the level before formal debate the commitment to plurilingualism mostly breaks down. Negotiations before plenary sessions take place in scheduled meetings of rapporteurs with individual members of the committee and of the formal committee as a whole. There are also unscheduled meetings, lobbying from pressure groups and individuals, as well as unstructured input through networks and socialising which feed into the process. Here communication is task driven and will be organised in the most effective way and not necessarily to respect the commitment to linguistic pluralism. MEPs will use whatever achieves their purpose, usually French and English.[10] MEPs who are not competent in French or English are forced to rely on assistants with language skills to help them interact in the less formal arena.[11]

My research also revealed a north-south split, which seemed to derive not simply from language but also from patterns of working and socialising and, most importantly, from common projects and concerns. Since, lobbying is an art which depends to a great degree on shared agenda and on seizing the occasion. MEPs report, not unsurprisingly, that they lobby in the languages in which they are competent and that they tend to look for support where they expect to share common aims, political allegiance and cultural background. For the most part, informal conversations to gain support for an issue or further a cause are limited by linguistic and cultural constraints. English and French appear to be assuming the role of *lingua francas* for the mainly Germanic north and the mainly Romance south respectively. This is not to argue, of course, that the languages of these dialect continua are mutually comprehensible, only that, according to respondents, the national groups often concert action in this way. One factor is undoubtedly the foreign language training received by Europeans in the recent past; French was the first foreign language for Spanish, Greek and Italian secondary school students when the majority of present MEPs were being educated.[12] In the north of the continent English has been the main foreign language in the various school systems for several decades. MEPs who worked within the context of EFTA have become used to English as a *lingua franca*.

MEPs interviewed suggested that this division results more from convergence of interest than language criteria, for there are several other cleavages which coincide with the linguistic divide. For example, the north of the continent tends to favour free trade; the south to be protectionist. Geography splits the continent, giving Mediterranean agriculture different concerns from the farming systems of the cooler north, and different lobbying networks as MEPs whose constituents have similar needs and worries tend to coordinate their action for maximum effect.

The two groups also reported different working patterns. The MEPs from the southern countries preferred to discuss business over lunch, usually taken in a restaurant away from the office; they were accustomed to work into the early evening. Northern MEPs reported greater tolerance for the lunch time meeting in the workplace with sandwiches and coffee and socialising outside the office tended to take place over a beer in a bar in the early evening. If this rather caricatural behaviour and these stereotypical patterns of association have any reality then they must be producing a cleavage in the Parliament with, for example, the olive oil lobby or those concerned with Mediterranean pollution meeting over lunch and communicating in French, and supporters of dairy farming or those concerned with North Sea fish stocks drinking a beer together in a bar after work and using English as their *lingua franca*. There is of course nothing set about these patterns and they could easily be broken. What it does mean, for the short term, is that the linguistic cleavage between French and English, north and south is reinforced by cultural patterns and common economic interests and has some reality in the European Parliament at the present time.

Evidence of this cleavage in the Commission is supported by the Quell survey, although she has evidence that the old divide of the French-speaking south and the English speaking north may be evolving. This may well be because her respondents were younger than Schlossmacher's and my own, and will have experienced the recent educational changes and the shift to English as the most widely taught foreign language. She finds quite strong evidence that English is the most used language in the Commission. It still remains true, however, that the trainees who report French as their first foreign language still tend to come from the southern Member States while those who report English as their strongest language mostly come from the north (Quell, 1997: 75).

An interesting point arises in a small scale study undertaken in the College of Europe, Bruges (O'Driscoll, 1996). O'Driscoll found that those who categorised themselves as highflyers and who had neither French nor English as their mother tongue perceived it necessary to acquire equally high levels in both languages. The main reason for this appeared to be a perception that English competence is now so widespread in the institutions that English is both a necessity and a commonplace. Those who wished to acquire a competitive edge needed to acquire high levels of fluency in French.

Thus we have *de jure* linguistic equality in the institutions of the European Union but *de facto* two *lingua francas*, French and English. Although, the two linguistic zones which result are not impermeable and a significant number of MEPs and most officials have competence in both French and English, the French/English dichotomy reinforces an undesirable north-south split. Naturally, the linguistic duopoly causes resentment and the Germans, in particular, react. For example, in the Summer of 1999, they boycotted informal meetings of ministers where German interpretation was not available.[13]

Delays, Prioritising and Loss of Meaning

The institutions of EU are faced with difficult choices. Already, before the hurdle of enlargement, the plurilingual regime is bedevilled by delay, choice or prioritising of information and loss of meaning.

In a bureaucracy and Parliament where, in theory, politicians, officials and populations can consult documents in any one of eleven languages, delay is inevitable as the translators work on the texts. In practice, delay is only a problem for some. Documents are usually available in French and English at a much earlier stage than the other language versions,[14] giving those with access to those languages longer to prepare their response than those who must wait for translations. In cases where no translator can work between certain pairs of languages, information originating in one of these languages must typically pass through English or French before becoming available in the other. Thus it is not unknown for EP committees to meet before MEPs of the lesser used languages (Eurospeak for Danish, Portuguese etc.) receive their versions of the necessary paperwork.[15] This leads in practice to reliance on the language skills of junior assistants for those MEPs who are unable to work in French or English.

Loss and change of meaning are endemic in such a system. A résumé from an assistant inevitably involves choice and paraphrase; the assistant plays a gatekeeper role with the possibility of prioritising or backgrounding material. This compounds the less than perfect situation already recognised by the official translation and interpreting service. The volume of work in the EU and the speed at which it must be undertaken have led to an acceptance that the service can only promise 'the best possible translation in time available'.[16] To mistranslation through time pressures, we must also add the loss of meaning that accompanies the loss of connotation and resonance of a word when it moves from one cultural and political tradition to another. The case of the word 'federalism' in the IGC which prepared the Maastricht Treaty reveals the various interpretations that can be lent to a word.[17] And finally, there is some evidence that mistranslation is also perpetrated knowingly and has been used to reconcile differences of opinions among Member States, permitting a choice of words which each can accept but which is not the most accurate translation. According to politicians and officials paying tribute to him, Emile Noel, secretary-general to the Commission from 1958–1987, was a past master at such formulations.[18]

Research in organisational theory (Jandt, 1995, Harris & Moron, 1987, Lord & Maher, 1993) illustrates how information may flow or be withheld according to the other interacting processes at work within organisations. Slow circulation of information, incomplete information, misinformation, disinformation, information withheld, concentric circles of networks and incomplete networks are to be found in any institution. A proportion of this can be explained by inefficiency. A proportion stems from the competitive strategies discernible in any organisation where highly ambitious people are pursuing careers and where coteries and factions are furthering group interests. The EU institutions are text book cases: a high number of extremely able and ambitious people in a complex and expanding situation are split by political orientation, national allegiance and divided into two camps with very different goals (supranational or intergovernmental Europe). Furthermore, there is the additional factor of the plurilingual nature of the institutions which adds another layer of difficulty, delay and scope for obfuscation. All this serves to explain why the informal networks of information in the institutions of the EU are likely to be both intricate and partial. It is inevitable that there will be blocks to transparency and free circulation of information.

In addition, organisational theory suggests that parallel information networks will relay relatively more inaccurate information in a multicultural situation than in a monocultural situation. And as the networks in the EU are multilingual as well as multicultural, the likelihood of inaccurate information being disseminated is increased. Language is also a major factor in the speed at which information travels round a complex network; routes of information flow depend on language networks. MEPs who had also been representatives of their national parliaments reported (Wright, 1996) that one of the major differences between national parliaments and the European Parliament is the fact that in the latter they do not know all the members, whereas in the national parliament they knew everyone at least by sight and name. This is in part because of the patterns of working – only a fraction of working weeks are spent in the parliament – but also because of fractures between linguistic groups. Not knowing a proportion of the members, even on the barest of terms, not socialising with them, not being able, because of linguistic insecurity, to pass a comment or share a joke in a lift means that information networks will be in concentric circles; it will be likely that elements of information will remain within discrete groups. To summarise, language, cultural norms of behaviour and adherence to common political or national goals are each significant. Intensive and extensive social intercourse between linguistic group members and the possibility of sharing social practices are as important in group formation as common goals and collective consciousness. In fact the former appear to be a prerequisite for the formulation and elaboration of the latter.

The key question in all of this must be whether plurilingualism promotes or hinders the democratic process within the institutions? Can the institutions of representative democracy function in a situation where representatives and bureaucrats come from different language backgrounds and where the community of communication necessary for decision making through negotiation and debate is achieved through translation and interpreting? The present linguistic regime is often attacked for its enormous cost but the budgetary burden would probably be borne willingly if translation and interpretation enabled the democratic process in a plurilingual context. But, at what point do the problems inherent in the system prove more of a disadvantage to speakers of the smaller language groups than the implementation of an agreed *lingua franca*?

The Contradictions of Plurilingualism

So, in the institutions, the principle of one single working language or a restricted number of languages has been firmly rejected several times, in favour of commitment to the absolute equality of all the official national languages of the Member States. However, the plurilingual regime demonstrably fails to deliver absolute equality to all language groups, advantaging some and disadvantaging others. Because there is a refusal to admit that two *lingua francas* are actually in use in all the institutions, there has been no discussion of whether these choices are the best possible nor is there coherent planning to ensure all politicians at EU level have access to them. The difficulty is, of course, that the subject is a minefield, touching national sensibilities and pride, as well as threatening entrenched interests.

> The story of the Danish proposal on the use of languages (1973) is revealing here; on its accession to the Union, Denmark was prepared to make the concession of not using Danish, and favoured restricting the number of languages to two – English and French – on condition that French-speaking members only spoke English and that English-speaking members only spoke French. This proposal was immediately rejected by the British and the French. (European Parliament, 1994a: 11)

The French and British revealed in their opposition to the idea the extent of their actual linguistic advantage and their expectation that it would be retained, if not increased.

In the short term it is likely that the policy of 'unity in diversity' will continue. But, as the European Union grows, expanding to the east and the south, the plurilinguistic regime will become ever more difficult to ensure in the institutions. There will tend to be two outcomes: increasing linguistic complexity will encourage use of the unplanned *lingua francas* in the bureaucracy of the Union. In the democratic institution, the Parliament, on the other hand, the commitment to diversity will struggle on. However, with its increasing numbers of delegates and increasing numbers of languages, this commitment will soon make it too unwieldy to be effective. Given that evidence shows that plurilingual arrangements are already breaking down, and that it is impossible to meet the requirements of such a linguistic regime without compromising quality, there needs to be some decisions on how the system will cope with enlargement. If only the five most likely countries from the applicants were to join the effect would be to push the number of official and working languages to sixteen and the pairs of languages to 240. Theoretically, the issue remains the same as before earlier accessions; practically the scale of the problem increases exponentially with each new additional language. Such gigantism would equal scelerosis. Scelerosis of the democratic institutions of the European Union might be to the satisfaction of those who want only a common market and a loose union of nation states, but, for those who seek to overcome the democratic deficit in an increasingly federal Europe, this linguistic problem is one of the major hurdles to overcome. Yet there is no solution which would be politically acceptable in all quarters in the foreseeable future.

Much hope is placed on the development of machine translation. EUROTRA and SYSTRAN are both in use within the institutions of the European Union for the translation of basic technical documents, documents where there is a high proportion of formulaic language and documents where absolute accuracy is not essential. It is used to produce a first draft which human translators refine. Machine translation appears to have only a limited capacity at the present time.

The Languages of National Minorities

Plurilingualism appears difficult to deliver, even in the Community institutions, the only place where the EU has jurisdiction and influence to require it. And were it to be achieved, the issue would still be contentious, because 'minority' linguistic groups are omitted. Present policies fail to satisfy because they mention only the official national languages. Minority linguistic groups are not only angry at being left out, they are also surprised, irritated, even outraged when political elites in Member States who in the cause of national homogeneity, had long suppressed or discouraged cultural and linguistic diversity within their own borders champion diversity at European level. There appears to be a certain lack of logic in finding plurilingualism divisive and disadvantageous at national level but a source of cultural capital within the EU. Numerous regional groups and linguistic minorities have pointed out the anomaly and used it in their own struggle for linguistic maintenance and cultural recognition. In France, the French government's new found commitment to linguistic diversity within the EU context amazed the Corsican, Basque and Breton militants who had only ever managed to wring very minor linguistic concessions from the French State (Blanchet, 1999; Breton, 1999).[19] In the UK, the point was picked up by Welsh and Gaelic speakers, whose languages had no place in the political process until very recently.[20] Throughout the rest of the Member States, the myriad linguistic minorities whose languages had been confined to the private domain, if not actively eradicated, reacted similarly. The recognition that it was an inalienable democratic right to use one's own language in parliament and in dealings with the state, and the political elites' passionate suppor' for European linguistic diversity became an arm to secure linguistic rights at a sub-national level. The militants in these groups exploited the opportunity presented by the apparent blessing of the national governments of the Member States for plurilingualism.

The contradictions are quite clear in numerous documents, including a COREPER document produced during the French presidency of the Union (January–June 1995), in response to the French wish to put European plurilingualism on the agenda. This document calls for the defence of European plurilingualism but makes it clear there is no case for it at national level. It states quite clearly:

> Les langues font partie du patrimoine de chaque peuple dont elles modèlent et expriment la culture et la pensée. Elles sont aussi, dans chaque pays un élément du lien social et un facteur d'intégration. (European Commission, 1995b: 4)

Here we have a strong expression of the Herderian belief in the association of languages and culture together with a weak expression of the Jacobin belief that one language and one people produce a cohesive state. This statement follows closely on the assertion 'Le pluralisme linguistique, un élément essentiel de l'identité européenne, une condition de l'avenir de l'Europe' (European Commission, 1995b: 3) and a footnote that 'ce mémorandum . . . ne concerne pas les langues régionales et minoritaires des Etats membres'.

However, such discrepancy and inequity were recognised by increasing numbers of MEPs, and militants from linguistic minority groups increasingly found the European Parliament a more receptive arena for their demands than national parliaments. Support for the languages of linguistic minorities grew in the context of the growing power of regions and the concept of regionalisation within the EU. It is this growing power of the regions which we shall now consider. If, as is claimed, devolution and autonomy have brought political power closer to the citizens, is there a significant linguistic dimension in this political development too?

Notes

1. Calvet makes a distinction between plurilingualism within the European Community and multilingualism which results from migration (Calvet, 1993).
2. There is some dispute about practice. Labrie (1993) believes that all four ~~—~~ may have been working languages. The discrepancy arises from the f an unpublished Protocol from 1952 in which the partners agreed four languages. However, actual practice between 1952 and 1958 seem to have followed this decision closely (John Pomian in on).

3. The situation in Belgium with its two/three official languages was not contentious since French, German and Dutch are all official languages in other Member States.

4. Mathematically there are only half that number of pairs but since translating and interpreting is usually from the foreign language into the mother tongue, French into German must be treated as a separate pair from German into French.

5. In anticipation, the Committee on the Rules of Procedure produced a report, 'The Right to Use One's Own Language' (European Parliament, 1994a), and the European Parliament reaffirmed its commitment to Article 217 of the EC Treaty, by passing a Resolution (European Parliament, 1994b).

6. Director of the Commission's Interpretation and Conference Services at that time.

7. This assertion derives from the raw statistics and hides the fact that the tendency to choose English or French as a *lingua franca* depends very much on personalities, social setting, composition of group and topic of debate, as I discuss later in the chapter.

8. See note 3.

9. One of Jacques Santer's first acts on taking over the Commission presidency in 1995 was to instigate press briefings in English as well as French, in recognition of a growing preference for English.

10. German is also used as a working language in this context but to a much lesser extent.

11. Thus, lack of language skills is only a drawback to some; the monolingual speaker of a language of lesser diffusion (e.g. Greek or Portuguese) is limited in a way that a monolingual French or English speaker is not. Interviewees observed that there are a number of very powerful monolinguals from these last two languages who appear not to have suffered at all from their linguistic limitations. There is also a tendency, mentioned by a number of respondents, that English/French monolinguals tend to impose their language on the group in which they are working.

12. French now appears to have been overtaken by English in the education systems of southern Europe. See Chapter 9. Thus the patterns of association noted which are dependent to an extent on foreign language competence acquired in the course of education may change in the future.

13. For example the imeetings of EU Trade and Industry ministers in Oulu in Finland on 2 and 3 July 1999.

14. For an explanation of the use of the 'vehicular' languages in drafting Directives see Heynold (1995: 11).

15. Information from interviews with MEPs 1996, Labrie (1993) and Jorna (1993). Jorna reported an MEP's complaint that 'You have to wait four months for a translation which is frustrating because you want to press on'.

16. The case of hurried and sometimes inaccurate translations is a problem mentioned by a number of writers on European institutions, e.g. Butler & Westlake (1995). A notorious mistranslation occurs in the very Regulation dealing with language use. The French version of Regulation No 1 Article 6 reads as follows:

Les institutions peuvent déterminer les modalités d'application de ce régime dans leurs reglements intérieurs (The institutions may stipulate in the[i] internal rules of procedure the way in which these rules on languages are to be applied).

The English version states:

The institutions of the Community may stipulate in their rules of procedure which of the languages are to be used in specific cases.

This very free translation of *modalités d'application* has led, of course, to discrepancies (cf. written question No 1576/79 by Mr Patterson, OJ No C 150, 18 June 1980, p. 17.)

17. For discussion of the connotations of this and other concepts in a number of European languages see Chilton (1996; 1998).

18. At a tribute to Emile Noel (24 October 1997) Sir Roy Denman (Director-General for External Affairs 1977–1982) told an anecdote about how 'droits' was translated as 'involvement' in the phrase 'workers' involvement' to make it acceptable to the British Conservative party. Denman also remarked that the Danes had often to be dissuaded from phoning up and pointing out such 'mistakes'.

19. This appears to be changing although a Jacobin lobby is fighting a rearguard action. The Poignant report (1998) recommended recognition of the minority languages of France and the signature of the European Charter for Regional and Minority Languages. The Cerquiglini report (1999) listed the languages that would be recognised under the Charter. At the time of writing (June 1999) the number was 76 and rising! Activists were disappointed since clearly the recognition of so many diluted the effect and limited what could be demanded. In addition the opposition mobilised and the Republican lobby invoked the Constitution in order to fight ratification of signature of the Charter.

20. Welsh and Gaelic have made strong progress in the public sphere. In Wales, education, local government, the Assembly, a part of the media, theatre and cinema, the Courts and a large number of public bodies and private enterprises now operate a bilingual regime. In Scotland, Gaelic is one of the official languages in the Parliament (Wright, 1999).

Chapter 8

New and smaller polities. Europe of the Regions.
Support for the lesser-used languages of Europe

The story of the centripetal forces at action in Europe in the 1990s is complex. In the east of the continent, the fracturing of the USSR and Yugoslavia are separate stories, bound closely to the history of the Russian empire in the first case and the decisions of the 1918 treaty makers in the other, and barely touched by Europeanisation. In almost all the other cases, however, the influence of European integration is an important factor. There is evidence (Mitchell, 1995; Peterson, 1995; Gripaios, 1995) that regions have found the umbrella of the EU an encouragement to bid for autonomy. All the advantages of being within the nation state are either already on offer from the European Union (access to sufficiently large markets for economic survival, redistribution of resources,[1] subsidies for poorer regions, presence or representation at negotiations at international level, pooling expensive research and development, single currency etc.) or being developed (defence, foreign affairs). To some analysts 'a Europe of the Regions has opened up the spectre of the redundancy of the nation state' (Newlands, 1994).

It is difficult to demonstrate any kind of connection in social and political movements, let alone cause and effect relationships, but it is an interesting coincidence that the increasing support for regionalisation by the EU has grown as demands for regional autonomy, even independence, have spread. For regions such as the Basque country, Catalonia and Galicia, Scotland and Wales, Wallonia and Flanders, the European context in which they sought and gained their various degrees of independence was influential. To this list of regions with devolved power or some degree of autonomy we shall probably have to add new names. The idea of greater independence is attractive to many in Europe. Demands range from minimal requests (Northern England has called for a Northern Assembly) to calls for total independence (in Northern Italy the idea of independent Padania is supported by a proportion of the population[2]).

Countries in Central and Eastern Europe hope that they too may becom

179

part of this organisation to gain access to the financial and structural support that would aid a successful conversion from the communist system to liberal democracy and the free market. In addition, the nationalism which has resurfaced in the wake of communism has been of the reductionist kind. A number of states have tended to form as or to fracture into ethno-linguistic groupings (e.g. the Baltic States, Slovakia and the Czech Republic). This process makes them quite small and even more needful of membership in an umbrella organisation.

In this analysis, the European Union becomes an agent in the continuation of the nineteenth century search for the congruence of cultural nation and political entity. Nations felt to be too small to constitute nation states under the old system of economic protectionism and sovereignty in matters of defence and security are now able to form new kinds of arrangements, and, under the protection of the treaties of the EU and within the general rapprochement brought about by European integration, to draw away from the states in which they find themselves. The resulting autonomy and devolution of powers are thus to be seen both as contributing to new configurations in European integration (Europe of the Regions) and as constituting another chapter in the European love affair with Wilsonian self-determination.

There are many reasons why this happened, one of which was a growth in the acceptance of the concept of subsidiarity, the idea that decisions should be taken as close to the citizen as possible. The arguments of the political elites of nation states to safeguard their own powers from being usurped by Brussels was seized upon by activists to push for the devolution of some political power to the regions. The intellectual poverty of advancing a principle as desirable and just at national level and refusing to recognise it as such at regional level was just as telling in this context as it had been in the case of the defence of plurilingualism in the European context.

So one spur to regionalism in the EU stems from the pragmatic seizing of chances and originated in the regions themselves. Interregional cooperation, fuelled by a host of independent initiatives, has grown piecemeal to become an important feature of economic life. Transnational cooperation between regions in the EU has increased with the recognition that areas with similar geographical realities, economic infrastructures, transport nvironmental threats have, at the very least, similar needs and can pool experience. More ambitiously, regions have t they can work together to set political agenda at EU level, ves the muscle that they lack when working separately. They can initiate research and development programmes that individually they could not afford to finance.

Transnational cooperation between regions started as early as 1957 with the Standing Conference on Local and Regional Authorities. The European Regional Development Fund (ERDF) was instigated in 1975. Regional problems continued, however, to be addressed through the medium of the nation state and using national criteria (Newlands, 1994) and the ERDF budget remained small compared to the funds managed within the CAP (Armstrong, 1996). However, the situation evolved. Regionalisation was given a boost in 1985 when the Council of European Regions (forty-five regions and nine regional associations) became the Assembly of European Regions (AER), with a secretariat in Strasbourg and close links with the Council of Europe. It was partly AER pressure at Maastricht that led to the creation of the Committee of the Regions, as part of the TEU. On the budget side, the ERDF was reformed in 1989 and given considerably greater funds and increased importance (Armstrong, 1996).

The integrationists at the Commission have encouraged regions to be autonomous or semi-autonomous actors, as a strategy for overcoming the power monopoly of the nation state (Peterson, 1995) and because they might be more malleable components in the integration process. Some of the most powerful personalities within the Commission have supported the regional approach as a means of tackling inequality. They have argued that a simple comparison of national statistics often masks grave regional disparities[3] and urge that regional problems, needs and structures be measured against EC rather than national norms.[4] During his period as president of the Commission, Jacques Delors proposed that regional and structural disparities be tempered using the ERD, the European Social Fund and some sections of the Common Agricultural Fund (Newlands, 1994). This policy made headway and, by 1993, structural funds to right interregional disparities accounted for 29% of the EU budget. To make sure that these funds would have an effect and not simply be used to replace national funding for regions, the EU insisted that this money should be additional to national finance. Such policies are likely to influence regions which have felt neglected by national governments and predispose them to European integration.

Moreover, EU regional organisation and structures give countries without regional infrastructure the framework on which to build should regional actors wish to do so. The European Charter of 1985 provided the legal and constitutional framework for local and regional self-government and the NUTS I, II and III categories imposed a European definition on regional entities. 'The EU is controlling and standardising the decentralisation of power and authority through which it can give competence to the regions' (Peterson, 1995: 7–8). The formal regional economic planning promoted by the EU leads to regions defining problems and needs in a comparable way in order for their bids for financial support to be assessed. The EU's requirement that regions coordinate projects leads to regional economic planning. Thus there is greater cohesion within the regions and greater comparability – at the very least in statistical and information gathering terms – across regions. And most importantly, in 1993 the Cohesion fund was set up (TEU, Article 130 d, 1992) to designate funds for regions which were disadvantaged. This is redistribution *in European terms and according to European norms.*

The Committee of the Regions

On 9th March 1994 the Committee of the Regions held it first meeting in Brussels, its member drawn from local and regional authorities. These 222 delegates were mostly elected local politicians or heads of local and regional authorites.[5] At present the CoR is only a consultative body, but like Parliament it may be able to extend its powers a little and it has ambitions to 'develop as a new European institution' (Pause, 1997: 3). It must be consulted in several areas of European Union policy: education; culture; public health; trans-European transport, telecommunications and energy networks; and most importantly economic and social cohesion. It may comment on land-use planning, agriculture and the environment.

In the first four years of its existence, the CoR published Opinions on a wide range of issues. In 1996 there were forty-six documents giving the view from the regional level on matters as diverse as voluntary service for young people, pollution of water, higher education, housing, the information society, safety at airports and fisheries. The Committee's interest stretched from detailed practical recommendations on communicable diseases, postal services and gas distribution networks to visionary declarations on racism, regional democracy and sustainable development (CoR, 1997a). Now, these issues are not particularly 'regional'. They would be the proper concern of any level of government. It would seem that the CoR is not confining itself to subjects which are local and only local.

One should beware of exaggerating the influence of the CoR, of suggesting that there has been substantial devolution of power to this institution, or of claiming that it has had an enormous economic impact. However, when its development is viewed against the background of pressure for autonomy and regional government from the regions themselves, it gains an added dimension. It then becomes one of the various strands in the devolution of power away from the nation state.[6]

The CoR may also prove to be influential in less easily monitored and quantified ways. New alliances and groupings within Europe will help to reformulate identification patterns. Anderson (1983) is very convincing on the importance of journeys and patterns of association in the creation of new political allegiances. He argues that the tours and encounters of young Indonesians within the geographical limits of the islands which were to become independent Indonesia contributed to an acceptance of the idea of the Indonesian nation. This process may now be at work in Europe as numerous categories of people journey inside the Union on business promoted and funded by the EU. The idea may be particularly relevant in the networks promoted by the CoR (CoR, 1997a). By grouping the Mediterranean zone (coastal regions of Spain, France, Italy and Greece), the Alpine zone (mountain regions of France, Germany, Austria and Italy), the Frontier zone (eastern regions of Germany, Finland, Austria, Italy and Germany), the Atlantic Arc (coastal regions of Portugal, Spain, France, UK and Ireland), and the Baltic and North Sea zone (UK, Netherlands, Denmark, Sweden and Finland), the CoR has imagined groups of communities which follow a different logic from networks established within the nation state.[7] They may come to have some enduring reality, since they have been conceived as alliances following geographical, structural and ethnolinguistic criteria and not the geo-political or administrative reasons of a nation state capital.[8] Sharing geographical features, they exhibit similarities in agriculture and industry, commerce and services, in environmental concerns and problems of transport infrastructure, climatic constraints and access to energy. They may be natural rivals but they will also be each other's best allies for lobbying for certain policies at EU level,[9] for sharing research costs and expertise in problems which concern only them and for cross-fertilisation of ideas and experience in restructuring. For reasons of self-interest, quite divorced from desire for European integration, many categories of people are likely to associate within these zones. The EU has made a conscious effort to promote a bottom up approach to the development of relations in this domain. Peterson (1995) believes that 'this new positively perceived regionalism' may rely on 'spontaneously conceived groups of professionals with sensitivity to mutual understanding' who will 'institutionalise anti-institutionalism'.

In contradiction to this 'Eurofederalist' optimism, which believes there has been general benefit from regionalisation and which sees transnational regional groupings as a growing and progressive force within the EU, of benefit to the poorer regions, there is a school of thought which finds regionalisation a worrying trend. Commentators such as Amin and Tomaney (1995) argue that many regional alliances link the powerful with the powerful. They cite as an example the Four Motors of Europe project which created a cooperation network between four of Europe's economically strongest regions: Baden Württemburg, Rhône-Alpes, Lombardia and Catalonia (FAST Monitor, 1991). They suggest that those who profit from regionalisation will be those who can use it to slide away from the redistributive policies of some European nation states. There may well be an element of truth in this. The desire for autonomy in Flanders, in Catalonia, in Slovenia was fuelled largely by a desire not to fund poorer regions in other parts of the nation state to which these regions belonged.[10] It is an important element in Padania's appeal for many Northern Italians. However, for the present argument, this divergence of views on who may be benefiting – the rich regions or the poor – does not really signify. Both camps admit that regional contact is happening.

The CoR is clear about what it is trying to do in promoting the new groupings. It declares that it sees national boundaries as a nuisance:

> A spatial planning and development policy does not acknowledge frontiers whether internal or external to the Member States and to the EU in its present configuration. (CoR, 1997b: 3)

It states that the determinants for the regional groupings were geographical similarity, similar structural concerns together with historical and cultural ties. In this last it claims that it is trying to undo some of the anomalies caused by national frontiers:

> (O)ver the centuries Europe has been sub-divided to such an extent, generally without consultation of the population affected and with no thought for their cultural ties, that it is high time to rediscover these ties and enable those who share them to express their opinions and their preferences. (CoR, 1997b: 3)

These three determinants are expected, individually or in combination to 'create a sense of belonging or common destiny'. It believes that 'the exercise has passed the point of no return' (CoR, 1997b: 4). The CoR may pay lip service in the final paragraph to the prior claims of national affiliations and the value of territorial cohesion, but, in the context of the earlier assertions, this recognition appears empty of meaning, a concession to national sensibilities for form's sake.

The Committee of the Regions is clearly ambitious. It wishes to be the natural guarantor of subsidiarity and 'for the principle to be applied at all institutional levels: European bodies and institutions, Member States, regions and local authorities' (European Commission, 1997b: 3). It wishes to extend the scope and power of weak local authorities by increasing the legal and administrative means and financing arrangements of those regions with less devolved power so that they can negotiate on equal footing with those regions which are in federal state arrangements (CoR, 1997b).[11] It sees a role for itself in solving the EU's democratic deficit. Its first president, Jacques Blanc, saw democracy served by proximity and called for:

> (P)olitical decisions (to be) taken by the political authority that is both closest to the citizens and most responsible to them. (Blanc, 1996: 1)

In many cases this will, of course, be the regional or local authority. It endorses the growth of transnational cooperation in place of international cooperation and insists at length that most policies work better where there is greater input from regional level.

Language and the Regions

The CoR is a young institution and some of the above is a wish list rather than reality. But even though it is in its infancy we might still ask how the growth of regional power and cooperation that it hopes for and promotes will affect language use in Europe. There may be two effects. The first will stem from the communication needs of speakers from different language communities coming together to work on common projects and to share information.[12] The second will occur because devolution of power to regions and the resurgence of regional identities may revive regional languages, long eclipsed by national languages in the public sphere.

There is as yet little thorough research on patterns of language use in interregional teams. However, working from reports from a selection of interregional projects[13] it seems reasonable to claim that although English and French are mostly used within regional cooperation they do not appear to dominate to the exclusion of all other languages as we have seen that they do in the Commission and to a lesser extent in the Parliament. This may be because the geographical proximity of some groups makes it possible for a language common to the area to be employed as *lingua franca*[14] or for communication strategies to be adopted which exploit the mutual comprehensibility of languages within a dialect continuum. It may also stem from the fact that the participants in Interreg initiatives are not necessarily people whose education will have included the acquisition of high level foreign language skills in the way that one might expect from bureaucrats at the Commission or even MEPs. Taking this together with the lack of funding that would guarantee translating and interpreting at all points, we should not be surprised by reports of attempts to communicate by using the mutual comprehensibility within dialect continua.

The new found self confidence within the regions themselves may well be a factor in an increasing desire to revitalise and revive local languages which had been allowed to fade. These languages have always been tarred as parochial and provincial. Speakers were made to feel that these languages denoted distance from the capital and thus lack of education, lack of engagement with the wider world and narrow, prejudiced, provincial attitudes. The novels of Stendhal, Gauthier, Sand and Flaubert in nineteenth century France and of Tomasi di Lampedusa and Carlo Levi in twentieth century Italy provide examples of the lampooning of provincial attitudes, and along with them, regional dialects and regional languages.

In some cases the use of regional languages was even seen as dangerous rather than simply amusing. Refusal to use the national language called into question the speakers' loyalty to the nation state. Bertrand Barère's famous attack[15] on Alsacien, Breton, Corsican and Basque is an extreme example of the fear and contempt felt by ruling elites for those they could not understand and whose loyalty they doubted. In some contexts such fears have proved to be well-grounded. Regionalists have sometimes aligned themselves with enemies of their nation state in order to further the regionalist project. This was the case in a number of the countries occupied by the Third Reich. Numerous less contentious examples show how loyalty and language use have been habitually linked in the context of the European nation state, and as we saw in the early chapters of the book, regional languages have often been eradicated in the cause of national cohesion. It is thus one measure of regional self-confidence and regeneration that we are witnessing a revival of regional languages across Europe.

This renaissance is not purely a European phenomenon. The so-called 'ethnic revival' has been a world-wide event.[16] In Europe, however, the revival has been particular because it has become enmeshed with Europeanisation as this process has transformed the way state and civil society interact. Language revitalisation has profited from the protective umbrella of the EU institutions and from the growing regionalist movement in which 'language constitutes the still most fundamental element' (Peterson, 1995: 8).

The European Union's Support for Minority Languages

In its involvement in the question of minority/regional language policies and planning, the European Community had no authority through the Treaties to involve itself, but did so none the less, as it had in the case of many other matters. The European Parliament was the prime instigator of action,[17] debating and passing a number of motions during 1979 and 1980 which culminated in the adoption of the Arfé Report and Resolution, which called for a Community charter of regional languages and cultures and of the rights of ethnic minorities. It asked, significantly, that Member States 'promote as far as possible a correspondence between cultural regions and the geographical boundaries of the local authorities' (EBLUL, 1994: 8). A parliamentary committee was set up in 1983 to examine how national education, the mass media, cultural projects and public institutions and social networks could accommodate regional languages, and what initiatives could be undertaken or aided by the Community. Parliament put pressure on the Commission to make funds available for such work. One of the Community's first actions was to fund research by the Istituto della Enciclopedia Italiana (1986) to provide an overview of the actual linguistic geography of Europe, define the term 'linguistic minority' and document the numbers of speakers of the regional/minority languages in the Member States. In 1987 the European Parliament passed another Resolution in this area,[18] increasing its support for what it was now terming the 'lesser used languages of Europe'. Seventeen recommendations asked the Commission as well as the Member States and the Council of Europe to fund and support a number of initiatives including educational programmes, the extension of minority language rights in the legal sphere, the creation of new media using regional languages, cultural and business projects using such languages and promotion of cross frontier contact where linguistic communities had been severed by political borders. These Resolutions did not have the force of law within the Community; they were simply an invitation to the Commission and to states to promote regional culture and languages. This meant, of course, that in the states where regional languages had always been an unpopular issue not a great deal happened.

However, the activists in the regions had found a new ally. In 1988 the sum of Community money designated for this area had reached a million ECUs[19]; by 1996 it was 4 million ECUs.[20] The money was being spent largely on education: teacher training, production of materials, grants and scholarships, visits and exchanges as well as documentation centres. The Community was instrumental in setting up the Bureau for Lesser Used Languages in Dublin to coordinate and manage exchanges and contacts within the minority communities and to sensitise the majority language speakers to the human rights angle of the language question.[21] The Community also funded the Mercator Network to disseminate good practice in education and culture, encourage cooperation among the various linguistic groups, keep the data on the area up to date and provide a focus for lobbying. Mercator works out of the Fryske Akademy and coordinates cooperation among a number of institutes and university departments. The Fryske bureau deals mainly with educational programmes; a centre in Wales is concerned with media, another in Catalonia works on legal issues and yet another in Paris deals with general matters.

In 1993, the Treaty on European Union officially included culture and education within the remit of the EU. The preamble and Article seemed to give a legal basis to the work carried out to promote and safeguard regional/minority languages. In 1998, however, the European Court of Justice ruled that the Commission and the Parliament could not fund projects in areas for which they had no legal basis other than their own statements. This included the 170 projects funded by the EU during the previous year in domain of minority languages. This recent development could have two outcomes. Although at first it appears to rein in EU activity in this area, it has also sparked a determination to create a legal basis for action in favour of minority and regional languages (Cresson, 1998). Although there has been a slight setback for the regionalists in this, it may in the long term regularise their situation and formalise the support minority languages gain from the EU.

What is actually happening is complex, the outcome is difficult to predict and there are no simple cause-effect relationships. Nonetheless, one would be justified in seeing the European dimension as a factor in the revitalisation of some regional languages. The European Charter for Minority Languages has been one manifestation.

The European Charter for Minority Languages

The idea of the Charter which had been raised in the Arfé Report was taken up by the Council of Europe and adopted in 1992. Six years later, in March 1998, 7 European states had signed and ratified the Charter, more than enough for it to enter into force. However, the Member States of the European Union were not well represented among these signatories. By March 1998, only Finland and the Netherlands had both signed and ratified; Austria, Denmark, Germany,[22] Spain and Luxembourg had simply signed without yet ratifying. The UK, France, Italy, Greece, Sweden, Portugal, Belgium and Ireland had not signed at that time. The reluctance to sign may stem in part from the way the Charter pushes regional/minority languages into the political sphere. The Charter reaffirmed support for the promotion of educational and cultural use of regional/minority languages, an issue which by the late twentieth century was relatively uncontroversial. Then, in addition, in Article 10, it pressed for their use 'within the framework of the regional or local authorities'. Such use would include:

> Article 10 2 (b) the 'possibility for users of regional or minority languages to submit oral or written applications in these languages.

> Article 10 2 (c/d) the publication by regional/local authorities of their official documents also in the relevant regional and minority languages.

> Article 10 2 (e/f) the use by regional/local authorities of regional or minority languages in their assemblies, without excluding, however, the use of the official language(s) of the State.

This was much more controversial.

The Charter also asked that regional/local bureaucracies ensure that citizens be able to interact with them, orally and in written form, in the regional/minority language. This was a step too far for some of those governments which had not yet signed. It would be another encouragement of the leaking down of powers, for which there was little support among these national governments.

Although the Charter was not a European Union initiative as such, the European Parliament threw its weight behind it and asked Member States to sign up. In 1994, the Parliament also produced its own Report and Resolution under the chairmanship of Mark Killilea,[23] in which it called for the official recognition of linguistic minorities and their protection by an appropriate legal statute in the Member States. European Union financing would be available for the teaching and promotion of their languages.

For the very centralised states, compliance with the Charter and the Killilea Resolution represented a complete break with their monolingual tradition and attacked the bedrock of the constitution. Such was the case in France where the philosophy of 'la République une et indivisible' had been reaffirmed in 1992 with a constitutional amendment which stated that the official language of the French state was French. French MEPs argued against the Killilea Resolution, arguing that its provisions would endanger the unity of each nation (Schwartzenberg, cited in EBLUL, 1994). However, even in this unpromising setting, the regional/minority language movement has made significant advances. Backed by the French committee of EBLUL, militants were able to mobilise thousands of demonstrators in the Basque country, Brittany and Alsace. In May 1999, the French government signed the Charter. At the time of writing the process of ratification is stalled, held up by a challenge from the Jacobin faction that it is unconstitutional to recognise the legal status of languages other than French. Despite this, events so far constitute a enormous shift in the French position.

The other nation states which tried to impose monolingualism from the centre have already made enormous linguistic concessions, if not always happily. Madrid has relinquished linguistic dominance in Catalonia on a remarkable scale. It is Castilian which now appears under threat in the Principat.[24] The British government has recognised Welsh as an official language within Wales. In some other Member States, recognition and rights on one side of a border have led to similar demands on the other. The Dutch government's ratification of the Charter and its recognition of Low Saxon created pressure for the German government to recognise Low German and ratify as well.[25] There is enough evidence ot suggest that the renaissance of regional/minority languages in Europe is a continent-wide phenomenon which is gaining momentum.

Language Revitalisation

Not all regional languages will regain the ground they lost to the official national language. The difference stems from the problem of critical mass, the moment when a language becomes viable again and starts to grow in numbers of speakers. For this to happen throughout a whole community, there seems to be a need for more than the commitment of language activists and the implementation of their strategies to strengthen language loyalty. For most families there have to be clear economic/social/political benefits accompanying a return to a language which had often been abandoned because it hampered social promotion and the realisation of career ambitions, and blocked interaction with the state and wider civil society. Some regional/minority languages in Europe have now come to fulfil these criteria. Welsh, for example, has gone from strength to strength in the last twenty years and is currently a medium of tuition and a subject of study in schools, is used in all forms of media including television and an artistically successful Welsh language film industry, is an official language in the Welsh Assembly alongside English and in a bureaucracy where the Welsh speaker can interact with the state through the medium of Welsh in most circumstances. This is very different from the situation twenty years ago when the use of Welsh was felt to be declining (Sharp, 1973). Then, to achieve social promotion through education and a prestigious career, it was only necessary to be fluent and literate in English. Now, the legal status of Welsh and the possibility of using it in so many domains of life has changed the balance in language choice. Instrumental reasons for choosing English and abandoning Welsh are less clear cut. Today, to be bilingual and biliterate in Welsh and English is probably the best way to serve ambition for those who wish to succeed within Wales.

It is when instrumental reasons join the integrative reasons of community, tradition and identity for retaining or regenerating a minority/regional language that the process is likely to succeed. Thus, where devolution and autonomy bring economic, political and administrative activity back into regions and where the EU gives moral, structural and financial support to that process, the likelihood of strong regional identity, increased local pride, the possibility of fulfilling one's ambitions without going to the capital and the relocation of lines of communication and infrastructure could all contribute to a regeneration of minority/regional languages that had been left for dead.

As a corollary to this, one might imagine that national languages could fade in some regions of European nation states. This would remain mere fancy were it not for one other social/political/economic trend which means the idea should be considered seriously. Because there has been a transfer of economic power and legal sovereignty to transnational corporations and supra/international organisations, increasing numbers of people have to learn to communicate on a global stage. As I discussed in Chapter 4, globalisation has meant the widespread adoption of English as a *de facto lingua franca*. Now, whereas this has been experienced as an imposition and an affront by large linguistic communities such as Francophonie who aspire to have their own language play the *lingua franca* role,[26] in small and formerly oppressed linguistic communities it may be regarded with more equanimity. Learning the regional/minority language together with English could serve all the communication needs of the individual, the first language fulfilling all the integrative motivations and giving access to roots, tradition, identity and community, and the second fulfilling some instrumental motivations and giving access to the wider world. There always remains the proviso that for this to actually happen the power of the nation state and its official language must really be on the wane. Political developments in regions such as Catalonia, Galicia and the Basque Region suggest that this could be the situation in some states.

However, the process is too young for predictions to be reliable. We know that political decisions may be made and in operation within a short time period, a truth we learnt from events in Eastern Europe, if we did not know it before. Other realities change much more slowly. Restructuring processes in social, cultural and linguistic domains must be measured in years and decades not weeks and months. At this stage, all we can say is that if the mesolevel of political and economic organisation becomes more significant, then it would be reasonable to expect more revitalisation of regional languages along the lines of the Spanish experience.

Notes

1. Armstrong (1996) compares redistribution within the EU with that within the US, Australia and Canada and shows how small the European programme is in comparison. This lack of access to funds pushes the EU to rely on policy formulation and limits its action to being a catalyst in regional redistribution.

2. In northern Italy, the *Lega Nord* hoped for a measure of independence for Padania. In 1994 it joined with Berlusconi's *Forza Italia* and the alliance swept to power in Lombardy and Veneto. The Berlusconi government reneged on federalism and the League withdrew its support, bringing the government down. The League has yet to recover from this ill-judged adventure.

3. This is the case, for example, in Italy and Germany, where internal disparities are particularly acute and where need for support can be lost in averages (European Commission, 1996).

4. Unemployment statistics are high in Spain and low in Denmark, Austria and the Netherlands. In every other member state figures are very variable between regions (European Commission, 1996a). It thus makes little economic sense to analyse the situation by country and EU statistics are presented by region.

5. The lack of democracy in this process has outraged many commentators. Lafont, for example, writes 'Quant à son mode de désignation, il passe toute espérance démocratique' (Lafont, 1993: 193).

6. Not all commentators agree with this analysis. Armstrong points out that convergence has been slow and may lead to a crisis of expectations. Amin and Tomaney (1995) would question whether a Europe of the Regions actually exists in any meaningful way. Even if it does have some reality, they argue that the Union's lagging and declining regions are probably best aided by policies conceived and managed at national level. They suggested that the disparity between the Golden Arc and the periphery was likely to grow and that EU policies would not be able to alter this. In the event, the first report of Economic and Social Cohesion was able to report that the gap between regions has narrowed 'significantly' (European Commission, 1996b: 5).

7. In an earlier document, Europe 2000, written before the 1995 accessions eight super regions were planned (European Commission, 1991).

8. The jury is still out on this issue. Gripaios (1995) asks whether the super regions are more coherent economic groupings than the nation state and finds that in purely economic terms this may not be so.

9. For the importance of lobbying in the EU see Ash and Tomaney (1995) and Mény *et al.* (1996).

10. This is a fairly general view Stone says:

    One of the forces behind the constitutional reforms has been the political dissatisfaction in Flanders over subsidising its poorer counterpart (Stone, 1994: 204).

    It is a problem that may well resurface as the principle of redistribution is accepted, albeit in a weak form, at supra-national level and as the enlargement of the EU to the east will demand structural funds.

11. As well as questioning the policies of the nation states, the CoR has not been reluctant to attack the EU where it sees the necessity. In the cultural field it points out that 'implementation of the "citizens" Europe through the strengthening of European identity may be problematic from the point of view of subsidiarity.'

The report, Citizens' Europe, includes the following observation: 'The CoR feels that citizens cannot adopt the European identity if the European dimension is not evident in their everyday life. There again if everyday life is Europeanised, the traditional local and regional identities of citizens could weaken. There are many examples which show that cultural identity cannot be given to or forced on people from above. Looked at from the cultural point of view the creation or accentuation of European identity seem somewhat questionable' (CoR, 1997c: 4).

12. Labrie (1993) recounts that Spain opposed allowing the CoR to set its own linguistic regime, fearing that Basque and Catalan representatives would demand to use their own language. The CoR must gain the approval of the Council of Ministers in this matter.

13. This evidence comes from verbal reports from participants in a German/Dutch transborder commercial venture, a Southern European distance learning project (Italy, Spain and Portugal) , an Interreg drought project (Portugal, Spain, Italy and Greece) and the Regio in Alsace/Bâle/Southern Germany. Participants report that some of the informal discussions in these groupings/projects take place with speakers using their own language/dialect and the other participants activating passive comprehension skills for languages very closely related to their own.

14. This language may be a national language or a regional language. Some cross frontier cooperation between Catalunya and Occitania has used Occitan and Catalan for working groups and reports (Le magazine de Midi-Pyrénées, 1997).

15. In his report to the Comité de Salut Public, Paris, 8 pluviose an II.

16. For a detailed discussion of the ethnic revival of the 1960s and 1970s see Fishman (1977a, b).

17. Labrie, 1993 deals with this question in great detail.

18. Known as the Kuijpers Resolution (J.O. C 318, 30 November 1987).

19. Answer to written question no 1187/88 asked by Juan Garaikoetxea Urriza (J.O C 180, 17 July 1989).

20. Reported in EBLUL, 1997. The sum was to be reduced to 3,675 million ECUs in 1997. EBLUL coordinated opposition to this cut.

21. The legal status of the Bureau is an independent limited company without share capital registered in Ireland. The second Bureau set up in Belgium has a similar status and is registered as an AISBL. Both institutions receive some funds from national governments and local authorities as well as from the EU.

22. Germany has since ratified.

23. Known as the Killilea Resolution (9 February 1994)

24. For a discussion of this see Strubell (1998).

25. Low German and Low Saxon are the respective German and Dutch terms for one language variety. See the debate on this in EBLUL, 1997.

26. More than most European linguistic groups, French speakers have experienced the relationship of language and power and know the benefits. The passion with which French is supported and anglicisation vilified can be seen as a narrow nationalist reaction bound up with pride or as a keen awareness of these multiple benefits. See Chapter 10.

Chapter 9

Language in the domains of defence, education and research networks

The second question posed in Chapter 5 asked whether linguistic change would be an inevitable consequence of the closer economic, political, defence, social and legal ties that the European Union has brought about between its Member States. This is what I would now like to consider. Although the EU is a polity *sui generis* which cannot be directly compared to the nation states of Europe, certain features of nation building have resurfaced in the European project. For example, there is a growing belief that common defence is possible and desirable, a commitment to a limited redistribution of wealth among the regions of the Member States, a sense of benefiting from a body of rights and a desire in some quarters to use education in the service of integration. Some of these will have greater linguistic consequences than others. Nation building projects, policies and activities from the national era can be divided into those which had profound language effects and those where the linguistic impact was only minimal. Those which may change language practice include conscription and citizens' armies, free and obligatory schooling, the journeys of administrators and functionaries and the deployment of various other state employees within a defined national space. The invention of national tradition, the reinterpretation of national history and the adoption of symbols may be connected to language shift but do not cause it. The redistribution of wealth and the development of a single national market can happen without major linguistic consequences.

In the domains which caused language change in the nationalist past is there any indication that there are similar developments in the European present? The pragmatic and ideological reasons for European integration were the pursuit of prosperity and the preservation of peace. Policies and projects in quest of the first aim are mostly those which have minor linguistic effects. However, cooperation in the defence field, educational initiatives to foster solidarity and understanding and the promotion of contacts between the peoples of the Member States parallel those policies of the nationalist era which have been seen to cause fundamental linguistic change. The particular interest at the present moment is to see if strategies designed to promote mutual understanding, cooperation and cohesion can succeed in a plurilingual context. If they cannot, how far is language a factor in their failure? If they succeed do they alter the linguistic landscape? Is the cession of some political power to the supra-national level causing a language shift similar in certain respects to that which accompanied the centralisation of power in the nation state?

Defence and Language Shift

History teaches us that the linguistic effects produced by armies may be profound. Urdu's very etymology betrays its birth as a *lingua franca* for military purposes. From the Turkish word *ordo*, meaning camp (the word which has also given us the English word 'horde'), the language has its origins in a *lingua franca* which evolved during the Islamic invasions and the establishment of Muslim rule in the north of India between the eighth and tenth centuries AD. The speech of the areas around Delhi, known as *khari boli*, was adopted by the Arabic, Pashto, Turkish and Persian-speaking invaders as the means of communication with the local population. In time, it became the *lingua franca* of the army itself, which, multilingual in origin, had need of a common idiom (Comrie, 1987). The language variety which then developed was considerably influenced both by its origins (*khari boli*) and by extensive borrowing and interference from Arabic, Pashto, Persian and Turkish. Urdu eventually penetrated the court, becoming the language of power and of literature and is now the official national language, and gradually replacing the other languages and dialects of Pakistan.[1]

The homogenising linguistic effect that armies can produce can also be seen in modern Europe. Conscription of all young men into a national (or citizens') army can be a melting pot experience which promotes shift from regional to national language. Once again, the French case provides a good example.[2] A period of military service has been obligatory for all French males since 1792. In France's citizens' army there was a conscious effort to suppress regional loyalties; regiments which retained close identification with a particular province constituted a danger for the 'one and indivisible Republic'. This desire to efface regional loyalties was realised in the context of the Napoleonic Wars; regiments suffered huge losses and were reorganised or amalgamated with no consideration for the geographical origins of the soldiers. In consequence, Napoleon's *Grande Armée* acted as a linguistic melting pot and the scale of language shift was significant because of the sheer numbers recruited from all sectors of French society. In the First

World War, this process occurred again. In the early days of the conflict, soldiers who had enlisted together from the same villages were put into the same regiments. After the terrible losses of the first engagements, regiments found themselves merged:

> Dès lors il était plus facile de parler la langue commune que tout le monde avait apprise à l'école que de se faire comprendre dans son patois natal. Ces regroupements décidés par l'Etat-major allaient porter aux patois un coup fatal, alors que la Révolution n'avait pas réussi à les ébranler. (Walter, 1988: 117)

Acquiring a language in such circumstances appears to have sealed its success; it would seem to have become part of an identity which could not be denied or forgotten (Baconnier *et al.*, 1985). The demobbed soldiers who returned to their villages in those areas of France where the regional languages had remained predominant in private and local life exercised a profound effect on linguistic change. Figures of prestige or pity, the old soldiers of 1914–1918 had lasting linguistic influence on their communities.

Is common defence likely to have a similar kind of linguistic influence in the European Union? Before attempting to answer that question there is a prior question which must be posed. Are there indications that there will be common defence for the EU and just for the EU? Certainly there are indications of widespread acceptance that Europe needs a common defence approach. There is some reason to believe that increased military cooperation has led to defence institutions that could be accurately labelled European. And, if integrated military initiatives and forces have not yet happened except in a very minor and piecemeal way, the psychological refusal to countenance such integration does seem to have been partly overcome.

A Common Defence Framework

Attempts to provide a common defence network for Europe have a long history. Early initiatives in the immediate post-war period foundered on French fears of loss of sovereignty and British commitment to US dominated NATO. The Six attempted to create some kind of common defence as early as 1951 (Forster & Wallace, 1996). However, the proposed European Defence Community (EDC) was blocked by the refusal of the French Assembly to ratify the Treaty (1954), which would have brought it into being. The French were anxious on two counts: they were reluctant to permit German rearmament as well as to cede any control of military power to a supra-national body. This led to the ultimate victory of the other European defence solution, the founding of the Western European Union (WEU), an organisation which was solidly intergovernmental and firmly subordinated to NATO.[2] The so-called Atlanticists who championed this policy were led by the British government. A rift in the continent's defence came when French opposition to Atlanticism caused them to withdraw their forces from NATO command during de Gaulle's presidency.

In 1970, after de Gaulle's departure, the European Community was able to return to the issue of cooperation on the political and security front. Discussions led to the establishment of European Political Cooperation (EPC), at the time of the accession of the UK, Denmark and Ireland to the EEC. The most important achievement in the early days of this initiative was that the institutions and networks of the EPC were central in the preparations for the Conference on Security and Cooperation in Europe (CSCE), which culminated in the 1975 Helsinki declaration. This agreement was significant in opening up dialogue between communist and capitalist Europe and in moving towards the guarantee of basic human rights throughout the continent. Despite this success, the general assessment of EPC is that, although it had developed a framework for European cooperation, its actual results were meagre (Forster & Wallace, 1996; Brittan, 1994; van Ham, 1997).

In the 1980s, European dismay at worsening Soviet-American relations led to renewed attempts to promote a European common position on defence.[4] However, not all Member States were ready to pool sovereignty in this area. In particular, the Irish with their culture of neutrality[5] were reluctant. Other members with a traditionally strong commitment to the Atlantic Alliance were unwilling to alienate the Americans and were therefore ambivalent about closer European cooperation:

> Warnings from Washington continued to accompany every gesture towards closer cooperation, with the German, Dutch and British governments in particular anxious to reassure the Atlantic hegemon of their prior loyalty to the Atlantic alliance. (Menon et al. in Forster & Wallace, 1996: 416)

After twenty years of EPC without much evidence of concrete cooperation except for a great increase in talking,[6] it is perhaps surprising how quickly the situation developed in the late 1980s and early 1990s. In the more relaxed atmosphere of the second détente (1987 onwards) the rigidity of the old polarisation relaxed and it seemed possible to envisage new alignments. Waever (1989) detailed the four new possibilities which presented themselves: the 'Common European House' metaphor of the Russians conceived Europe as stretching from the Atlantic to the Urals; Milan Kundera and others argued for Europe from Portugal to Poland; a third group believed in the pre-eminence of the CSCE with the two superpowers still dominating defence in the area; the fourth idea of Europe was that of the European Community. In 1989, Waever tended to dismiss the Community as irrelevant, arguing that 'the interdependence of security dynamics is so high that any process of Europeanisation has to be conceived in all-European terms' (Waever, 1989: 293). Nonetheless, by the time of the Maastricht Treaty on European Union and in the light of the political events of the late 1980s and early 1990s, the prospect that there might be these 'conflicting Europes' (Waever, 1989: 299) had waned and the idea of common and independent European defence under the auspices of the European Community had come to seem a quite logical development and was becoming more widely accepted. The French, in particular, had ambitions to establish a European defence policy within the WEU as a way of resisting US 'hegemonical tendencies' in Europe[7] (Sjursen, 1998: 106).

The inclusion of political and security matters[8] in the intergovernmental conference (IGC) leading up to Maastricht came about through the pressure of external political events. The crisis in Yugoslavia revealed the weakness of Europe in general and the EU in particular faced with the need to react to a European emergency. Leon Brittan termed the situation 'institutional confusion . . . ruthlessly exposed by the Yugoslav crisis (Brittan, 1992). The Balkan situation together with the crumbling of Soviet hegemony, the reunification of Germany, instability in the Middle East and the likely contraction of US involvement in Europe led to a desire to strengthen the political arm of the Community.

The European Parliament voiced what were general European concerns on the perceived instability of the post-communist world and found it a reason to strengthen European Union defence:

> Alors que les événements en Europe de l'Est bouleversent quotidien-
> nement les équilibres nationaux, n'est-il pas opportun de relancer la
> coopération militaire au sein de la CEE? (Verwaerde, 1990)

Other perceived threats both from within and without the Community motivated a number of governments to seek closer cooperation. The prospect of a strong and reunified Germany was a spectre for those with historical reasons for fearing the resurgence of a dominant Mitteleuropa. Colmès voiced a fear prevalent in France when he asked his readers in *Le Point* 'L'Allemagne va-t-elle dominer l'Europe?' (Colomès, 1992). Else-where, a feeling that Muslim fundamentalism on the other side of the Mediterranean posed a threat increased feelings of insecurity in the

Member States geographically close to these problems (*Le Monde Dossiers et Documents*, 1991; Gomez, 1998).

The Atlanticists had to recognise that, in the post-communist world,[9] the US might be less willing to fund European defence, through its NATO commitment. The declarations of the Reagan and Bush administrations made it quite clear that there must be 'a redefined transatlantic bargain to reflect the end of western Europe's security dependence' (Transatlantic Declaration 1990 in Forster & Wallace, 1996).[10] The Clinton administration promoted closer European cooperation saying quite unambiguously that the 'new security must be found in Europe's integration' (USIS-Defense Special File 13 January 1994 in van Ham, 1997).

The TEU took the first steps in this domain. Article J4.1 stipulates that the EU's Common Foreign and Security Policy (CFSP):

> shall include all questions relating to the security of the Union, including the eventual framing of a common defence policy, which might in time lead to a common defence.

Article J4.2 of the TEU requests:

> the Western European Union (WEU), which is an integral part of the development of the Union, to elaborate and implement decisions and actions which have defence implications.

Of course, none of this was a completely new departure. The de Gasperi proposals of the 1950s[11] had covered some of the same ground. The difference came in the widespread acceptance of the idea of the European Union as an entity to be protected, even if all matters to do with defence remained the province of the intergovernmental Council of Ministers rather than the affair of the supra-national Commission.[12]

The Amsterdam Treaty (1997) attempted to push the process forward. Article J.2 requires that Member States move towards a common foreign policy by:

- defining the principles of and general guidelines for the common foreign and security policy;
- deciding common strategies;
- adopting joint actions;
- adopting common positions;
- strengthening systematic cooperation between Member States in the conduct of policy.

These are manifest steps towards this goal and are backed by exhortations for the signatories' 'mutual political solidarity' and 'a spirit of loyalty and mutual solidarity' (Article J1.2), which remind the reader of the discourse of nation building and reveal that the countries in the consortium (or at least the treaty writers) see themselves as constituting far more than an alliance for their own defence in the old European balance of power model. In addition, the discourse in the Treaty gives an indication that the EU had aspirations for the role of international policeman, in the American mould. The protection and consolidation of democracy, the rule of law and respect for human rights were central to the document, (Article J1); the EU's ambition to become their main guarantor in Europe and the prime instigator of humanitarian and rescue tasks, peacekeeping and crisis management was evident (Article J7.2).[13]

Common Defence Institutions and Actions

So what have the various EU treaties actually brought about in the way of common defence institutions and actions for the Member States that may affect language use?

The criticism of EPC was that it was merely a talking shop. At first it was an intermittent talking shop relying on the foreign ministry of the country holding the presidency to convene meetings and suffering from the inability of the smaller countries to respond to all the pressures. This problem was partially relieved by the creation of an EPC secretariat, composed of seconded officials from the Member States, and a secure communications network (COREU) to link their foreign ministries. Direct links between foreign office desk officers increased enormously, with the effect that the intermediary role of national embassies was virtually eliminated (Forster & Wallace, 1996). By 1990, EPC was clearly a successful network for exchange of information and for consultation, although it did not have the teeth to be more than that. By the provisions of the SEA the head-quarters of the EPC were brought to Brussels.

Similarly, the CFSP was unlikely to progress further than a super-diplomatic function unless it acquired the military capacity to implement the decisions taken by it as a body. When the common foreign and security policy was formally established in the Maastricht Treaty, the WEU was adopted as 'an integral part of the development of the European Union', designated to formulate and implement defence and military aspects of policy. However, in 1992, the WEU was a quasi-moribund body. A new and more extensive role for the WEU had been discussed in the Rome summit in 1984 and the Reykjavik Summit in 1986, culminating in the WEU statement, a 'Common

Platform on European Security Interests', in October 1987. However, little had happened. For the WEU to have any effect it had to be revitalised. In January 1993 its head-quarters were relocated in Brussels for symbolic as well as strategic reasons. WEU officials established working relationships with the European Council, COREPER and the secretariat of the CFSP. The terms of the EU and WEU presidencies were synchronised. The WEU has grown in importance since Maastricht, expanding in terms of personnel and research groups. The Petersberg Declaration (June 1992) suggested a potential role for the WEU within Europe and set out the means by which this could be achieved. When, in January 1994, NATO endorsed an independent European security and defence identity, the way was open for a strengthening of the WEU. Member States recognised that a potential force would need a central planning agency to allow it to prepare contingency plans for both its defence and peacekeeping roles, forces upon which it could call, and a structure to ensure the necessary command, control and communication arrangements. A planning cell, a contingent of forces answerable to WEU (FAWEU) and a command structure are now in place.[14]

The exact position and future of the WEU are still under discussion because of continuing clashes between Community and Atlantic visions of Europe. Apologists for the former wanted the WEU to become the defence arm of the EU; those supporting the second wanted the WEU to become the European pillar in a reformed NATO. FAWEU troops became 'double-hatted' which meant they were designated by the Member States as employable by either organisation. Then the Blair administration led a veto on a EU-WEU merger at the Amsterdam summit. This seem to have destroyed the short-term prospects for any defence dimension for the CFSP, but as the Kosovo crisis began, the question of a European Security and Defence Identity resurfaced again. The NATO summit in April 1999 outlined plans to allow a EU force access to US military assets, including satellite intelligence, as well as NATO's planning capabilities, in any future regional conflicts where the US wished to remain uninvolved.

There is a fundamental difficulty in creating a defence force with intergovernmental command. Who would control such an army? In NATO, responsibility is clearly intergovernmental; however, the execution of an agreed policy is directed by a supranational command structure. The US dominated this organisation and provided leadership. The WEU and the CFSP too are organised at intergovernmental level, but there is plenty of opportunity for fudge, lack of decision, uncertainty and unpredictability in a situation where agreement would have to be reached by all the members and where there is no acknowledged state which provides leadership. One might speculate whether in the distant future and in a scenario which called for immediate decisions on action this would continue to be the case. At what point would a government want to relinquish operational control of its assets to multi-national control? Once control has passed to the multi-national commander then the nation's role becomes one of logistic supplier to its allocated forces and they cannot be subject to national micro-management (*Flight International*, 9 September 1992).[15] On the one hand, the diversity of European reactions to the crises in Yugoslavia (1991–1992) and Iraq (1998) showed how difficult it was for the EU to orchestrate common action where different national reactions were at odds; on the other hand, in the Kosovo crisis, the EU governments at the Cardiff summit (June 1998) responded swiftly and unanimously in terms of verbal warnings, even if the subsequent action was organised under the aegis of NATO. In the Kosovan crisis a European defence and security identity did seem to be developing among the European NATO states, in that a kind of collective responsibility restrained individual governments from breaking ranks even where it was clear that both they and their populations had grave reservations about the bombing strategy adopted by NATO. In its defence pillar the EU possesses embryonic institutions which can build on this experience of solidarity and collective responsibility.

At the present time, the position of the WEU as the defence pillar of the EU is undermined by the anomaly that it includes countries which are not in the Union, but does not include all those which are. The ten full members of the WEU are the Member States of the EU except for Ireland, Denmark, Finland, Austria and Sweden (these have observer status), six associate members (Norway, Iceland, Turkey, Czech Republic, Hungary and Poland) and an ever-growing number of states with the status of associate partnership. These are the countries who expect to join the EU in the next decade. This 'variable geometry' and the association of non EU countries compromise the strengthening of the WEU-EU relationship and may block the final merger of both organisations desired by integrationists, although the neutral states have softened their commitment ot non-intervention in the past decade and alignments are liable to change (Hill, 1996).

While it has proved difficult to achieve an all-encompassing common European defence through top down strategies; piecemeal, practical cooperation has, however, flourished under the umbrella of the EU. Once again small incremental instances of collaboration have been successful in furthering the integrationist cause. These include the Eurocorps (with forces from Belgium, France, Germany, Luxembourg and Spain), the UK/Netherlands Amphibious Force, the Multinational Division-Central (with forces from Belgium, Germany, the Netherlands and the UK), the Franco-British European Air Group.

The Eurocorps, founded as a result of Franco-German rapprochement in a common Defence Council (1988), has the highest profile. This brigade brought together troops from France and Germany, in the first instance, to work as one fighting unit. It has provoked nationalist reaction[16] but at the same time had immense symbolic importance as an actual example of transnational defence cooperation. Politicians invested it with immense significance:

> Eurocorps is the central building stone for a European defence. We are creating an instrument for a joint foreign and security policy of the Europeans. At the end of the road Europe's unification will be waiting. (Volker Rühe quoted in *International Herald Tribune* 6–7 November 1994)

As did political analysts:

> In a fundamental sense and in terms of a genuinely autonomous Western European defence union the Franco-German institutions can be regarded as the only, albeit tiny, nucleus for a multilateral European army. (Rummel & Schmidt, 1991: 271)

It is likely that the development of common defence and peace-keeping at the operational level will continue and may well contribute to the development of common defence structures which will ultimately be irreversible. Hill notes:

> the gradual increase in the number of states wishing to associate themselves with the Eurocorps, and the willingness of the neutral states to soften their commitment to non-intervention. (Hill, 1996: 83)

And, if we assume that cooperation will continue and perhaps strengthen, we can expect this domain to have an impact on language. The higher echelons of command have been dominated by French and German, and the other national groups have had to accommodate. This has caused some difficulties. Among the French some of the officers have learnt German in school because of the prestige accorded that language in the French education system. Among the ranks, there are few who have the language before enlisting except for the French-Alsatian bilinguals. On the German side the linguistic situation is even more problematic among the ranks because of the low educational level of the recruits (*Courrier International*, 1996). However, when Julian Garcia Vargas proposed the use of English because of the inadequate French and German skills among the forces, the French were outraged and English has been formally banned (*Libération*, 10 April 1996). The Dutch-speaking Belgians have demanded that Dutch be included as a language of command (*Libération*, 19 November 1993).[17] So far without success.

Within the army command there is some concern about the consequences of the multilingual regime. François Clerc (commander-in-chief in 1996) complained that thought had been given to compatibility of weapons but not to compatibility of language. He suggested that going to war with comrades one was not sure of understanding added to the risks and that the Eurocorps practice of writing down orders in both languages to lessen the risk of misunderstanding would not work in the midst of action. He underscored the need for a community of communication in an army by stating that 'il ne peut imaginer avoir besoin d'un interprète pour transmettre un ordre' (*Courrier International*, 1996).

Neither of the historical case studies described at the beginning of the chapter is directly comparable to that of the Eurocorps, nor to any of the other common projects in existence nor to future forces which might be organised by NATO or WEU. However, there are similarities in that any army must have channels of communication and these will develop in response to need. As Clerc made clear, no fighting force could adopt the language policy of the institutions of the EU with its policy of equal status for each of the official languages. Whereas government might be able to envisage working in eleven languages and functioning through translation and interpreting, this is not an option for an army when engaged in any kind of military activity. Clerc's reproof to the Dutch was that they should not 'confondre un état-major militaire avec un parlement' (*Le Monde*, 18 November 1993).

The UN provides a precedent for the EU in that although it uses six official languages within its organisation,[18] in its multinational peacekeeping forces there has been an overwhelming tendency to adopt English unofficially as a *lingua franca* for ease and speed of communication.[19] NATO reinforces this precedent: command and contact are also largely monolingual, although the official documents of the alliance are published in both French and English, both texts being equally authentic and of equal status[20] and there is provision of interpreters for those who do not wish to use either English or French within the formal meetings of Foreign Ministers.[21] If the Eurocorps survives, it will probably move to a monolingual regime. At the present time, without the involvement of other states that language will probably be French.

In Weber's definition, the state has the monopoly of violence. Those who were least convinced that the Member States of the EU would achieve any kind of federal union or would be prepared to cede any more sovereignty evoked Weber, citing the lack of a purely European common defence organisation as one convincing reason. Writing in 1982, Stanley Hoffmann suggested that were such an organisation to arise then the balance might be tipped towards integration:

> (A) common defence regime would be much more damaging for the nation-state than the economic and monetary regimes achieved so far. These have strengthened the nation-state more than they have dispossessed it. A defence Community would require a leap towards more powerful central institutions; here, the relation between Community and states is a zero-sum game. This is another reason why so little has been undertaken. (Hoffmann, 1995: 225)

Are the steps towards a defence component in the CFSP an indication that the balance has been tipped towards integration? Should these processes continue, the resultant army controlled by or even closely linked to the European Union would need to reconsider the EU's commitment to multilingualism. To refuse to do this would be unthinkable; a common fighting force without a *lingua franca* would be a new departure. What it could actually mean in practice would be difficult to predict since even the multilingual forces of the Habsburg empire adopted a form of German as a *lingua franca*.[22]

Education and Identity

Free and obligatory schooling became the norm in Western European nation states in the late 19th century.[23] There was a complex agenda behind this drive to universal education: first and foremost it was fuelled by industrialisation's need for a more educated workforce; secondly it was a means of socialising citizens to be part of their nation state and to provide the literate workers necessary for its bureaucracy; and thirdly it reflected the growing importance of the individual's role as a participant in increasingly democratic societies.

In France, the precept of six or seven years[24] free education provided by the state and obligatory for all had been brought before the Convention in three projects elaborated successively by Condorcet, Talleyrand and Daunou (Mayeur, 1981). The implementation of the idea actually took some eighty years to realise. As in all the industrialising countries, the needs of industry and commerce were a strong motive for universal education. At the same time, nation building in the infant republic was equally important. In the IInd Republic, Carnot called explicitly on teachers to 'contribuer pour leur part à fonder la République.'[25]

In the IIIrd Republic, French republicans set out to wrest the moral function of education from religion and make it the business of the state. The arguments for secular education were humanist, democratic and patriotic.[26] The story of the confrontation of the Catholic church and the French state has been well documented (cf. Capéran, 1967) and need not concern us here. It is sufficient to note that the ultimate victory of the secular movement gave France a public elementary school funded by the state and staffed by state employees[27] which could be employed as:

> an instrument of social control (which) could lead the people to a community of patriotism and beliefs'. (Moody, 1978: 98)

The aphorism of the *Ligue de l'enseignement* sums up attitudes:

> Who controls the schools directs the world; and those who control the schools of France, rule the country. (quoted in Moody, 1978: 96)

Of all school subjects, the study of French national history lent itself best to the nationalist project. A school of historians based at the Sorbonne is noted for its contribution to building the subject and to giving it a national dimension. Michelet with a literary and romantic approach to national history dominated the subject in the mid-19th century. The next generation of historians introduced study of the modern period and scientific method. Although Monod, Lavisse, Seignobos believed in archival research and argued that history should be based on documentary evidence, their concern for a scientific approach did not lead to conflict with the political classes who demanded a single and unified national story that could be employed to encourage a cohesive and patriotic people.[28] Both the monarchy and the Republic had been highly centralised with the result that the national archives on which research was to be based told the story of the Franks, the French monarchy, northern chivalry, northern feudalism, the Parisian based ruling class, not the parallel stories of the kings of Provence, the royal family of Brittany, the House of Savoy. Thus the aims of both the academic and political worlds were in accord.

Lavisse, perhaps the most influential of the Sorbonne group by virtue of his position as professor of history at the Sorbonne, director of the *Ecole normale supérieure*, advisor to several ministers of the *Instruction publique* and prolific author of both scholarly and educational texts, makes clear use of history in the service of promoting national cohesion and patriotism. In his primary textbook which sold millions of copies (Prost, 1968), he told French school children that they should love France 'parce que son histoire l'a faite grande' (Lavisse, 1902). To foster this pride he advised his trainee teachers to recount 'les Gaulois et les druides, Roland et Godefroi de

Bouillon, Jeanne d'Arc et le grand Ferré, Bayard et ces histoires de l'ancienne France' (Lavisse, 1895: 40).

Not only were Parisians and Northerners the subject of this official, national history, it was their construction of events which prevailed. For example, the interpretation by which the Albigensian Crusade was the invasion of what is now the south of France by the north was suppressed, and IIIrd Republic school children learned that the intervention of the French king was essential because:

> une secte d'hérétiques, nommés Albigeois, . . . désola le midi de la France par de sanglantes entreprises. Ils parcouraient les villes et les campagnes, massacrant les catholiques, brûlant les églises et les couvents. (Melin, 1895: 41)[29]

The idea of the essential unity in French society is a continual refrain, expressed on numerous occasions and in numerous different contexts. Ferry made the point in the discussion of what moral code to teach. By definition it must be:

> la bonne vieille morale de nos pères, la nôtre, la vôtre, car nous n'en avons qu'une'. (Ferry speech in Sénat 10 June 1881, J.O., p. 807 quoted in Prost, 1968: 196)

Education proved a very effective tool in assimilating the children of the diverse traditions of France and building a culturally cohesive nation state. The individual's sense of community at the regional level was weakened and refocused at national level. This is in fact an ongoing process and the present curriculum continues to neglect and obscure the diversity of regional histories in France:

> Les instructions officielles de 1985 mettent l'accent sur l'histoire nationale. L'histoire locale est bien absente et c'est dommage. (Marchand et Terrier, 1992: 7)

Europe and Education

The French were not alone in employing such methods, although they were undoubtedly among the most successful. Political elites in the other European nation states used the same strategies with greater or lesser effect. Given this legacy, we might expect European integrationists to adopt, or to try and adopt, similar strategies to promote European identity and cohesion. There are, of course, four brakes on any such attempt. Firstly, the immense power of national loyalty and identity will be a counterweight. Secondly, the parents of pupils today are more sophisticated than the largely illiterate parents of the 1880s and their children less easily manipulated. Thirdly, the commitment to respect cultural diversity contained within the preamble to the TEU[30] forces Europeanists to be more circumspect than their counterparts in the heyday of nationalism. Fourthly, the principle of subsidiarity deprives the Commission of both the funds and the authority to implement programmes and it must work through the national education systems.[31] Despite these restraints, there has been a clear attempt to use education to 'build a citizens' Europe' and allow 'society . . . to acquire a new awareness of its European identity' (Couloubaritsis *et al.*, 1993: 13). Jean Monnet recognised the power of education. Of European unification, he said 'Si c'était à refaire je commencerais par l'éducation' (cited in ESHA, 1990).

The first concrete expression of the role the Community hoped to play in education came in the Resolution of the Council and Ministers of Education 9 February 1976. This called for the sharing of information on Member States' education systems, assessment of comparability, and the improvement of language teaching. The Stuttgart Declaration of 19 June 1983 recommended cooperation between institutions of higher education and the development of European awareness through knowledge of European culture and history. The Fontainebleau Declaration of 25 June 1984 reinforced the idea of promoting the concept of the European citizen through education. The 1985 Adonnino Report clearly recommends education as a tool of unification. The authors advised that 'all young people should be *trained* to become fully fledged European citizens' (European Commission, 1985, my emphasis). In response to the Adonnino report and in the context of preparations for 1993 and the implementation of the Single European Market, pressure to Europeanise the curriculum grew, aided by European funding.[32] On the 24 May 1988, a Resolution was adopted in the EP which called for a European dimension to education. This set out to:

> strengthen in young people a sense of European identity and make clear to them the value of European civilisation and of the foundation on which the European peoples intend to base their development today, that is in particular the safeguarding of the principles of democracy, social justice and respect for human rights.[33]

This was reaffirmed in Article 126: 2 of the Maastricht Treaty, which called again for a European dimension in education, gave a commitment to the promotion of all the Member States' official languages as foreign languages in the Community's schools and colleges and recommended student mobility as a means of achieving such aims.

The European Dimension in the School Curriculum

The reaction to the call to 'Europeanise' from teachers and educational managers in the Member States' education systems was mostly very positive. During the period leading up to the introduction of the Single European Market there was particular enthusiasm. Even in the eurosceptic UK there was a flurry of activity to respond. The following exhortation to British college principals:

> Can you encourage all staff to 'think Europe' in their teaching, by:
> * drawing examples from other EC countries;
> * using EC terms associated with their specialism;
> * generally exciting their students about Europe?

was not atypical (APC, 1989: 25). There were numerous conferences on 'Delivering the European Dimension',[34] new professional journals devoted to the subject[35] and countless small initiatives by schools, colleges and local education authorities to promote 'European Awareness'[36] among their students and pupils.

In Britain, the Education Reform Act made no provision for the European dimension and so dampened this enthusiasm to some extent. The Conservative policymakers had felt that Europeanisation would weaken British national identity (Morrell, 1996; Macey, 1990). In contrast, the post-SEA euphoria has continued in many other Member States and the European dimension has flourished (ESHA, 1990).

Nowhere has this been more evident than in the rewriting of history to highlight a common European past. In some of the works published there is a clear reinterpretation of the past in order to build Renan's 'common legacy of memories' for Europeans.[37] This was undoubtedly the aim of *The Origins of European Identity*, a history text book, commissioned and published by the Commission and setting out to provide

> secondary school teachers and students in the twelve countries of the Community with a work aimed primarily at charting a common pool of information on the (sic) European identity and encompassing the main thrust of ideas and the essential features of European civilisation. (Couloubaritsis *et al.*, 1993: cover)

The book is interesting in its unabashed attempt to replicate the strategies of the nationalist era. The very first sentence, 'Our first duty is to love Europe', echoes Lavisse's call to French school children, 'Tu dois aimer la France'. There is uncritical acceptance that Europe was and is pre-eminent in most domains and a chauvinist approach redolent of nationalist historians. There is an attempt to instil a pride in being European which sometimes appears to be attempting to replace narrow state nationalism with a 'continentalism' which could be equally unpleasant. The following extracts which the authors choose to quote illustrate the point:

> Europe made the world by discovering and arousing each of the continents in turn out of its slumber. It created the world trade system and spread its machines and its ideals over the Earth. (de Rougement quoted Couloubaritsis *et al.*, 1993: 167)

and

> When formed by Nature, our part of the world was given no title to that glorious preeminence which distinguishes it today. Our small continent, possessed of least territorial wealth is rich only in ideas . . . however, such is the power of the human spirit: this region, endowed by Nature with nothing but vast forestland, became peopled with powerful nations and acquired the wealth and rich pickings of two worlds, this narrow peninsula, appearing on the globe as merely an Asian appendage, has become the metropolis of the human race. (Valéry quoted Couloubaritsis *et al.*, 1993: 168)

and

> In the final analysis, however, Europe has always condemned them (the murders of Socrates and Christ) as scandalous errors. And we still continue to believe, even more than ever, that freedom of thought and respect for humanity are consubstantial in Europe, such that Europe ceases at the point where either of these commandments is broken. (de Madriarga in Couloubaritsis *et al.*, 1993: 179)

In fairness, Couloubaritsis *et al.* caution against a return to the closed patriotism of earlier times and argue that no one who is not also a 'citizen of the world' will ever be a true European of the twenty-first century. However, against the background of their uncritical celebration of the world-wide impact of European ideals, this seems inadequate. The effect of Europe's cultural imperialism is well-documented (cf. Said, 1994).

The authors attempt to rewrite the old diverse national histories as one. Of course, within the restricted geographical space of Europe, links and influences are inevitable. These are highlighted. Where events, beliefs or practices divide the peoples of Europe, such divisions are pushed to the background. The main interest of the work, however, is the list of authors; this was not the idea or the work of minor figures. Emile Noël, secretary-general of the Commission for nearly thirty years and then president of the prestigious European Institute in Florence is one of the collaborators.

This book is not alone in the bookshops of the Member States. Throughout the 1980s, the shelves labelled European History took on a new appearance. Alongside the histories of France, Germany, Italy, UK etc. which had always constituted the majority in such a section, titles appeared which showed that the authors' perspective or focus was European rather than national.[38]

The parallels between the role of history education in nation building and that of the promotion of a common European heritage in the unification of Europe founder, however, when it comes to the implementation of policy. The national education ministries have the budget and the power to choose which history courses are taught whereas the Commission can only rely on exhortation and small amounts of pump-priming funding to promote any initiatives.

The other major difference is in the language medium used for this activity. Nineteenth century national education systems consciously used the national language as a strategy for national linguistic unification. This is not replicated in Europe with its commitment to linguistic diversity. The European Interuniversity Press published *The Origins of European Identity* in the nine languages which were official in the EU at the time of its publication.

Language Education for European Integration

Even if there is absolutely no question of working towards linguistic homogeneity in Europe, there is still a strong desire for a community of communication. The second element in Article 126 of the Maastricht Treaty concerned language education to facilitate transnational contact. It was recognised from the outset of the European project, that integration and unification would make little headway where citizens remained bound within their national groupings because of language. So policies for improving foreign language skills in the various populations were an early feature of Community educational involvement. There were two prongs in this policy: foreign language provision in the class room was to be extended and made more effective[39] and contacts and exchanges among national groups were to be built up.

The LINGUA programme introduced in 1990 was intended to 'improve language competence throughout the 12 Member States'. It would do this by the in-service training of teachers and trainers, by supporting language students in higher education, by helping personnel in SMEs acquire the languages they need for trade and commerce, by promoting school and youth exchanges and developing foreign language teaching materials. However, even if all these strategies proved successful, and general foreign language competence did improve, this policy would still not ensure communication among the populations of the Member States, because LINGUA had as its brief the promotion of *all* the national languages and sought particularly 'to encourage the teaching and learning of the less widely used languages of the European Community'. There was no suggestion that one or more languages might be designated as *lingua franca*(s). The Commission, influenced by the commitment to linguistic equality in the institutions and reluctant to wound the sensibilities of any national group, could not and would not act otherwise in this matter. This commitment to plurilingualism in language education means that the language issue is polarised between, on the one hand, an impracticable idealism which would have school children learn several languages and participants in multinational groups each use their own language relying for comprehension on the foreign language competence of the others.[40] And on the other, a brutal, hard-headed acceptance of the laws of the market which makes English, because of its use in intercultural communication throughout the world and for access to scientific, technical and academic knowledge, the most valuable language to acquire.

In this unequal struggle, LINGUA is unlikely to be able to influence behaviour profoundly. EU money may persuade the odd group to learn some Danish or Portuguese in order to take a funded trip to the countries of the target language, but it does not appear able to sustain such learning.[41] This should not surprise us. The miserable results of language learning within the classroom unsupported by any clear extrinsic or intrinsic motivation are well documented (Gardner & Lambert, 1972; Rubin, 1981; Seliger, 1983; Byram, 1989). Language education which has as its sole purpose European integration is unlikely to ensure language acquisition. For most people there has to be demonstrable material advantage (extrinsic motivation) to repay the effort necessary for language acquisition. Where there is clear reward, where mastery of a foreign language gives access to knowledge or brings economic advantage, then it is more likely that large numbers of people will develop foreign language competence.

This explains why, at the moment, despite all Commission efforts to the contrary, the education systems of the EU are providing tuition in one foreign language to the virtual exclusion of all the others. In the school year 1996–1997 89% of all EU secondary school children were reported to be learning English (Eurydice, 1998). This showed an increase on the 1992–1993 figure of 88% (Eurydice, 1996), which was itself a jump from the 83% recorded in 1991–1992 (Eurostat, 1994). In addition the 1998 report shows that 26% of non-anglophone pupils at primary level are now learning English.

The dominance of English is strongest in the countries in the Germanic continuum/in the north of the continent. The 1992–1993 figures show that 100% of Swedish secondary school children were learning English. The figure was over 90% in Denmark, Germany and Finland, over 80% in the Netherlands and Austria. The percentages fell to 71% in Belgium, 66% in Italy and Luxembourg, 64% in Greece and 52% in Portugal. From the southern, Romance continuum, only Spain and France reported that more than 90% of their secondary pupils were learning English. In the primary sector Finland led the English-learning league with 64% of pupils with Spain second at 63% (Eurydice, 1998). The Eurydice report noting the dominance of English remarks that:

> The other official languages of the EU feature less in the curriculum and are selected less often by pupils. (Eurydice, 1998)

French is the only real rival for English, with 32% of non-Francophone EU secondary school pupils learning it in 1996–1997 (Eurydice, 1998). This percentage has remained constant since 1992–1993. The statistics break down as follows: Luxembourg 100% of secondary school children learn French, as do 98% of Dutch speaking Belgians, 70% of Irish pupils, 44% of Greek and 44% of Portuguese. No data was available from the UK for that year.

In only four countries were there significant numbers learning German: Denmark 67%, Luxembourg 100%, Dutch 61% and Sweden 42%. Only the French had a significant number of secondary school pupils learning Spanish (29%) (Eurydice, 1996).

The trend towards English as the first foreign language is illustrated by the Spanish case. Here there has been a remarkable and unexpected shift from French to English. In 1985–1986, 28.5% of Spanish secondary pupils were learning French (reported in Calvet, 1993). The 1998 Eurydice report shows that this figure has now dropped to 8%. This mirrors the rise in English from 71.1% (reported in Calvet, 1993) to over 90% (Eurydice, 1996).

Citizens of the anglophone countries do not appear from these reports to be enthusiastic foreign language learners. Among EU Member States, only Ireland and the UK do not have a foreign language on the primary curriculum. And as a final comment, it is interesting to note that the accession countries appear to be reinforcing the trend towards English. For example, the Czech republic reports that, in the school year 1996–1997, 48% of its primary school children were learning English (Eurydice, 1998).

Thus, by virtue of being the most frequently taught foreign language in the education systems of the EU, English is on its way to becoming the unofficial second language of the European Union. The EU policy to promote diversity seems not to have been able to withstand market pressures from parents and pupils who see the acquisition of English as necessary for the realisation of their educational and professional ambitions. The great difference between this phenomenon and the imposition of a single national language on nation states stems from the fact that English is learnt only as a *lingua franca* for utility and access to knowledge and markets; there appears at present little likelihood that English will replace any learners' mother tongue as a first language and learners' competence in the foreign language may remain quite limited both in sophistication and in the domains in which the learners can operate. Bearing in mind these significant differences, one can still argue that European education is reproducing some of the effects of national education. It is creating a community which can communicate, even if only in school pupil English.[42] This has, of course, provoked reaction. The 'unacceptable domination of English' has been attacked from many quarters, not least by academics in the linguistic disciplines.[43]

Moreover Siguan (1996) has pointed out that this situation is unlikely to remain stable. As individuals expend immense effort to acquire and perfect a foreign language and less time mastering their own and acquiring high levels of mother tongue literacy, there may come a point when the balance tips towards the foreign language which then becomes the dominant idiom for the individual. We see this among immigrant children where it signifies imminent language shift and it is an alternative scenario to stable diglossia in countries where English language skills in the population are very high. Then a conscious effort would be needed to maintain the national language.

Other Parallels to Nation Building: Taxation and Networks

The organisation of economies on a national scale had immense effect on the relationship of citizens to the nation state. The symbol of the national currency and the protection of the domestic market contributed to a sense of belonging. When the nation states became welfare states and prosperous citizens were taxed so that all could have access to health and education services and rights to unemployment benefit and a retirement pension, this sense was heightened and the relationship of citizens with each other strengthened. Taxpayers may or may not have accepted willingly the extent of welfare provision that they were expected to provide; what was not open to discussion were the beneficiaries. These would be the co-nationals. Where the national group was reasonably cohesive this solidarity was not usually questioned.

Now the EU has taken on a small part of the redistributive role of the state. It collects VAT charged on goods and services by the Member States (a maximum of 1.24% of their VAT revenue in 1996). Secondly, each country donates a share of its Gross National Product (a maximum of 1.22% in 1996). Thirdly, the EU collects customs duties from non-EU countries on imported goods. These resources are then redistributed within the EU to support regions, social groups or industries which are in difficulty or to promote transnational ventures and cooperation. Lesser developed regions, sectors of the economy and social groups which are in need receive European aid through the European Regional Development Fund, the European Social Fund, the European Agricultural Fund and the Financial Instrument for Fisheries Guidance. Together with Community Initiatives, which target specific causes of deprivation, such funding may have long-term consequences for European identity. These mechanisms may make Europeans responsible *as Europeans* for each other.[44] Thus the feelings of responsibility that we had for others less fortunate within *our* community which were factors in the development of national cohesion and the building of national identity are being reproduced at European level. There is, however, little linguistic effect from redistribution of wealth as such. It can be effected without the need for large-scale transnational contact.

Networks: The Exchange of Information and the Pooling of Research

On the other hand, where tax is used to promote collaboration among Europeans in economic, social, political, defence, judicial, scientific and academic sectors, there may be a major impact on the individual's language repertoire, encouraging more widespread use of those languages which function as *lingua francas* and making their acquisition a prerequisite for jobs which entail networking at EU level.

Collaboration in European Community networks has come into existence from pragmatic need as well as integrative idealism. European Research and Development programmes first grew from the necessity of finding partners for research in areas where the costs could not be borne by the small European nation state. European nation states have a tradition of pooling resources in order to compete with the US or Japan. particularly in the aerospace industry (Picq, 1990), with research organised bilaterally by governments or companies. However, in many of these collaborative projects there was a history of poor relationships; partners appeared to have been hampered by linguistic and cultural differences which were never confronted and projects were at the mercy of changing national policies (Wright, 1986; Muller, 1989). Collaboration tended to last only for the duration of a project and partners retained a tendency to return to cut-throat competition among themselves at the drop of a hat.[45] The necessity to overcome this failing and plan long-term cooperation became more pressing as the Community's share of the market in the new technologies fell (Swann, 1995) and as analysis suggested that the SEM might benefit Japan and the US rather than the fragmented European market where replication and duplication of innovation wasted precious resources (Macioti, 1988).

In 1985 the European Community pledged itself to establish a European Technological Community involving far more extensive collaboration in high technology research than had hitherto been attempted in Europe. The Community promised funding for joint research and development programmes in areas such as information technology, communications, new industrial technologies, energy, biotechnology and environmental issues where research is very costly and where avoiding wasteful replication would be beneficial and where the pooling of human talents might be productive. There were early teething troubles, caused in part by the UK government under Thatcher who argued that the larger part of Research and Development funding should come from industry.[46]

However, the Commission's stance prevailed with most of the Member States. By 1988 (supra) state-funded research programmes organised across the European Community were mushrooming in number and size. For example, Esprit, regarded as the flagship of European technological co-operation in information technology, moved to a second and much larger phase in 1989, involving some 5,500 researchers throughout the twelve nation bloc, with a budget of 1.6 billion Ecus over five years for collaborative research projects. The original budget was increased because of the very enthusiastic response from industry and because of the high number of viable projects. The programme brought together the biggest players in Europe: 200 researchers and technicians from Siemens AG and Teg-Telefunken Electronic GmbH of West Germany, Philips of the Netherlands, France's SGS-Thomson Microelectronics, and Britain's Plessey Company Plc came together in a 90 million dollar project on high speed silicon bipolar circuits, used in telecommunications and consumer electronics; Ing C. Olivetti e C. Spa of Italy, Bull SA of France and ICL of Britain worked on the development of cheaper and more versatile computer workstations.

Esprit was only one of several research initiatives which the EC introduced to prevent European industry trailing behind competitors in the US and Japan. Under the umbrella of the Framework Programmes, the principal instrument by which the European Community stimulated research, encouraged collaboration and ensured the dissemination and the exploitation of European discoveries, transnational teams worked on all the new technologies: telematics, language engineering, biomedicine, nuclear fission. There was also finance for environmental, climatic, population, energy and transport issues.

The integrationists in the Commission saw the Framework programmes which were extended and formalised by the SEA as a motor for integration. This tended to happen because, as the Community took on the role of financing and promoting research in these areas, national governments were disposed to withdraw financial support whenever they needed to cut budgets,[47] seeing the Community scheme as replacing their funding, not as additionality. Thus research teams from universities and research institutes were forced to consider the Community as a major source of funding and, industry looking for state support had to turn to European consortia underpinned and organised by the Commission.[48]

Although the Commission only contributes about 1/30th[49] of total public funding for research it has a disproportionate effect because of the way it targets the money geographically and because of the sectors it chooses to support. For example, in 1992 the twelve Member States, as individual national governments, allocated the equivalent of 50,000 million Ecu to R and D 87% of this expenditure, however, came from just four states (Germany, France, Italy and the UK), and France and the UK spent 35% and 43% respectively on research in the defence sector. In addition, nearly 7% of the total budget was spent on space research. In contrast, the Commission spread its 1,800 million Ecu budget throughout the twelve Member States and funded research into land use, control of pollution, production of energy and industrial production and technology. It had no defence expenditure and only 0.36% of the total went to the exploration of space. The effect of EU action was proportionally more important than the actual sum might suggest because it promoted R and D in less favoured but essential areas, encouraged the dissemination of findings throughout the Member States, and through its funding rules ensured that industry and state funded research were coordinated.[50]

As Community rules demanded that all the research that it supported be 'European' in the sense that partners be drawn from more than one member state, teams of researchers were by definition multinational and almost always plurilingual. Language use in this context is elaborate and complex, and the level of language ability needed for effective interaction is great since researchers are required to conceptualise and theorise in a second language. If the Framework research teams have been able to manage linguistic difference, it is probably because there was already a tradition of using English as a *lingua franca* for disseminating research findings in scientific conferences and papers and a custom that non-English speaking science students study English in order to communicate within the scientific community. The Framework programme used this tradition to accommodate the plurilingual nature of the research teams and further promoted it. Despite the possibility of submitting research proposals in any language, research groups were encouraged to submit their research proposals in English to simplify the evaluation process. Research teams felt that their chances of being accepted were enhanced if they used English and so they tended to do so.[51]

It would, of course, be erroneous to imagine that all transnational research collaboration happens solely or even chiefly under the aegis of the Community. In parallel with the growing force of research teams organised under the European umbrella, it has also become normal practice for companies in high tech industries to collaborate on a global scale. For example, Siemens started cooperating in 1992 with the American IBM and the Japanese Toshiba companies in memory chip research. Such global cooperation is also governed by the traditions of scientific linguistic culture and English is again likely to be the working language of the project teams.

However, there may well be differences between European and global collaboration in terms of identity. The drawing of boundaries round the Member States is bound to promote a sense of community. Given the rules for funding, it is only from among the EU states that partners can be found for the various European initiatives.[52] It is evident that the strict funding rules of the Community which have created purely European teams on European multi-sites have produced the travellers who replicate in a certain way the administrators described by Benedict Anderson (1983). He argued that the awareness of boundary and frontier contributes to identity and that the journeys made by functionaries to the borders of the state – and no further – helped to fix the concept of the nation state, the idea that it comprised just this geographical territory and no other. The search for collaborators for European funded schemes and the visits for collaborative work are within defined borders – the fact that these institutes are eligible, but not those; that these nations can provide collaborators, but not those – contributes to building the concept of the European Union. The difference between global and European collaborative ventures may thus reside not so much in language use but in patterns of identification with funding from

Brussels and its attendant rules giving a character to research teams that will be different in kind from that of bilateral cooperation between multinationals.

And if boundaries are not yet clearly defined for these travellers, the reason lies mainly in the fact that they have been ever-changing and that this is likely to continue. The regular admissions of members to the EU mean that there is a constant need to relocate the limits of within and without, and that, therefore, in the short time of the existence of the Community it is unlikely that its *actual* borders have impacted greatly on the European imagination in physical terms. However, the majority of Europeans are used to boundary change. Only a minority of European states have the same frontiers at the end of the twentieth century that they had at the end of the nineteenth. The full impact of the European space will only be felt after a period of stability. At the moment it may be that mental maps are more important.

More Journeys: Students

The importance of research networks has had an impact on the education of the next generation of researchers. Student mobility and transnational education have as part of their brief the preparation of future researchers for European collaboration. It is no longer simply the linguists who are sent on European journeys to hone their language skills in the higher education institutions of other European countries; in increasing numbers, students of other disciplines are also spending a proportion of their education in a different Member State and in a different language environment.

There are several schemes to promote language learning, student mobility and closer contact between young people and the coordination of educational practice. The first set of initiatives was monitored by Eurydice, the EU's education and youth policy information network. Set up in 1980 to provide information on cooperation programmes and information on Member States education systems, it was able to demonstrate the importance of exchanges for integration and the use of analytical comparisons for dissemination of the best practice in the EU.

Comett which started in 1986 was concerned with fostering university and enterprise cooperation, transnational exchanges, training courses and training packages in the area of advanced technology. By its second phase (1990–1994) it was achieving 5000 student placements, 100 staff exchanges, 1,300 courses, and producing 800 packages of training materials annually, which in turn contributed to the training of 100,000 individuals. By 1994 one million Europeans had benefited directly from it.

Tempus (Trans-European Mobility Scheme for University Studies) was targeted at the former Warsaw Pact countries and the former Yugoslavia. JEPs (Joint European Projects) would link universities in these countries with institutions in the EU states to promote the development of higher education in central and eastern Europe, foster research and provide mobility grants for individuals.

Petra was set up to allow young people who had left the education system to be included in European initiatives for contact and collaboration. It provided vocational training for young people, a transnational placements network and vocational guidance in relation to the single market (Educational and vocational guidance in the European Community July 1993 European Commission). The Leonardo da Vinci programme which replaced it in 1995 continued in the same vein arranging transnational work placements for young trainees and job seekers, as well as undergraduates, postgraduates and those in work. The aims of the programme are firstly technical – 'cooperation in respect of the transfer of technological innovation' – and cultural – 'transnational exchanges to improve language skills' (Johnson et al., 1997: 25).

One of the best known of the initiatives is the Erasmus programme which allocates grants to individuals and links universities in consortia with the aim of increasing students' understanding of other European countries and cultures and improving their language skills through a period of study in another Member State. The scheme has been very successful in attracting students and participation has become a commonplace. Launched in 1987, mobility organised within the Erasmus programme rose from 27,000 study placements in 1990–1991 to 64,000 in 1993–1994 (Socrates, 1997).[53] By 1996, the figure had risen again to 80,000 (Erasmus, 1998). In 1998–1999, 200,000 students were expected to participate[54] (Erasmus, 1998). A handful of universities and exchange students in 1987 had grown to 1,600 participating universities from 24 countries by the academic year 1998–1999 (Erasmus, 1998). Funding had also increased from 64 million Ecu in 1990–1991 (European Commission, 1990) to 11,625 million in 1998–1999 (Erasmus, 1998). EU policy is that in the long term 10% of all students in all disciplines will be involved in such an exchange.

Since 1995 the Erasmus scheme has been organised within the Socrates programme which also includes Comenius which focuses on school education and provides the framework for joint project work between schools in different Member States, Lingua which is concerned solely with promoting foreign language learning and teaching at all educational levels and Arion which allows educational experts in the Member States to network and exchange information and experience.

ECTS (European Credit Transfer Scheme) which started in 1989 was a refinement of Erasmus' student mobility. By this scheme, trans-national cooperation between higher education institutions allowed periods of study abroad to count towards the final degree in the home institution. A system of credit transfers guaranteed recognition of courses among participating universities and gave students the possibility of moving institution knowing that modules would be coherent and would build on prior study in the first university. An integrated study programme was assessed by a common grading system.

These European Union schemes have broadened from their early focus which was to promote knowledge of the other Member States. Now there is a desire to promote knowledge about the European Union itself. Jean Monnet Fellowships allow researchers to spend one year at the European University Institute Florence, which houses all the documents pertaining to the founding and development of the EU. Robert Schuman Scholarships allow postgraduates to research at the Commission or Parliament. Jean Monnet professorships at universities in Member States are financial incentives to encourage studies 'concentrating entirely on European integration at undergraduate or postgraduate level' (Johnson et al., 1997: 26).

The effects of these student journeys, work placements, joint projects and collaboration for identity is likely to result in the growth of informal networks of 'Europeans'. The contact and the period of residence may well have long-term effects for identification, with those who have had happy experiences in their study period and who have retained links being predisposed to both that Member State and the idea of European integration.[55] At the same time, we should also remember that there are students who did not have positive experiences and Karl Krautsky's cynical observation that the railways were the great breeders of national hatreds could be adapted to apply in this instance.

There will also be linguistic outcomes to this mobility; students who hitherto ceased learning another language at the end of secondary school or before, now continue in order to achieve the linguistic competence necessary to study in the language of another Member State. Such students, at the end of their period of study in the other language will have achieved a mastery of it which is likely to remain with them throughout their adult life. However, it should be noted that student mobility in Europe is not multidirectional. Students are going to study in the Member States whose languages are commonly taught as foreign languages in their secondary education systems. This is shown by the list of regions[56] which reported the largest numbers of EU students in the 1994–1995 academic year – eastern

France, eastern and western Austria, south east England, Wales, East Anglia, Northern Ireland, London and Paris (Eurydice, 1996) and by the constant struggle recorded in all the Erasmus documents to keep a balance between the receiving and the sending countries (Socrates, 1997; Ainsworth, 1999).

The level of language competence necessary to take part in schemes such as Erasmus, ECTS or the various projects of the Leonardo da Vinci programme is high. Acquiring a new language not learnt in school within a short time span is theoretically possible but few students have chosen to take up the offers of intensive language courses which would allow study in the countries with less widely spoken languages. Student mobility is thus linked to the availability of courses in English, or to a lesser extent, French and German. This strengthens the position of English as the most commonly spoken second language and increases the numbers with competence in French and German. Language is key in the process: it constrains choices of destination and promotes the linguistic domination of the 'big three' – English, French and German.

Conclusion

It could be argued that the equivalent of the French Third Republic melting pot policies where public employees were sent to other parts of the country is the system of transnational educational exchanges organised and funded by the Commission, which sends large numbers of young people to other parts of the Union, or the research teams which must be multinational to access funding at European level. Both of these societal phenomena may be reinforcing the tendency for English to be the second language of Europe (and to a lesser extent the relative vitality of French and German compared to the other languages of Europe). Foreign language competence is pivotal to the success of research networks and educational exchanges. Programmes to improve language skills had to be integrated into all the other initiatives to make them possible.

The language effects of common defence, may be less clear. The practice in the UN and NATO of using English as the military *lingua franca* promotes that language in some arena, while the refusal of the UK to be part of Eurocorps means that French and German are the languages of command and exercise in this initiative.

The attempts to use education to build awareness of a common heritage and to promote those parts of the European past which bind Europeans together rather than cast them as traditional enemies has been done with respect to the linguistic and cultural diversity upheld in the TEU, and in itself may not have an effect on language use.

Promoting European unity while preserving diversity and respecting cultural difference and linguistic plurality may be difficult. Extensive contact between the populations of the Member States as citizens are increasingly educated in each others' universities, brought together in research teams and organised as transnational armed forces will have a linguistic effect. Sociolinguistics has taught us that when languages are in close contact there are consequences for both the speakers and the languages, and that the necessary linguistic accommodation always takes place. Those who need to communicate find ways of doing so. If at the same time educational policies succeed in breaking down national chauvinism and historic prejudice, the psychological impediments to language learning also begin to disappear. We should expect the kinds of European integration described here to have, in the long term, profound effects on patterns of language use in Europe.

Notes

1. Both in Pakistan itself and among the Pakistani diaspora (Wright, 1993).
2. Eugen Weber (1979) catalogues the various forces for linguistic change and their interaction. He finds the role of conscription to have been critical. Emmanuel Le Roy Ladurie's work on conscription records shows the variety of languages and dialects spoken by those entering the armed forces.
3. The West European Union was eclipsed by NATO, whose domination of European defence in the Cold War era meant that 'high politics' was virtually out of the hands of the Europeans for decades (Williams, 1980).
4. These attempts occurred both within the EU and in Europe as a whole. For example, the London Report 1981 expanded foreign policy consultations to cover security questions; the Genscher-Colombo plan called for the coordination of security policy and the adoption of common European positions; the French relaunched the Franco-German defence talks; the six monthly WEU meetings of foreign and defence ministers were revived in 1983 (Forster & Wallace, 1996: 415).
5. When Sweden, Austria and Finland joined in 1995 the number of non-aligned nations increased.
6. And always under the shadow of NATO domination.
7. This has perhaps weakened with the French rapprochement to NATO in the 1990s.
8. Suggested by the Belgian government and supported by President Mitterrand and Chancellor Kohl and agreed by a majority at the Strasbourg European Council in July 1990 (Forster & Wallace, 1996).
9. The changed security environment has had a number of effects: the erstwhile enemy camps have been able to cooperate; the disappearance of an eastern frontier to be defended means that NATO has been able to expand to the east, opening its membership to former Warsaw pact countries.

10. There is a strong US sentiment that Europe got its defence cheaply in the past and a desire to make Europe, under whatever umbrella, rely less on the US. On the other side, in Europe there has been, in some quarters, a disinclination to make European defence a purely European affair because of the enormous costs involved. This may now be overcome by NATO's leasing and lending some of its installations.

11. The Italian prime minister, Alcide de Gasperi, had put forward a plan making the EDC the first step towards the setting up of a European political community. According to commentators (e.g. Varsori, 1992), the Italians had harboured a long-standing desire to protect their interests within a supra-national organisation. In 1948–9 they suggested transforming the OEEC into a more powerful instrument of political and economic cooperation. Franco-German rapprochement appeared threatening; NATO appeared to be sidelining the Italians; a European supra-national organisation seemed attractive.

12. The Commission has the right to make policy proposals on CFSP matters and a separate directorate-general (DG1A) has been set up to provide expertise in this area (van Ham, 1997). However, the framework set up at Maastricht makes CFSP one of the three 'pillars' of the Union, separate from the first pillar (the EEC, Euratom and ECSC) and the third pillar (Justice and Home Affairs) and keeps control firmly with the Member State governments and cooperation reliant on consensus rather than qmv (van Ham, 1997).

13. This mirrors developments in the WEU. The Petersberg Declaration laid down that in addition to its traditional collective defence role 'military units of WEU of the Member States, acting under the authority of WEU, could be employed for: humanitarian and rescue tasks; peacekeeping tasks; and tasks of combat forces in crisis management, including peacemaking (Petersberg Declaration, WEU Council of Ministers, Bonn, 19 June 1992).

14. In terms of its performance, the WEU has not been overly effective so far. At the time of the Gulf War, the WEU seemed the obvious co-ordinator for concerted European action because NATO could not act outside its defined area of action. This did not happen and the Member States who took part in the conflict did so as separate sovereign nation states. The conflict in former Yugoslavia provided a further opportunity for cooperation which was not realised. Indeed in the early stages of the conflict between Serbia and the secessionists, the incoherence of EU reactions may well have fuelled the conflict. In particular there is some feeling that Germany's unilateral recognition of Croatia accelerated the descent to war. As the fighting spread and it became clear that there were terrible abuses of human rights, the Europeans as a group still failed to achieve the consensus necessary to act and it was left to the UN to take the initiative in organising peace-keeping in the area. In 1996 this role was taken over by NATO. In 1999 it was again NATO and then the UN that intervened in Kosovo. The EU, as an organisation, had failed to act effectively in a conflict bordering its own territory and the global organisations had continued to be necessary for European security.

15. An example from the Gulf War exemplifies the tensions this provokes. The then Italian minister of defence, Virginio Rognoni, refused to relinquish control of Italian air force Tornados until a specific mission had been assigned to them. The USA would not give them a mission until they were under its control. The impasse lasted for some time until common sense prevailed (*Flight International*, 9 September 1992).

16. The reports in the French press on the occasion of the fiftieth anniversary of the end of the war and on the 14th July 1995 Bastille Day march which included German soldiers from the Eurocorps illustrate this. It was the first time German soldiers paraded on the Champs-Elysees since Hitler organised a World War II victory parade in 1940, and the move was widely-criticised in resistance circles and by some politicians (AFP 7 July 1994; *Le Figaro*, 14 July 1994; *Le Monde*, 14 April 1994; Lamassoure, 1994; *Humanité Dimanche*, 16 July 1995).

17. Delcroix, the Belgian minister, also suggested that if Dutch could not be added to the working languages, then French should be abandoned and English replace it as a *lingua franca* that greater numbers were likely to know. The strength of feeling among the Flemish community was noted:

> Les Flamands qui n'ont pas oublié que leur mouvement nationaliste et d'émancipation est né dans les tranchées de 14–18 où leurs grands-pères mouraient sans comprendre les ordres donnés en français, jubilent en écoutant le langage musclé de leur ministre (*Libération*, 19 November 1993).

18. Arabic, Chinese, English, French, Russian and Spanish. See Chapter 4.

19. Source UN desk officers UN Headquarters New York. They confirmed that although the two 'working' languages for missions were French and English 'official communication was in English most of the time' as were most other interchanges. Examples of French use were available (e.g. among French/Spanish/Arabic speaking forces in the Western Sahara mission) but were much fewer in number.

20. For example, the text of the treaty which established NATO in 1949, North Atlantic Treaty, 1949 Washington DC. Article 14. English quickly established itself *de facto* as the language of command and contact, following French withdrawal from NATO command structures and US domination of the organisation.

21. Text of the report of the Committee of Three on non-military cooperation in NATO, 1956. Paragraph 91. (NATO, 1976).

22. Ärarisch Deutsch.

23. Jules Ferry, *ministre de l'Instruction publique* in France's Third Republic, introduced legislation in 1881/2 to make primary education obligatory and free. In Britain the 1870 Elementary Education Act introduced the idea of compulsory education but left implementation to local decision. Ten years later the Mundella Act made schooling compulsory throughout England and Wales to the age of 10. In Germany the constitution of the Weimar Republic (1919) formalised compulsory school attendance from 6–14, although this had been general practice in most German states for several decades. Denmark had been the first state to make primary education compulsory (1739) but as the whole cost had to be borne by the parishes it was not implemented in all areas (Samuel and Hinton, 1949).

24. Depending on the child's sex.

25. Circular 6 March 1848.

26. For example, Lockroy, in the Chambre des Députés (17 December 1880, J.O., p. 12481), wondered whether priests who had renounced all human attachments, who were outside the great democratic debate, who ultimately were answerable to a foreign power,

sont bien faits pour élever des enfants qui doivent se mêler, le bulletin de vote à la main, au grand mouvement des idées, qui sont faits pour être maris, pour être pères de famille et enfin pour devenir les citoyens d'une grande République (cited in Prost, 1968: 212).

27. Peguy's celebrated description of the _instituteurs_ was 'the black hussars of the Republic'.
28. Renan's speech _Qu'est-ce que'une nation_ made it clear that a nation needed 'la possession en commun d'un riche legs de souvenirs' (Renan, 1882).
29. The temptation for teachers to pass on local interpretations of history instead of the official national tale was lessened by the practice of sending teachers to work outside the district of their birth.
30. The preamble expresses the Member States' desire 'to deepen the solidarity between their peoples while respecting their history, their culture and their traditions'.
31. TEU Article 126: 1.
32. The _Europe in the Schools_ programme, coordinated by the Eurydice Europe Dimension Department.
33. The Community expected this to involve:

    adjusting curricula, focusing courses on themes of European integration, learning at least two foreign languages, twinning arrangements with schools and local authorities from various Member States, cooperation with other schools in Europe on specific projects and experience of life in a multicultural society. (_Education and Training_, 5 June, 1992: 12)

34. For example 12th UK CEE National Conference, 6 November 1990.
35. EDIT (European Dimension in Teaching) First Issue Spring 1991, published under the umbrella of The Central Bureau for Educational Visits and Exchanges.
36. For example in 1989–1990 the Central Bureau sponsored 16 European Awareness Development Projects with LEAs in England and Wales.
37. The Council of Europe also promotes the European dimension in curriculum. The following advice comes from a workshop organised by the Council for Cultural Cooperation of the Council of Europe and the Georg-Eckert Institute for International Textbook Research on History and Social Science Textbooks, which concluded:

    (1) Textbooks should present a proper balance of local, regional, European and world history and geography. Cooperation among the 12 States of the European Community, the 24 Council of Europe countries, the wider Europe presupposes awareness of Europe's cultural heritage and cultural intellectual interpenetration. History should no longer be presented mainly from a national point of view. The greater European context of development has to be brought out.

    (2) Prejudices with regard to other peoples and regions have to be overcome, but good textbooks need not necessarily be free from underlying assumptions (e.g. the assumption that parliamentary democracy is something positive).

    (_Council of Europe Education Newsletter_, 2 and 3, 1990, p. 4)
38. Evidence for this is clearly shown in the changes in the relative weight of sections in catalogues (various 1980s and 1995) from major publishing houses France, Germany, Italy, Netherlands and UK.

39. By the school year 1994–1995 all Belgians, Germans and Dutch learnt a foreign language to 18. All the other Member States had legislated for compulsory foreign language education to the end of compulsory education at 15 or 16 years, Irish to 14. (Eurydice, 1996).

40. Conferences of language specialists in the last three decades have issued recommendations that school children learn at least two European languages besides their own. E.g. Colloque international «Langues et Coopération européenne» 17–20 avril 1979, Palais de l'Europe, Strasbourg; European Language Council Launching Conference 3–5 July 1997, Université de Lille. The reports of multilingual groups using their own languages and relying on passive comprehension are not always documented. It is apparently a not uncommon occurrence in the Romance continuum (Private communication at Istituto de Lingue Straniere, Facoltà di Economia e Commercio).

41. For example, in the early Lingua programmes, UK projects which undertook the teaching of Danish seemed assured of acceptance. A number of local education authorities took advantage of this additional funding and proposed and organised exchanges with Danish schools. Danish classes for participants did not continue past the date of the visit and British pupils reported that they had not been able to use their basic Danish because of the English language skills of the Danes (Private communication from Birmingham ML advisors, 1989).

42. Eurobarometer 44 (fieldwork Oct–Nov 1995) suggests that 49% of all EU citizens have some competence in English. Of these 16% are mother tongue speakers and 33% those who report that they speak English well enough to take part in a conversation. The equivalent scores for French were 16% mother tongue speakers and 15% other EU citizens with competence in French. For German the figures are 34% with 9%. As the foreign language level is self reported the actual competence is unknown and comparisons across countries very difficult and unreliable.

43. It is understandable that language professionals should wish to conserve the diversity of foreign language provision in the curriculum. The European Language Council, bringing together language professionals from the universities and funded in part by the Commission was set up in 1997 with protection of this diversity within higher education as one of its aims. Many in this organisation oppose the domination of English. Nonetheless in its conference debates and working parties English still dominates. A much smaller proportion of the work is carried out in French and German. See also Chapter 10.

44. This reliance is likely to increase with European Monetary Union which reduces the financial independence of Member States. For example, EMU stops governments unilaterally changing interest rates to stimulate or rein in the economy. So if individual economies are in recession, governments are reliant on strategies at EU level and support from other Member States. These funds are under review and set to change slightly from 2000 onwards (EC, 1997a).

45. The Airbus and Ariane projects proved, after teething troubles, to be exceptions and survived.

46. Both British industry and other Member States were angry at this stance. In 1987 Westland Aerospace called on the government to invest £7m in the European Ariane V space project. Without this funding, Westland was to be excluded from

£30m of work, building advanced composite materials for the Ariane V launch vehicle. The British government's investment in the project of £700,000 was insufficient to qualify British industry in the race for contracts (*Sunday Telegraph*, 18 October 1987, p. 4). Britain's hardline attitude to European collaboration meant that it dropped out of major European space programmes. The British government cut their contributions to the European fusion programme (JET) which in the mid 1980s was leading the race to exploit the source of energy that drives the sun. As JET's host, Britain's lack of commitment had far-reaching effects, among which the loss of leading scientists to competing projects was felt to be the most serious (Highfield, 1988).

47. For example, in 1988 the Italian state was forced to cut back the role it played in whole sections of the economy. Researchers looked to Europe to make up the shortfall (Reuters, 30 August 1988). For example, in 1988 the British Government withdrew funding to the Hotol (Horizontal Take-Off and Landing) vehicle project. Kenneth Clark, Trade and Industry Minister, said that it was up to British Aerospace and Rolls-Royce to attempt to obtain backing for the scheme from international bodies such as the 13-nation European Space Agency (*Financial Times*, 26 July 1988, p. 44).

48. For example, H B van Liemt, chairman of DSM, Netherlands, asked for more support on research funding from the EC to allow the chemical industry to compete. Van Liemt argued that the European chemical industry's leading role in innovation can be maintained only if the state – *at whatever level* – continues to invest heavily in research (*Financieele-Dagblad*, 7 June 1988, my emphasis).

49. 1992 figures. Funding has increased since, as the figures for the Framework programmes illustrate.

    | 1984–1987 | 3.7 billion Ecu |
    | 1987–1991 | 5.3 billion Ecu |
    | 1990–1994 | 6.6 billion Ecu |
    | 1995–1998 | 13 billion Ecu (estimate) |

    Source: Statistics in Focus Research and Development, 1997/1

50. In these shared cost actions the EU puts up 50% of funding as does industry.

51. This widepread belief was confirmed by documentary evidence in the information pack distributed during briefing on Fourth and Fifth Frameworks by Commission representatives at Aston University, October 1997.

52. Covering both the European Community and the European Economic Area in some cases.

53. The Synthesis Report for Student Mobility includes Lingua students in this figure.

54. The 1998–1999 figures also include students from 9 applicant states to the EU but do not include Lingua exchanges. In addition there is some imprecision in the figures because statistics are gathered by the different Member States according to slightly different criteria and including slightly different categories of HE institution. However, despite the fact that different sources produce different totals for mobility, all sources show a steady increase (Socrates, 1997).

55. Students also seem to have acquired European frames of reference outside the limits of these schemes and to be fuelling the tendency to mobility in certain

kinds of casual labour, such as hotel and bar staff, construction and farm workers. Although the statistics for casual work are notoriously incomplete and unreliable, it does appear to be the student population which is particularly active in transnational seasonal work (Romero, 1994).

56. NUTS 1 regions.

Chapter 10

Conclusions

From the preceding chapters a number of apparent rules and relationships emerge. Firstly, a community of communication appears to be an element in group formation. Although it is rarely a sufficient reason on its own for a group to coalesce, a common language, or at least a set of allied dialects, seems one of the basic organising principles for the construction of societal groups. In the context of nationalism, a common language may exist prior to nation building. If it does not, efforts are usually made early in the process to encourage the adoption of one common language for the whole nation. While the linguistic cleavages between nations which result from this are conducive to intergroup conflict, the communities of communication which this process creates are the cement of intragroup solidarity. The impossibility of communication with the 'others' and the incomprehension that results can be used to build a discourse which makes them outsiders, strangers and, where necessary, enemies. Of course, we do not have to fight those we do not understand and we do not necessarily live peaceably with those that we do, but the impossibility of communicating can contribute to the polarisation of two groups. The lines between enemies with different languages are clearly drawn on linguistic grounds and language difference reinforces whatever other sources of discord there may be. It reduces contact to the single channel of diplomatic negotiation through interpreters. It limits exchange between the two populations to the formal and the mediated. It allows the distancing and stereotyping which contribute to enmity. The recognition of this is a constant refrain in the writings of the founders of the various branches of the European movement.

On the other hand, a single community of communication helps create solidarity in the group, allowing it to think of itself as an entity. The duties of communal life in the modern state are perhaps easier when performed for those with whom we can communicate. Conscription, citizens' armies, the redistribution of wealth to support health care, pensions and education for all members of a society have been more easily accepted and organised in cohesive societies than in fragmented. People accept the pain of taxation for the needs of a community which they recognise as their own (Compass 9 March 1998). People submit to the priority of the state's needs above the individual's where a strong nationalist ideology has shaped them.[1] People can be brought to accept the need to share in the sacrifices of war, when they feel a part of a whole. All of this is is more easily effected in a single community of communication. A community of communication allows the organisation of the procedures necessary for the public life of a democratic polity. It permits all citizens to participate in the debate which constitutes the political process. It allows the communication circuits of forums and associations. It permits the elaboration of a discourse which makes war necessary, just and heroic. To summarise, in the organisation of the nation state system, language and language difference have played a central role both in defining the nation and in drawing the lines between nations.

However, the world of sovereign nation states is evolving. Power is clearly leaking away from the nation state. The influences of globalisation and Europeanisation have transferred some authority, duties and rights from the national level to supranational, transnational and international organisations. A number of commentators (e.g Bull, 1977; Held, 1991; Jessop, 1994) predict that this leakage of power away from the nation state will continue. Globalisation in the economic, political, legal, cultural and technological spheres makes it virtually impossible for the nation state to remain isolated. Those states which have conducted policies of economic isolationism have not prospered. The absolute sovereignty of the state is no longer respected. Groups which have tried to protect themselves from cultural intrusion have often found that their own young have played the role of Trojan horse, adopting and promoting aspects of so-called global culture. Technology makes economic and cultural isolation increasingly difficult to maintain as both people and ideas circulate more easily than in the past. The monolingual communities of communication and the fragile homogeneity achieved by the European nation states continue to exist but they are under constant threat of change: citizens have increasing need for transnational contact and thus must cross linguistic boundaries; even citizens who do not travel are subject to the influence of other languages with the end of state monopolies in broadcasting, the growth of cable and satellite TV and the mushrooming of global information networks and, most importantly, massive post-war migration brought people from former colonies and from the developing world to work in the European labour market and to influence communities of communication.[2] The linguistic effect of the early stages of globalisation has been a monumental increase in the use of English, both as the vector which has transmitted the political, economic and cultural philosophies of globalisation from the largely English-speaking free market economies to the rest of the world, and as a *lingua franca* permitting the day to day realisation of globalisation.

The European Union is in a singular and paradoxical position. It both contributes to and provides a brake on globalisation. The regional grouping that it has achieved is part of globalisation, part of the ever-increasing tendency for economic, political, legal and technological issues to be dealt with transnationally. However, at the same time, the Union is also a conscious attempt to provide an economic competitor for the Pacific Rim and the Americas, and halt globalisation in terms of US hegemony. Secondly, the European Union both contributes to greater world security and poses a potential threat to it. The EU had its genesis in the need to overcome dangerous nationalisms and to safeguard peace among European nation states with a history of conflict. However, as a powerful economic entity which closes its borders to immigration and protects its markets from outside competition, it provokes fear in those outside the grouping that it may become 'Fortress Europe', concerned to maintain its own prosperity at the cost of poorer regions. Certainly, some analysts perceive the new fault lines in terms of religious-cultural cleavages and there are signs that Christian Europe and the Muslim world sometimes perceive each other in terms of 'enemy' (Huntington, 1996). Thirdly, the European Union is concerned to safeguard linguistic and cultural diversity and fight the market forces which have brought about creeping anglicisation and americanisation. In many ways, it is well placed to fight this cause. Europe's languages are standardised, Europeans are literate in their national languages and there is a long tradition of their use in national political and cultural life. At the same time, however, the EU brings together numerous groups for transnational, inter-cultural cooperation in increasing political integration, in the single market, in the technological transfers, in the defence structures and in the educational exchanges it has fostered and organised. In much of this contact, there has been little thought given to safeguarding the linguistic diversity which is its official policy, and English is frequently used as the *lingua franca* which permits contact. Only a limited number of other national languages also play a *lingua franca* role, principally French and German.

This conflict between the twin ideals of achieving lasting European unity and peace while safeguarding national diversity is nowhere more apparent than in this last paradox, the question of how Europeans communicate with each other. How could it be possible to safeguard linguistic and cultural differences while promoting solidarity? There are few models for this. In the cause of cohesion, nationalists chose to eradicate difference, suppress local autochthonous languages and promote national language and culture. This process still continues. In the era of the mass migrations of the twentieth century, European host societies which are inclusive have usually demanded cultural and linguistic assimilation as the price immigrants must pay for their inclusion. Where there has been recognition of incomers' cultural difference, this has been either tokenism or an expression of the host community's desire that the immigrant group maintain its language and culture in order to be able to return to the country of origin once the economic reasons for its presence no longer exist.

In the minority of cases where the state has respected the cultural and linguistic difference of autochthonous groups, the nation has not been so cohesive and political structures have tended to loose federalism. Multilingual Switzerland is, as I argued above, only an exception to a certain extent. Other bilingual states, such as Belgium, have exhibited marked centrifugal tendencies. In the former empires of Europe, rulers accepted group difference, and cultural and linguistic particularity in those groups not close to the ruling centre could be tolerated as long as they remained loyal. But the empires were feudal, and democratic participation in the life of the state was not required. As models they have little to say to us today. If European unification is to be plurilingual, multicultural and democratic, there is very little at all in European history on which to build; neither the old empires, nor the tradition of *Gastarbeiter* nor the existing bilingual states provide convincing blueprints for reconciling respect for difference and promotion of cohesion in the process of European integration.

This résumé of the main arguments of the book returns us to the central dilemma. It is clear that there is a pressing need to find a way for all Europeans to associate if the European Union is ever to become more than a trading association run in an autocratic way by plurilingual patrician technocrats, if it is to develop the democratic structures which would give it political legitimacy and if it is to give meaning to its policies of free movement. The difficulty is how to do this. There are two intractable problems. Firstly, which languages to promote to ensure such association and, secondly, how to persuade Europeans to acquire them.

Motivations for Language Learning

Let us deal with the second point first. Here we need to take into account the work done on motivation in language learning, since the situation of the European Union differs from that of the nation state in the nineteenth century and no language can be imposed. Europeans have to be persuaded of the need to acquire another language. The accepted orthodoxy in Second Language Acquisition is that there are two main kinds of motivation: instrumental and integrative and that most successful language learning occurs where both types are in play.

It is not difficult to mobilise arguments to show the instrumental advantage of learning languages for both individual and societal benefit. The circulation of information and ideas within the Union depends on individuals learning the languages that ensure exchanges, flows and pooling of ideas in technological, scientific and political domains. In the economic domain Europe provides companies with an enormous single market, only limited by the ability of company employees to communicate with collaborators and consumers across linguistic borders to market their products. Member States and companies need individuals to build the bridges; individuals will usually benefit professionally from playing this role. The motivation to undertake language learning for these reasons is evident.

Instrumental motivation may be very strong, fuelled as it is by the need to acquire information or sell goods or to gain the jobs which carry out these functions. The process is principally bottom up as parents demand that their children learn the language(s) they perceive as most likely to lead to employment or as those in employment work on acquiring the language(s) they need.

However, the most efficient solution of these evident communication needs is not the teaching and learning of all eleven state languages in the education systems of the EU, which remains the official Commission policy, given form by the Lingua programme. And all the available evidence suggests that instrumental motivation works to promote English as the main foreign language learnt in Europe. The position of English is continually strengthened as individuals make a rational choice to learn English because comparatively it gives them the best return in the number of interlocutors they can contact and in the number of domains they can access.

However, when we turn from instrumental to integrative motivation, the issue becomes more confused. A number of groups within Europe are promoting the learning of the other languages of the member states as a way of furthering the integration process and breaking down barriers and building bridges (cf. Vlaeminck, 1997). They differ from those motivated purely by instrumental concerns in that there are more complex and covert forces at play.

The first group are the idealists who see the time and effort given to acquiring the language of the other as the clearest indication of good will:

> une signe de politesse pour attester à une autre communauté linguistique le profond intérêt que l'on ressent pour elle. Aucun autre geste n'en rendrait un temoignage plus généreux et plus digne de foi. (Weinreich, 1993)

Idealists hope that the Europeans will benefit from the solidarity between national groups that may accompany interest and understanding, and that the shared identity that results from contact and friendship will ensure peaceful coexistence. The individual European is expected to benefit from access to the language borne culture of the other and can expect intellectual pleasure, enjoyment and enrichment. Such motivation is usually 'sold' top down through the education system as part of a package to promote the European ideal, responsible citizenship and peace on the continent. In this interpretation no language is preferred and all are promoted.

The problem with the commitment to full plurilingualism is that the sheer number of languages within the present EU and the even greater number that enlargement will introduce into the system (even if one limits consideration to the official languages of Member States) mean that such a policy would lead to individual enrichment through bilateral contact but would not contribute to building a community of communication. The argument that plurilingualism can deliver European communication was true only for the Community of Six when there were just four official languages, and then only within limits. Zapp (1979) suggested that if each language group split its school children into three sub-sets and had each learn one of the other three languages in school, the four language groups could communicate in the following way:

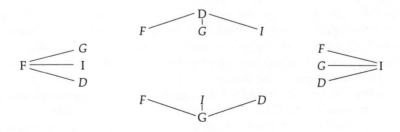

Key overleaf

In this model, the mother tongue speakers of any one group can communicate with a third of the rest who learn that language as a foreign language in school. When these same individuals use the foreign language they have learned, they can converse with its mother tongue speakers and those for whom the language is also a learnt foreign language. Thus any individual can communicate with a very large proportion of the others, either using one of the interlocutor's mother tongues or a third language as *lingua franca*.

If Member States were to have school children learn two of the three other languages, the communities of communication would mean very few pairs of citizens would be unable to communicate.

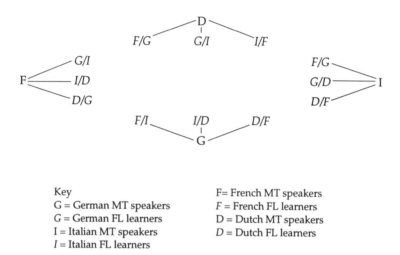

Key
G = German MT speakers
G = German FL learners
I = Italian MT speakers
I = Italian FL learners

F= French MT speakers
F = French FL learners
D = Dutch MT speakers
D = Dutch FL learners

However, with accessions of new states, the addition of each extra language makes the model less workable. What works in a theoretical way when the number of languages involved is small, could not work with a larger number of languages in the model. In the present situation of eleven official languages, a similar policy would fragment rather than unite the EU and would fail to provide the community of communication which would support a democratic forum.

Finally, such a policy would not work in reality because, although many would recognise plurilingualism as an honourable, egalitarian and fraternal idea, it neglects the basic rule of language planning in that it takes no account of individual wishes. It relies on directing parts of the population to learn certain languages regardless of the integrative or instrumental motivation they might or might not feel. It would require massive social pressure, even coercion, to ensure the working of such a system, and that cannot be an option. Khubchandani, analysing the Indian situation, makes a crucial point about language planning in democracies:

> Language planners have to remember certain basic tenets for introducing changes in language behaviour, such as 'changes envisaged have to be in tune with wider social trends' . . . and 'there has to be a functional justification for learning a skill'. (Khubchandani, 1983: 107)

Even some of the supporters of plurilingualism recognise this and the utopian nature of such a strategy:

> Il faut se montrer très réaliste. En effet, toute tentative visant à imposer par la force l'apprentissage de certaines langues plutôt que d'autres, ou toute tentative reposant sur l'idée que l'augmentation du nombre d'étudiants «de langues moins enseignées» peut se faire grâce à la réduction du nombre des étudiants «des langues les plus enseignées» est vouée à l'échec. (Siguan, 1996: 186)

The fault with the plurilingual policy initiatives is that they only address integrative motivation. Respect for all the languages of Europe and the inclusion of all of them in the school curriculum is in the mainstream of the language and peace tradition, our need to know and understand our neighbours, to learn and respect their culture and traditions for peaceful coexistence. Such policies disregard instrumental motivation which is more closely linked to personal advancement? Where they direct young Europeans to learn languages of the smaller language communities, they are doubly at odds with it.

The idealists who support European plurilingualism, have often used their own experience to develop policy; members of a cosmopolitan, European intelligentsia, their education proves that it is possible to be polyglot. We should beware, however, of extrapolating from their linguistic achievements and imagining that they can be made general. The intellectual European polyglot has put much time and effort into the acquisition of language; for this to be commonplace all Europeans would need to give the same time and effort and have the same interest and intellectual capacity. This is idealism; we are not all fascinated by language; we do not all have the same intellectual abilities. In addition there is a class factor. European polyglots tend to come from a cosmopolitan background which fosters language learning. The biographies of famous multilinguals, such as George Steiner, Isaiah Berlin, Otto von Habsburg, etc. reveal how much contact they had as children with linguistic groups outside their own. This takes language learning from the classroom and puts it into the real world. For the majority, the education system tries to replicate this contact in the form of school trips and exchanges. The influence of the two experiences is not really comparable. Drawing a parallel with the Indian experience[3] again, we might note what Khubchandani says:

> Skilful mastery over several sharply insulated standard languages is a remarkable feat which only a few motivated professionals can be expected to achieve. To expect it of every individual appears to be an expensive and futile exercise. (Khubchandani, 1983: 107)

It seems that plurilingualism presents difficulties whether it means that individual Europeans will learn different foreign languages chosen from among a wide variety or that a single individual will learn a minimum of two foreign languages. The first alternative fails to recognise the lack of motivation which would accompany any language learning that did not clearly meet the communication needs of individuals as they themselves perceive them. The second ignores too many realities, most importantly, the improbability of both individual and education system according the time, effort and money needed to acquire competence in more languages than they believe necessary. The aim that we are all going to learn a number of languages will remain the hope of a small number of idealists, but is ultimately unattainable.

The second category of support for plurilingualism comes, perhaps not surprisingly, from the language professionals. Language teachers are one of the few groups who have openly debated the question of communication and Europeanisation and who have issued unequivocal statements that learning the language of the other Member States in the EU is a cornerstone of European integration.[4] In pursuit of this aim, they call, predictably, for more language teaching in the curriculum, for an earlier start to language learning, for more contact between language groups whether virtual or real, for the development of new and better pedagogical methods and for the best exploitation of all the new technologies. On the more difficult subject of which languages to teach in order to achieve better communication among Europeans, the teaching profession is close to the position of the idealists, calling for more diversity in the range of languages offered and for two foreign languages as the norm for all secondary school children. A German educationalist maintains that:

A European incapable of speaking at least two foreign languages remains a foreigner even within their (sic) own continent, and a teacher who does not master at least three, even if his subject is biology, may still be able to teach well in German but he will not be a good European teacher. (Lenzen, 1996: 25)

A Catalan advises that:

Le premier principe est de veiller au maintien de la variété tout en élargissant au maximum la capacité de communiquer des Européens . . . Il n'y a rien de bien nouveau dans tout cela, et l'Union européenne elle-même a souvent exprimé le désir de voir dans un futur assez proche, tous les citoyens d'Europe en mesure d'utiliser plusieurs langues outre leur langue propre ou principale. (Siguan, 1996: 186)

The academic desire for diversification in the foreign languages offered within the curriculum and for the study of two foreign languages to be the norm, is echoed by the education policy makers in the Commission. Since the 1980s this has been the Commission position, expressed clearly in a White Paper (European Commission, 1996c). Commentators note:

La Commission européenne envisage la promotion du plurilinguisme. (Muylle, 1997: 30)

La Commission européenne propose au nom de l'Union européenne que chaque citoyen devrait en plus de sa langue maternelle connaître deux autres langues. (Lenarduzzi, 1997: 38)

This policy that all Europeans should acquire two languages during their education is unlikely to be adopted throughout the EU. In some Member States there would be resistance to the reorganisation of the curriculum if the number of foreign language classes increased.[5] When the policy of two foreign languages was first discussed at Commission and Council level, the UK under the Thatcher government refused to agree, seeing the policy as contrary to national interest. The Irish have not been so overtly antagonistic but the low levels of language learning noted above indicate they would be unlikely to wish to undertake more. Those opposed to the two foreign language policy argue that language learning demands much classroom time. More time devoted to language acquisition would reduce the time available for other subjects. The need to prepare young people for an increasingly complex technological world sits uneasily with according greater time to language learning. To use the Indian parallel again, the Delhi government has expressed a view that too much time and too many resources were being spent on acquiring the second and third language in school and that much of this was wasted because of the limited success of the programmes (Kubchandani, 1983).

One strategy for solving the time problem is to use the foreign language as the medium for teaching other subjects, rather than as a subject itself. This goes some way to solving the lack of space in the school day, although evidence from other societies which have longer experience in doing this shows that success is not assured. For example, the Hong Kong education system has been struggling to maintain the trio Cantonese/English/ Mandarin and has found that, political pressures and considerations apart, the simple pedagogical difficulties of achieving this are immense (Wright, 1997b). There are still time demands on the curriculum as pupils acquire basic knowledge of the foreign language, and for those who have difficulties with it, lack of fluency has implications for successful learning of other subjects.[6]

Moreover, where the difficulty of the undertaking is allied to a lack of motivation on the part of the learner the project is doomed to failure.

The third category promoting plurilingualism includes the groups who do not wish to see their own languages disappear as international media. Were one language to dominate, these groups are very aware of the material advantages such a position would confer on the speakers of that language. The advantages are financial (societies which already use the *lingua franca* are spared the costs of acquisition, translating, dubbing and interpreting), political (those who have this language as mother tongue are advantaged when presenting, defending or countering policy[7]) and educational (fewer resources, less time need be spent on foreign language acquisition in the curriculum). Other advantages are less clear cut and are linked to prestige. Traditionally it has always been the language of a dominant power group which has been adopted in plurilingual situations. Much intangible but very real benefit may accrue from this association. In addition, for those languages which find themselves excluded from the international sphere, there may be negative effects at the level of the very structure of the language. For example, if certain domains are treated exclusively in the *lingua franca*, the other languages cease developing the vocabulary and syntax to deal with these subjects. This is apparently already happening in branches of science because of the dominance of English (Zapp, 1979; Denison, 1981; ELC, 1997).

The plurilingualists never envisaged true plurilingualism. Depending on how a language is defined, it is possible to list as many as 120 languages spoken in Europe as a whole, 40+ in the present European Union,[8] without taking into account the languages of the linguistic minorities constituted by recent immigration. The plurilingual camp is not suggesting that

Europeans should learn all the languages of their continent. The languages envisaged for a role in European polyglottism are only the official languages of the Member States. Then as we examine the rhetoric, it becomes clear that EU plurilingualism only really means French and German in addition to English, with Italian and Spanish in some cases. The other national languages are much less likely to be taught as foreign languages in the education systems of the Member States. The regional languages are never considered in this context. Of course, the five dominant languages have distinct advantages over the others. They are standardised and have the dictionaries and grammars which make it possible to acquire them in the classroom, which is not always the case with regional languages. They each have established literary traditions and give access to a cultural heritage, which already has international recognition. They are the languages of large numbers of citizens and give access to important communities of communication, with all the implications this has for motivation linked to economic advantage. They are the languages of the largest Member States within the European Union and as such have the most influence in political terms. They are thus the languages of the dominant linguistic groups at the level of their own nation states and at the level of the supra-state.

It seems then that the policy of unity and diversity intends only limited diversity. It is evident that the prime motivation for many in the French speaking world is the defence of French through this strategy. When *Le Monde* publishes a debate on the matter, the idealist plurilingual stance, e.g Weinreich's argument that

> la maîtrise de trois langues, à savoir la langue d'origine et de deux langues étrangères en plus doit être reconnue comme minimum d'une «europhonie» sans laquelle cette fameuse maison communautaire serait construite sur un terrain de sable. (Weinreich, 1993: 21)

finds itself alongside more overt expressions of support for French.

In the pluralist camp, the position of French is to be defended and educational choice extended perhaps to Italian, German and Spanish. Very few are proposing the inclusion of Catalan, Greek, Portuguese, Finnish etc. or the policy of learning the *langues de proximité*. In much of the writing on this subject, the hegemony of English is excoriated and constitutes the prime reason for battling for plurilingualism in the foreign language curriculum, the media and transnational contacts (Huyghe, 1993; Cercle, nd; ELC, 1997; etc.). However, this camp fails to recognise that the hegemony of the big five might be just as unacceptable to speakers whose mother tongues still remain excluded.

These reasons may explain why there has been little success so far in promoting plurilingualism. The literature is either explicit on this (Olbert, 1979) or the problem is implicit in that there are continual calls for the introduction of the two foreign languages model rather than reports of success in doing so (Vlaeminck, 1997; Zwarts, 1997). However, although the plurilingualists may not have been able to persuade the education ministers of the Member States to introduce diversity into the language curriculum, the time allotted to foreign languages within the various education systems has been increased and all school children now learn one of the languages of another Member State in the course of secondary education,[9] even if this is, increasingly, English.

In summary then, the campaign to improve language learning has been partially successful, more learn languages and for longer, but to a very large extent the choice of languages tends to be very restricted. This should not surprise us. After all, within the Community institutions themselves, a forum where the EU can control and influence language policy and practice (far more so than in the education systems of the Member States where the European Union has no jurisdiction), plurilingualism is not working and French and English dominate. It seems that everywhere market forces are at work and thus sowing the seeds for an unplanned European *lingua franca*.

Lingua Francas

A planned *lingua franca* is theoretically a possible solution to the communication problems of Europe. Objectively and logically, one single language agreed to by all Member States and learned *in addition* to the mother tongue would construct the community of communication which the European integrationists need to advance their project. Realistically, bringing all parties to agree to adopt any of the national languages of a Member State as a *lingua franca* would be impossible. For all the major contenders to be the sole working language of Europe there are strong grounds why they would not be adopted unanimously in a formal policy.

The main contender for the role of European *lingua franca* is English, since it appears to be imposing itself without any formal institutional support. However, it is highly unlikely that there would be acceptance of English in all parts of the EU. There is and will continue to be ferocious opposition to English domination for a number of very deeply felt reasons. Firstly, English links the EU to the US, and for many, the French in particular, one of the basic reasons for the EU was to provide an alternative to American hegemony. English is perceived as the language of capitalism in general and of free market, Reagan/Thatcherite theories in particular, which reduces its appeal to 'socialist Europe'.[10] English serves as a vector for American culture, rejected by parts of Europe as unwelcome Coca-Cola cultural imperialism.[11] Secondly, English is the national language of the Member State least committed to integration, of the most reluctant and least enthusiastic Europeans, which makes it difficult for those committed to Europe to accept English as a *lingua franca*. Lastly, there is already resentment of the Anglophones for the reasons of material advantage that already accrue to the group possessing the unofficial *lingua franca*. In addition, they do not play fair: they allocate fewer resources to foreign language acquisition, large numbers remain monolingual, expecting others to accommodate to them and at the same time they profit from the English language industry as English speaking teachers selling their skill in their mother tongue to those driven by market forces to acquire it. For all these reasons English will be rejected by some parts of the European Union. This is already clear from the plurilingualists' arguments. Plurilingualism is not just promotion of diversity, it is also a reaction against creeping anglicisation.

However, the advantages that English confers will probably overcome the lobby against it, as new generations come to make decisions on what to learn. English has the advantage that it is not only developing as a *de facto lingua franca* for Europe, it plays this role throughout the world and so gives the individual who learns it a tool for international communication. It has become a *lingua franca* for the domains of science and technology, of international police-keeping, of international commerce, of transnational corporations. In terms of utility, it repays the immense personal effort needed to master a foreign language. Its success feeds its success because as more people learn English it becomes ever more useful in its role as *lingua franca*. And because it has assumed a role in globalisation and is the official language in many states, there are some who argue that English is losing its narrow identification with a single culture and nation and has a neutrality conferred by the fact that there are more speakers of English as a second language than there are mother tongue speakers of English.[12]

The aggregated influence of those who have chosen English as a language of contact to further their personal projects weighs heavily against those who are trying to preserve the linguistic eco-diversity of Europe. It is proving difficult to persuade people to follow the ideal of plurilingualism rather than pursue what they perceive as the personal advantage of learning English.[13] It is revealing that the support for English as a *lingua franca* does not come exclusively from its own mother tongue speakers.[14] In the Member States where there are already high levels of English language competence,[15] the personal investment that individuals have made in acquiring English predisposes them to accepting its role as a European *lingua franca* and they see no need for any other.[16] They do not want to lose the advantage that they have acquired through effort.[17] Even in France, where the opposition to 'le tout-anglais' has traditionally been strongest, one can find an acceptance of this position. Claude Allègre, the French minister of education in 1997, said that the battle against English had been lost and called on the French to 'cesser de considérer l'anglais comme une langue étrangère'.[18] This caused a storm of protest in sections of the francophone world which are fighting English hegemony.[19]

French is the only other serious contender for the role of *lingua franca*, although this appeared more possible in the past than now. If, in the early days, the Community had ever decided to adopt a *lingua franca* , it would have been French. Luns, the Dutch signatory to the Treaty of Rome, suggested French as the sole working language of the institutions just before the first enlargement (Lavenir, 1994). Otto von Habsburg called for French to be adopted in his book *Bientôt l'an 2000;* the *Comités pour le français* which exist in many European countries show there would have been widespread support. Within France, the *Comité pour la langue de l'Europe*[20] promoted French in this role:

> Le choix d'une langue officielle de l'Europe, destinée à marquer son indépendance et son unité; cette langue ne pouvant être que la langue française, que son passé, sa place dans le monde et sa position intermédiaire entre langues romanes et germaniques, désignent naturellement pour jouer ce rôle. (Camus & Ficquelemont, 1979)

If French has lost out to English in this contest,[21] the reasons are mainly the reasons for English dominance already cited. However, there is also the point that French has a tradition of purism and hyper-correction which tends to make second language speakers of French insecure[22]; they feel under great pressure to use the language 'correctly'; there are no equivalents to the simplified forms of international English. As Posner says:

> (French) has the great advantage of having established itself as the language of all Frenchmen, and of some others, and of being eminently teachable, because strictly codified. The corollary of this is, however, that its purist intolerant stance has resulted in many speakers of French,

both as a mother tongue and as a second language, suffering from severe linguistic insecurity. (Posner, 1994: 27)

In the search for a means to allow Europeans to communicate, would two *lingua franca*s prove a solution? What if French were to be used alongside English? This would be a compromise between unworkable plurilingualism and monolithic English. It would defuse francophone opposition. On the other hand, it encourages the undesirable north–south split already noted among MEPs in the European parliament and advantages two of the traditionally dominant groups of Europe.

German too has to be considered as a contender for the role of *lingua franca*. Up until the present time there has been no question that German could or should have this function. Reticence on linguistic matters is in keeping with Germany's general approach of remaining low profile in certain political domains, which is a legacy of the Second World War. The political class is of course correct. German would not be tolerated as a *lingua franca* while the generation which remembers the Second World War and the supremacy of German in conquered territories is still alive. If it is true that a *lingua franca* cannot be imposed in the European situation, this is doubly true for German at the present time. However, the number of those who experienced the War is dwindling and future economic and demographic realities may radically alter the linguistic landscape of Europe, allowing German to develop a dominant role in an incremental, unplanned way. Already German is the language group with the largest number of mother tongue speakers in the present EU. Enlargement will bring states in the Union which have pockets of mother tongue German speakers (e.g. Poland, Hungary). German investment in these economies has been significant and will have all the linguistic effects one can expect where a strong economy invests in weaker neighbours. The opening of borders after the fall of communism has already encouraged a bilingualism of proximity through small scale trade and easier contact between the German-speaking countries and Poland, the Czech Republic, Slovakia, Hungary and Slovenia. In each of the states of Mitteleuropa the tradition of learning and using German, which was eclipsed by the political events of the twentieth century, could be revived. The financial weight of Germany within the EU must have an effect on its influence in the long term. As the integration of the British and German stock markets, which began in mid-1998, progresses, it will be interesting to see which language is used for contact between the two. Linguistic practice will reflect, as it usually does, economic and political dominance. In the short term English is likely to dominate because of its global utility. However, if in the long term

Germany comes to be the senior partner, this would be a further reason why German might come to play a greater role in European transnational contact.

Other, and Less Likely, Solutions

Solutions to European communication problems are linked to geopolitical visions (Treanor, 1997). Nationalists defend the right of their national language to be the *lingua franca*; the Community and the linguists support an idealistic plurilingualism; optimists hope for a universal language.

The solution of reviving an ancient language on the model of Hebrew was considered briefly. Patija and Van der Hek, proposed the adoption of Latin to the EC Parliament in 1974 but the idea was rejected. No matter what other advantages and disadvantages Latin might present, it would not find supporters in Protestant and secular Europe. Its long association with the Catholic church would prevent its universal acceptance.

There are also the artificial languages, Volapük, Esperanto, Interlingua and Interglossa etc., which could be adopted as a *lingua franca*. In one way they are ideally suited to the role since they are not the languages of European nations or states. However, this is not to say that they are culturally or linguistically unaligned; they have each been used to carry the message of various political and religious movements, in particular an idealistic internationalism or utopian socialism. Because of this the planned languages currently have a poor image. At best they are associated with unfashionable idealism and unrealistic optimism. At worst their supporters are stereotyped as faintly ridiculous eccentrics. They are popularly dismissed along with naturists, vegans, pacifists as well meaning but not to be taken seriously.

Nonetheless, in September 1993 representatives of the European parliament heard evidence from experts in the area of planned languages on the feasibility of introducing a 'neutral inter-ethnic' language as a step towards a Citizens' Europe (Erasmus, 1994). The idea has not received serious consideration from the decision-makers. On a superficial level the political classes join the rest of the population in rejecting the constructed languages as products of naive internationalism. At a deeper level there is perhaps a very real fear that a non-national language adopted as a *lingua franca* for the European Union might unleash a number of effects unacceptable at the level of the nation states. In an ideal world some wholly idealistic solution like Esperanto would solve most of the linguistic problems of the European Union and not only in its institutions. From its adoption onwards, young citizens in the various education systems would be socialised to accept a diglossic situation. In adulthood they would use their mother tongue for their linguistic needs in their immediate environment and for local democracy, and the planned language for access to the wider society outside their linguistic frontiers and to participate in the community of communication of a European-wide democracy.[23] No section of the EU would reject Esperanto in the way that it would reject English. None of the objections would apply. This scenario is, of course, most unlikely to happen. The majority of the citizens of Europe are unlikely to invest time and effort into learning a language which has as yet few speakers. Without massive institutional support and a campaign to win hearts and minds, Esperanto is unlikely to spread. It does not have the base from which to grow in an organic way, gathering momentum. This is a circle which it is difficult to break. The Esperantists' strategy to overcome this argument has been to promote Esperanto as an introduction to foreign language acquisition in primary schools,[24] arguing that a language which is wholly regular gives students language awareness and facilitates the learning of other languages (Wentzlaff-Eggebert, 1997). If this argument were to be widely accepted, the position of Esperanto could change radically.

Communities of Communication

The successful realisation of European integration presupposes profound but not inconceivable societal change, not least in the composition of communities of communication. For most Europeans there would be two: the supranational community of communication, however this was realised, and the national. For the large minority that is already bilingual there would be three: the supranational community of communication, the national and the local. This would present a greater change for those in the previously monolingual first group than those previously bilingual. These latter already understand diglossic situations. Not that this new situation would be traditionally diglossic with a prestige language fulfilling all official functions and a non-prestige language or dialect used for all private functions. If a *lingua franca* developed or could be agreed upon, this would be, theoretically, simply an *auxiliary* language replacing the national language only at the supranational level. The auxiliary language would allow the democratic debate necessary for the functioning of the European Parliament, the exchanges necessary for transnational cooperation, and the free movement of labour throughout the Union. If in certain circumstances it shared the economic (e.g. international commerce) and educational (e.g.

transfer of science and technology) function with the national level, it would not dethrone the national language completely. The national community of communication would continue as before, even if slightly diluted because political power would no longer be concentrated solely at that level. The national language would retain its democratic function. It would be the language of much education, and the language of social intercourse and civil society. It would be the language that maintained a link with national heritage and traditions.

However, as all opponents of a single *lingua franca* have foreseen, language is not just a passive reflector of power relationships but an active agent. Were any national language to become the language of Europe *de facto* or *de jure*, there would be several effects that many would find undesirable. Firstly, as discussed above, such a position would confer immense material advantage on mother tongue speakers and the resulting hierarchy would cause justifiable resentment in a polity where groups have come together freely for mutual benefit.

Secondly, a *lingua franca* might allow one world view to dominate. Those who fear this, argue that we are socialised into society through learning and sharing concepts elaborated by group members in the group language. If we were to be socialised into European society through the medium of one language rather than plurilingually, the view of one community might dominate. Zapp suggests that this is already the case where English dominates:

> L'anglais est le moyen d'expression d'une communauté concrète; le signifié de la langue étrangère enseignée est en grande partie repris tel qu'il existe dans les sociétés de langue anglaise. Ceci a pour conséquence une orientation dirigée uniquement vers les pays anglo-phones sans que les autres pays puissent apporter leur contribution. (Zapp, 1979: 91)

Thirdly, the languages themselves would not be unaffected by the new linguistic realities. They would be permeable to new terms and structures used in the *lingua franca* and, as Denison has shown in his study of German-English contact, it is likely that there would be convergence. This would be experienced with great pain in those linguistic communities which have purist tendencies; it would obstruct the comprehension of pre-twenty-first century texts, if languages changed significantly. It would represent a rupture with traditional culture for the linguistic communities wherever it happened.

Fourthly the vigour of national language might weaken in areas where local/sub-national languages are strong and provide the medium for public life. It could be envisaged that a national language could be relegated to a minor role and squeezed out of many functions where the supra-national *lingua franca* and the local language together fulfilled all the requirements of public and private life in the community. Such development could be conceivable in the case of Catalan, for example. Catalan has a democratic function at the local level, is the carrier of Catalan culture, permits social intercourse and builds civil society. At present it shares a political, economic and educational function with the national language. But if Catalans were ever to exchange their secondary identity, becoming Catalan-Europeans rather than Catalan-Spaniards, then the position of Spanish would inevitably weaken.

Finally, the more successful the *lingua franca* the greater the dangers of creating the monolith which the plurilingual camp has traditionally feared (Trim, 1979). On the one hand, it would be difficult to undermine the national languages of Europe. They have deep roots in public life. Their prestige comes from association with national histories. They are codified, have grammars and dictionaries. Their speakers have acquired literacy in them. With such strengths it is most unlikely that a *lingua franca* could replace them. In theory a *lingua franca* would only have limited functions that would not affect the national languages. On the other, as Siguan (1996) argues, this state of affairs only holds true when speakers do not master the auxiliary language as well as they master their mother tongue and where the politico-economic situation does not evolve.[25] Using English as an example, he envisages a situation where the pressure on the individual to maintain a competitive edge demands ever greater mastery of English for all those ambitious for any kind of prestigious work. It is possible that the time and attention given to acquiring competence in English may eclipse the efforts made to achieve high levels of literacy in the mother tongue. With a population competent in two languages, domains of use become fluid. Sociolinguistics teaches us that where there are two or more languages for any function, all but one usually disappear in that function (Romaine, 1989). A classic diglossic situation then arises with the mother tongue increasingly relegated to the private and local domain. There are inevitable semantic and structural consequences for a language if it is never employed to express complex political, scientific or technical ideas. Its speakers feel less and less secure when they use it in such domains.

So, my conclusions seem to be the following. History teaches us that where a community of communication is necessary for economic and political purposes it evolves. This would suggest that, if European integration progresses, a community of communication will develop along with it. European integration has usually happened in a 'top down' way and if this is also the case in the linguistic domain, this community will be established by educating the next generation to be personally trilingual, in a variety of national languages. However, this does not seem to be happening and citizens are resisting the solution proposed by the Commission and language professionals. Ignoring the policy of 'unity in diversity', increasing numbers of Europeans are choosing to acquire English as their first foreign language. The pressure is incremental and as each individual European decides to learn English the reasons to do so grow stronger for the others, as the English speaking community grows. This is an organic societal movement which has evolved 'bottom up' because individuals have decided it is in their interest to learn the language. However, a vigorous rearguard action is being fought against this tendency and respected authorities state unequivocally:

> Cette proposition (l'anglais comme langue auxiliaire de communication hors des frontières de chaque état) a bien peu de chances d'être acceptée, que ce soit en tant que décision formelle de la Communauté, ou en tant qu'attitude collective adoptée par les Européens eux-mêmes. (Siguan, 1996: 184)

There is little general discussion about these issues. There is minimal interest. The French press gives space to a discussion of creeping anglicisation but the terms of reference are national prestige and identity not Europeanisation. In the north of the continent it becomes progressively easier to use English in all kinds of situations and there seems to be societal acceptance of this with minimum discussion. In the English speaking west there is little awareness of or interest in the issue at all. This is an omission that deserves to be studied. Language would appear to be a key element in the construction of any Union which progresses beyond a free market. Difficulties in communication will restrict integration; ease of communication speeds the process. The societal effects that accompany the adoption of English as a *lingua franca* need to be discussed, and by everyone.[26] Our difficulty is, of course, that we do not have a Europe-wide community of communication where this can take place.

Notes

1. Clausewitz recognised the force of nationalism. In his estimation this ideology returned warfare to the 'absolute' war carried out by barbarian hordes who fought as a whole people to gain territory and living space and who were, because of the total commitment of their effort, difficult to contain or defeat.

   The danger to the adversary had risen to the extreme . . . War, freed from all conventional restrictions, broke loose, with all its natural force. The cause was the participation of the people in this great affair of state. (Clausewitz, 1997: 34)

2. Post-war migration has meant that few urban areas and no capital cities have remained monolingual in the state language. Every European city has a proportion of its population constituted by recent immigration. These peoples' resistance to linguistic and cultural assimilation may well be seen to be as important a factor in the crumbling of 'one state, one language, one people' nationalism as Europeanisation. It is an immense subject, a parallel story to the one I have told and deserves a book of its own to do justice to its complexities.

3. Khubchandani makes the telling point that it is dangerous to extrapolate from the success of the 'easy-going grass-roots multilingualism of illiterate societies', where personal multilingualism fulfils everyday communication needs, to suggest that all students of publicly monolingual societies will acquire oral fluency and literacy in prestige languages for with which they see no pressing personal need.

4. For example in a number of conferences which have brought together language teachers and policymakers to underscore this relationship: Langues et construction européenne, Paris, 6–8 December 1974; Langues et coopération européenne, Strasbourg, 17–20 April 1979; Eurosla, University of Essex, 24–26 November 1989; European Language Council Launching conference, Lille, 3–5 July 1997 are notable examples. There have been many others; the European Commission, the Council of Europe, UNESCO and organisations such as Cercles have played a role in promoting and organising these gatherings.

5. De Broglie presents the argument that English should be a compulsory foreign language but forbidden as the first foreign language in an education system (de Broglie, 1986). It is likely that the anglophone Member States would resist this.

6. This problem is not unknown of course. All societies which switch language for secondary/higher education have experience of it. The point here is that it has not traditionally been a European problem, since most European education systems use the national language as their medium. It has been a problem for children of migrant groups and has been felt to be a factor in under-performance (Skuttnab-Kangas, 1984)

7. This is the opinion of the European Parliamentary Committee asked to examine the case for the Right to Use One's Own Language: 'Switching to another language is a mistaken concession to colleagues of a different native language. Anyone who has taken the trouble to learn a foreign language knows that genuine multilingualism is a rare phenomenon. Most of us have full mastery of our mother tongue only. Clearly those allowed to speak their own language are in a *politically* stronger position. Being allowed to speak your own language is an advantage over those who are obliged to muddle along as best they can in another language. Conversely, those who are not allowed to speak their own language have handed over a *weapon* to political opponents with a different mother tongue (European Parliament, 1994a: 10) Italics in original.

8. For further information and a discussion of this see Wright & Ager (1995).

9. With some provisos. Some systems permit those with learning difficulties to opt out. Some systems permit the teaching of the languages of the country of origin of migrant groups provided that a EU language is offered as an alternative.

10. Cf. Lockhard (1996).

11. For example, *le comité pour la langue de l'Europe* predicts that Anglo-American culture will eclipse continental European. They call upon non-English speaking Europeans

> résister à la diffusion progressive de l'anglo-américain qui finira par réduire à rien les langues européennes et les cultures dont elles sont le véhicule. (Camus & Ficquelemont, 1979)

That they do this in French in the same text that calls for French as the language of Europe underscores that some of the anti-English rhetoric is not a fight against hegemony in general but against a particular hegemony.

12. Discussed and convincingly refuted by Pennycook (1994).

13. There is some evidence that there are complexities in this although they do not invalidate the general argument. It appears that both German and French may be chosen as foreign languages to differentiate the learner from the mass learning English (although English will still be learnt). This is true in France where parents who are aware of this strategy choose *collèges* which teach German as a first foreign language. This has a tendency to group middle class children in the same school and has a streaming effect in a comprehensive system. The mass of parents choose schools with English as a first foreign language judging that language to be more useful and not knowing whether their children will be in streams which take second foreign languages. The parents choosing German expect their children to be able to take English later (Bayrou, 1990). In the elite universities which traditionally produce the entrants to the European institutions fluent French is considered the differentiator; fluent English is considered the basic requirement (O'Driscoll, 1996).

14. It is difficult to find overt popular support in the UK for English as the language of Europe. Whether this is from lack of interest or a belief that it will just happen pragmatically is difficult to say. The poor record of foreign language learning in England indicates that either of these two reasons is feasible. The political class is well aware of the economic and political advantages but Churchill's forthright recognition of the advantage is rare:

> I am very much interested in the question of Basic English. The widespread use of this would be a gain to us far more durable and fruitful than the   annexation of great provinces. (Churchill cited in Pennycook, 1994: 107)

15. In the north of the continent there are high levels of expertise not only among academics and the power elites who have transnational contact but throughout all educated sectors of society, fostered in part by the tendency for higher education to be in English. Where language communities are too small for translation to be profitable in specialist subjects, higher education tends to use English as a medium. Usage tends to creep, since if information is accessed in a certain language it is sometimes easier to process it in the same language rather

than move to the mother tongue with all the difficulties of finding appropriate terms that this might cause.

16. On the other hand those who have invested heavily in acquiring French as a foreign language are often hostile to English. The articles attacking creeping anglicisation are often in French but not always by native speakers of that language (e.g. Weinreich, 1993; de Gorter, 1979; Olbert, 1979; Siguan, 1996, etc.).

17. Would it be too cynical to see some parallels with the situation in India that Pattanayak describes? Here knowledge of English is used as a filter for the political elites:

> English serves as the distinguishing factor for those in executive authority, no matter how low the level is, and acts as a convenient shield against the effective participation of the mass of the people in the governmental process. (Pattanayak, 1969: 63)

18. Speech 30 August 1997.

19. See, for example, readers' letters in *Le Monde* following the speech, in particular that from Jean Larose of the Université de Montréal in which he makes the point:

> il est naïf de ne pas donner un sens politique à la domination de l'anglais. (*Le Monde*, 1 December 1997, p. 15)

20. Which was, significantly, an off shoot of the association *Défense de la langue française* and composed of members of the French Academy, French academics and French politicians.

21. The contest is not just in the European arena, but in France itself. The legislation within France (1992 amendment of the constitution and 1994 Toubon act) to protect French from English borrowings and to exclude English from the public domain has not had complete success. Denison (1981) makes the point that language academies have greater or lesser success depending on whether they reflect the public mood or not. Going against what is happening organically is never successful and this appears to be the case in this context. The Toubon law is being flouted in a number of domains, particularly the language of colloquia and conferences in France.

22. See Jernudd and Shapiro (1989) for a full discussion of language purism and in particular the way that a lack of tolerance declares out of bounds some ways of being 'other'.

23. This diglossic organisation of Europe would allow those languages which are not national languages to regain ground. The move from a regional language to a national language has sometimes been prompted by economic considerations, access to power networks etc. A European *lingua franca* for all citizens makes it much easier to retain loyalty to a language of lesser diffusion. A constructed *lingua franca* is a language for certain functions only and allows coexistence in the way that English or French may not.

24. For example in the Eurom 4 project financed by the Commission and with pilot projects in Rome etc.

25. Although this has not yet occurred, a recent report from the Swedish Language Academy shows that there is a growing awareness of the danger that Swedish may disappear in certain domains, eclipsed by English (Swedish Language Council, 1998).

26. My own research provides an example of the problem about which I am writing. I can access the English, French and German communities of communication. For the debate that takes place outside these forums I am dependent on informants. I cannot immediately take part and this skews both reporting and discussion.

Bibliography

Adorno, T. (1974) *Minima Moralia, Reflections From a Damaged Life* (trans Jephcott). London: New Left Books.

Ager, D. (1990) *Sociolinguistics and Contemporary French*. Cambridge University Press: Cambridge.

Ager, D. (1996) *Language Policy in Britain and France*. London: Cassell.

Ager, D. (1997) *Language, Community and the State*. Exeter: Intellect.

Ainsworth, K. (1999) The Erasmus Programme: A question of language. MSc Sociolinguistics Dissertation, Aston University.

Allum, P. (1995) *State and Society in Western Europe*. Oxford: Polity Press.

Amin, A. and Tomaney, J. (1995) *Behind the Myth of the European Union*. London: Routledge.

Ammon, U. (1994) The dominance of English in Europe. *Sociolinguistica* 8, 1–13.

Ammon, U. (1997) Language spread policy. *Language Problems and Planning* 21 (1).

Andersen, S. and Eliassen, K. (eds) (1996) *The European Union, How Democratic Is It?* London: Sage.

Anderson, B. (1991) *Imagined Communities* (first edition 1983, second edition 1991). London: Verso.

Andrew, M. (1991) *The Birth of Europe*. London: BBC Books.

APC (Association of Principals of Colleges International) (1989) *Vocational Education and Training for the SEM* 1.

Arendt, H. (1962) *On Revolution*. New York: Viking.

Aristophanes (1995) Knights. In C. Rodewald (ed.) *Democracy, Ideas and Realities* (pp. 89–92). London: Dent.

Aristotle (1988) *Politics* (trans. Jowett). Cambridge: Cambridge University Press.

Armstrong, H. (1996) European Union regional policy: Sleepwalking to a crisis. *International Regional Science Review* 19 (3), 193–209.

Armstrong, J. (1982) *Nations before Nationalism*. University of North Carolina Press.

Ash, A. and Tomaney, J. (1995) The regional dilemma in a neo-liberal Europe. *European Urban and Regional Studies* 2 (2).

Baconnier, G., Minet, A. and Soler, L. (1985) *La Plume au Fusil*. Toulouse: Privat.

Bagdikian, B. (1983) *The Media Monopoly*. Boston: Beacon.

Bainbridge, T., with Teasdale A. (1995) *The Penguin Companion to the European Union*. London: Penguin.

Bankowski, Z. and Scott, A. (1996) The European Union? In R. Bellamy and D. Castiglione (eds) *Papers presented at the 22nd Conference of the UK Association for Legal and Social Philosophy*. Aldershot: Avebury.

Barbour, P. (ed.) (1996) *The European Union Handbook*. Chicago: Fitzroy, Dearborn.

Barnes, I. and Barnes, P. (1995) *The Enlarged European Union*. Harlow: Longman.

Barnet, R. (1994) *Global Dreams, Imperial Corporations and the New World Order*. New York: Simon and Schuster.

Barnet, R. and Müller, R. (1974) *Global Reach, the Power of the Multinational Corporation*. New York: Simon and Schuster.

Barret-Ducrocq, F. (1992) *Traduire l'Europe*. Paris: Payot.

Barth, F. (ed.) (1969) *Ethnic Groups and Boundaries*. Boston: Little, Brown.

Baudrillard, J. (1985) *Le miroir de la production, ou, L'illusion critique du matérialisme historique*. Paris: Galilée.

Bayrou, F. (1990) *La décennie des mal-appris*. Paris: Flammarion.

BBC (1996) From our own correspondent, BBC Radio 4. 10 February.

Bealey, F. (1988) *Democracy in the Contemporary State*. Oxford: Clarendon Press.

Beck, U. (1997) *The Reinvention of Politics*. Cambridge: Polity Press.

Begg, P. and Begg D. (1994) *Economics Work Book*. Maidenhead: McGraw Hill.

Beheydt, L. (1994) The linguistic situation in the new Belgium. In S. Wright (ed.) *Languages in Contact and Conflict, Contrasting Experiences in the Netherlands and Belgium*. Clevedon: Multilingual Matters.

Bell, D. (1973) *The Coming of Post-Industrial Society*. New York: Basic Books.

Bellamy, R. (1996) The political form of the constitution: The separation of powers, rights and representative democracy. In R. Bellamy and D. Castiglione (eds) *Constitutionalism in Transformation*. Oxford: Blackwell.

Bellamy, R., Bufacchi, V. and Castiglione, D. (1995) *Democracy and Constitutional Culture*. Lothian Foundation Press.

Benveniste, E. (1969) *Le Vocabulaire des Institutions Indo-européennes*. Paris: Editions de Minuit.

Bideleux R. and Jeffries I. (1998) *A History of Eastern Europe: Crisis and Change*. London: Routledge.

Birch, A. (1993) *The Concepts and Theories of Modern Democracy*. London: Routledge.

Birnbaum, P. (1991) Le nationalisme à la française. *Nationalismes, Pouvoirs* 57, 55–69.

Blanc, J. (1996) Interview. *Regions and Cities of Europe* 7.

Blanchet, P. (1992) Langues et démocratie. In P. Blanchet (ed.) *Nos Langues et l'Unité de l'Europe*. Louvain-la-neuve: Peeters.

Blanchet, P. (1999) What is the situation of a Provençal speaker as a French citizen today? In P. Blanchet, R. Breton and H. Schiffman (eds) *Les Langues Régionales de France: Un État des Lieux à la Veille du XXIe Siècle*. Louvain-la-neuve: Peeters.

Bloch, M. (1939, 1940) *La Société Féodale* (2 vols). Paris.

Bloed, A. and Wessel R. (1994) *The Changing Functions of the Western European Union*. Dordrecht: Martinus Nijhoff.

Boer den, M. (1966) Justice and home affairs, cooperation without integration. In H. Wallace and W. William (eds) *Policy-making in the European Union*. Oxford: OUP.

Boer den, P. (1993) Europe to 1914: The making of an idea. In K. Wilson and J. van den Dussen (eds) *The History of the Idea of Europe*. London: Routledge.

Bourdieu, P. (1991) *Language and Symbolic Power*. Cambridge: Polity.

Boutros-Ghali, B. (1996) Foreward. In T. Weiss and L. Gordenker (eds) *NGOs, the UN, and Global Governance*. Boulder and London: Lynne Rienner.

Boutros-Ghali, B. (1999) Plus de repos pour les bourreaux. *Le nouvel Obervateur* 18–24 March, 35–7.

Boyle, B. (1993) The democratic deficit of the European Community. *Parliamentary Affairs* 46, 458 – 477.

Brass, P. (1994) Elite competition and nation formation. In J. Hutchinson. and A.D. Smith (eds) *Nationalism*. Oxford: Oxford University Press.

Braud, P. (1980) *Le Suffrage Universel Contre la Démocratie*. Paris: PUF.

Braudel, F. (1986) *L'Identité de la France*. Paris: Arthaud.

Breton, R. (1999) Solidité, généralisation et limites du modèle jacobin de politique linguistique face à une nouvelle Europe. In P. Blanchet, R. Breton and H. Schiffman (eds) *Les Langues Régionales de France: Un État des Lieux à la Veille du XXIe Siècle*. Louvain-la-neuve: Peeters.

Breuilly, J. (1982) *Nationalism and the State*. Manchester University Press.

Breuilly, J. (1993) *Nationalism and the State* (2nd edn). Manchester University Press.

Brittan, L. (1992) Speech at Camberley Staff College, 11 October.

Brittan, L. (1994) *The Europe we Need*. London: Hamilton.

Broglie, G. de (1986) *Le Français Pour qu'il Vive*. Paris: Gallimard.

Bromley, S. (1993) The prospects for democracy in the Middle East. In D. Held (ed.) *Prospects for Democracy*. Oxford: Polity Press.

Brown, G. and Yule, G. (1983) *Discourse Analysis*. Cambridge: Cambridge University Press.

Bruckmüller, E. (1993) The national identity of the Austrians. In M. Teich and R. Porter (eds) *The National Question in Europe*. Cambridge: Cambridge University Press.

Bryce, J. (1921) *Modern Democracies*. London: Macmillan.

Budd, S. and Jones A. (1992) *The European Community – A Guide to the Maze*. London: Kogan Page.

Budge, I. (1993) Direct democracy, setting appropriate terms of debate. In D. Held (ed.) *Prospects for Democracy*. Oxford: Polity Press.

Bull, H. (1977) *The Anarchical Society: A Study of Order in World Politics*. London: Macmillan.

Burgi N. (ed.) (1994) *Fractures de l'Etat-Nation*. Paris: Kimé.

Burke, E. (1905) *Reflections on the French Revolution* (With 'The Substance of Mr. Burke's Speech, in the debate on the Army Estimates, the 9th day of February, 1790'). London: Methuen (originally published 1790).

Burrows, B., Denton, G. and Edwards, G. (1977) *Federal Solutions to European Issues*. London: Macmillan.

Butler, D. and Westlake, M. (1995) *British Politics and European Elections*. London: St. Martin's Press.

Byram, M. (1989) *Cultural Studies in Foreign Language Education*. Clevedon, Multilingual Matters.

Caire-Jabinet, M.-P. (1994) *Introduction à l'Historiographie*. Paris: Nathan.

Calvet, L.-J. (1993) *L'Europe et ses Langues*. Paris: Plon.

Camartin, I. (1985) Les relations entre les quatre régions linguistiques. In R. Schläpfer (ed.) *La Suisse aux Quatre Langues*. Genève: Editions Zoé.

Camus, P. and de Ficquelmont, G. (1979) Le Comité pour la Langue de l'Europe. *Le Monde*, 25 May.

Capéran, L. (1967) *Historie Contemporaine de la Laïcité Française*. Paris: Nouvelles Editions.

Carnot Circular (1848). 6 March.

Carnoy, M. (1993) Multinationals in a changing world economy, whither the nation-state? In M. Carnoy *et al.* (eds) *The New Global Economy in the Information Age*. Pennsylvania State University Press.

Carrère d'Encausse, H. (1978) *L'Empire Éclaté*. Paris: Flammarion.

Cartier, J. (1545) *Brief Recit et Succincte Narration de la Nauigation Faicte es Ysles de Canada*. Paris: P. Roffet and A. Le Clerc.

Cassen, B. (1994) Parler français ou la langue des maîtres. *Le Monde Diplomatique* (p. 32). April.

Cassen, B. (1995) Le mur de l'anglais. *Le Monde Diplomatique* (p. 22). May.

Castells, M. (1993) The informational economy and the new international division of labor. In M. Carnoy *et al.* (eds) *The New Global Economy in the Information Age*. Pennsylvania State University Press, 1993.

Castiglione B. (1900) *Il Libro del Cortigiano*, 1528. *The Book of the Courtier*. Done into English by Sir Thomas Hoby, anno 1561. With an introduction by Walter Raleigh. London: David Nutt.

Castiglione, D. (1995) Contracts and constitutions. In R. Bellamy *et al.* (eds) *Democracy and Constitutional Culture*. Lothian Foundation Press.

CERCLE (Comité européen pour le respect des cultures et des langues en Europe) (Ambrosi M., Bortoli G., Bourdieu P. *et al.*), Open letter to national governments and the EU calling on them to safeguard plurilingualism, http://Persoweb.francenet.fr/~mbonnaud/cerclefr.html, nd.

Cesarani, D. and Fulbrook, M. (eds) (1996) *Citizenship, Nationality and Migration in Europe*. London: Routledge.

Chilton, P. (1996) *Security Metaphors, Cold War Discourse from Containment to Common House*. New York: Peter Lang.

Chilton, P. (1998) The role of language in human conflict. In S.Wright (ed.) *Language and Conflict: A Neglected Relationship*. Clevedon: Multilingual Matters.

Chirac, J. (1997) *Discours Inaugural au VIIe Sommet de la Francophonie*. 14 November. Hanoi.

Clausewitz, C. von (1997) *On War* (trans. Graham). London: Wordsworth.

Clemens, W. (1991) *Baltic Independence and the Russian Empire*. New York: St Martin's Press.

Clyne, M. (1997) *Undoing and Redoing Corpus Planning*. Berlin: Mouton de Gruyter.

Cocks, Sir B. (1973) *The European Parliament*. London: HMSO.

Coffey, P. (1995) *The Future of Europe*. Vermont: Edward Elgar.

Colchester, N. and Buchan, D. (1990). *Europe Relaunched*. London: Hutchinson.

Colomès, M. (1992) L'Allemagne va-t-elle dominer l'Europe? *Le Point* 1014 (p. 19) 22 February.

Committee of the Regions (1997a) *Summary of Consultative Work 1996*. CdR 99/97. EN.

Committee of the Regions (1997b) *Opinion on Spatial Planning in Europe*. CdR340/96 fin.

Connor, W. (1994) A nation is a nation, is a state, is an ethnic group, is a . . . In J. Hutchinson and A.D. Smith *Nationalism*. Oxford: Oxford University Press.

Conservative Party (1994) *A Strong Britain in a Strong Europe*. London.

Constant, B. (1988) *Political Writings* (trans. Fontana). Cambridge University Press.

Comrie, B. (1987) *The Major Languages of South Asia, the Middle East and Africa*. London: Routledge.

Cooper, R. (1989) *Language Planning and Social Change*. Cambridge University Press.

Corbett, R. (1993) *The European Union*. London: Longman.

Coulmas, F. (1991) European integration and the idea of the national language. In F. Coulmas (ed.) *A Language Policy for the European Community: Prospects and Quandaries*. Berlin: Mouton de Gruyter.

Couloubaritsis, L., de Leeuw, M., Noël, E. and Sterckx, C. (1993) *The Origins of European Identity*. Brussels: European Interuniversity Press.

Council of Europe (1990) *Education Newsletter*, 2 & 3: 4.

Cresson, E. (1998) Speech at the Colloquy for Lesser Used Languages, Brussels. September.

Crowley, T. (1996) *Language in History*. London: Routledge.

Crystal, D. (1985) *A Dictionary of Linguistics and Phonetics*. Oxford: Blackwell.

Crystal, D. (1987) *The Cambridge Encyclopedia of Language*. Cambridge University Press.

CSCE (1992) *Helsinki Declaration*. Helsinki: CSCE.

Culler, J. (1986) *Saussure*. London: Fontana.

Delors, J. (1985) Speech to the European Parliament at Strasbourg. 14 January.

Delors, J. (1989) Speech to European Parliament at Strasbourg. 17 January.

Delors, J. (1992a) Reconcilier l'idéal et la nécessité. Speech to the College of Europe in Bruges, October 1989. In J. Delors *Le Nouveau Concert Européen*. Paris: Odile Jacob.

Delors, J. (1992b) *Aide aux Régions d'Europe*, CC-73-92-950-FR-C.

Delouche, F. (1992) *An Illustrated History of Europe*. London: Weidenfeld and Nicholson.

Denison, N. (1981) English in Europe with particular reference to the German-speaking area. *Europäische Mehrsprachigkeit, Festschrift zum 70 Geburtstag von Mario Wandruszka*. Tübingen: Max Niemayer.

Denman, R. (1997) *Missed Chances: Britain and Europe in the Twentieth Century*. London: Indigo.

Dentith, S. (1995) *Bakhtinian Thought*. London: Routledge.

Département fédéral de l'intérieur suisse (1989) *Rapport sur les Langues*.

Dessemontet, F. (1984) *Le Droit des Langues en Suisse*. Québec: Conseil de la langue française.

Deutsch, K. (1966) *Nationalism and Social Communication*. Cambridge, MA: MIT Press.

Deutsch, K. (1979) *Tides Among Nations*. London: Macmillan.

Deutsch, K. and Foltz, W. (eds) (1963) *Nationbuilding*. New York: Atherton Press.

Dezelay, Y. and Garth B. (1995) Merchants of law as moral entrepreneurs, constructing international justice from the competition for transnational business disputes. *Law and Society Review* 29, (1): 27–64.

Diamond, L. and Plattner, M. (1993) *The Global Resurgence of Democracy*. Baltimore: John Hopkins University Press.

Dinan, D. (1994) *Ever Closer Union?* London: Macmillan.

Dryzek, J. (1990) *Discursive Democracy*. Cambridge University Press.

Dubois (1887) *Introduction à la Nouvelle Grammaire Française* (3rd edn). Amersfoort.

Duby, G. (1987) *Le Moyen Age 987–1460*. Paris: Hachette.

Dunbabin, J. (1985) *France in the Making 843–1180*. Oxford: Oxford University Press.

Dunn, J. (1992) *Democracy, the Unfinished Journey*. Oxford: Oxford University Press.

Duverger, M. (1991) L'Europe balkanisée, communautaire ou dominée? *Pouvoirs* 57: 129–42.

EBLUL (European Bureau for Lesser Used Languages) (1994) *Contact Bulletin.* Spring, pp. 1–5.

EBLUL (European Bureau for Lesser Used Languages) (1997) *Contact Bulletin.* Spring, p. 6.

Eco, U. (1995) *The Search for the Perfect Language.* Oxford: Blackwell.

Education and Training (1992) European education and training, No. 5 (June): 12.

Education, Information and Sport Committee (1980) Working document PE64.563. 8 April.

Edwards, G. and Pijpers, A. (eds) (1997) *The Politics of European Treaty Reform.* London: Pinter.

Edwards, G. and Regelsberger, E. (1990) *Europe's Global Links.* London: Pinter.

Edwards, J. (1985) *Language, Society and Identity.* Oxford: Blackwell.

Edwards, J. (1994) *Multilingualism.* London: Routledge.

Eide, E. and Solli, P. (1996) *From Blue to Green – the Transition from UNPROFOR to IFOR in Bosnia and Herzegovina.* NUPI UN Programme.

ELC (European Language Council) (1997) *Synthesis Reports of Thematic Network Project in the Area of Languages.* DGXXII and Université de Lille.

Erasmus, H. (1994) Le problème de la communication et des langues dans l'Union européenne. *Context* 6.

Erasmus (1998) Erasmus programme in 1998/1999 (press release). 25 May.

ESHA (European Secondary Heads Association) (1990) *ESHA magazine* 2.

Euripides (1975) The suppliant women. In C. Rodewald (ed.) *Democracy, Ideas and Realities* (pp. 82–3). London: Dent.

European Commission (1985) A people's Europe. *Bulletin of the EC*, Supplement 7.

European Commission (1990) *Memorandum on the Rationalisation of Vocational Training Programmes at Community Level*, Com (90) 334 Final.

European Commission (1991) *Europe 2000 Outlook for the Development of the Community's Territory.* Brussels: Office for Official Publications.

European Commission (1995a) *Commission Report for the Reflection Group Intergovernmental Conference 1996.* (CC-89-95-357-EN-C). Brussels: Office for Official Publications.

European Commission (1995b) *Mémorandum de la Présidence sur le Pluralisme Linguistique dans l'Union Européenne.* (SI (95) 46-4034/95). Brussels: Office for Official Publications of the European Communities.

European Commission (1996a) *European Economy, Annual Report for 1995*, no. 59. (CM-AR-95-001-EN-C). Brussels: Office for Official Publications of the European Communities.

European Commission (1996b) *First Report on Economic and Social Cohesion.* Brussels: Office for Official Publications of the European Communities.

European Commission (1996c) *Teaching and Learning: Towards the Learning Society.* (96/C 195/01). Brussels: Office for Official Publications of the European Communities.

European Commission (1996d) *Frontier Free Europe.*

European Commission (1997a) Agenda 2000: For a stronger, wider union. *Bulletin of the EU*, Supplement 5.

European Commission (1997b) *Committee of the Regions.* (No GF-01-96-535-EN-C). Brussels: Office for Official Publications

European Economy (1990) One market, one money – an evaluation of the potential benefits and costs of forming an economic and monetary union. *European Economy* 44 (CB-AR-90-044-EN-C).

European Economy (1994) The economics of EMU. *European Economy*, Special edn 1/94 (CM-60-90-208-EN-C).

European Parliament (1990) *Report of the Committee of Institutional Affairs on the Principle of Subsidiarity* (Giscard d'Estaing Report).

European Parliament (1994a) *Report on the Right to Use One's Own Language.* (Rapporteur Marc Galle, PE 207.826/fin.nl).

European Parliament (1994b) *Resolution on the Right to Use One's Own Language.* (OJ C 205/528).

European Parliament, UK Office (1997) *A Citizen's Guide to the Institutions of the European Union.*

Eurostat (1992) *Education in the EC during the 1980s*, no. 1/92.

Eurostat (1994) *Year Book 1993.* Brussels: Office for Official Publications of the European Communities.

Eurostat (1995) *Basic Statistics of the European Union.* Brussels: Office for Official Publications of the European Communities.

Eurostat (1996a) *Year Book 1995.* (CA-81-93-2-4-EN-C). Brussels: Office for Official Publications of the European Communities.

Eurostat (1996b) *Migration Statistics 1995.* Brussels: Office for Official Publications of the European Communities.

Eurydice (1996) *Key Data on Education in the EU.* Brussels: Office for Official Publications of the European Communities.

Eurydice (1998) *Key Data on Education in the EU.* Brussels: Office for Official Publications of the European Communities.

Farrar, C. (1992) Ancient Greek political theory as a response to democracy. In J. Dunn (ed.) *Democracy, the Unfinished Journey.* Oxford: Oxford University Press.

Federal Trust (1995) *Network Europe and the Information Society.* London: Federal Trust.

Feraud, E. (1992) Le provençal comme moyen de communication et la vie économique. In P. Blanchet (ed.) *Nos Langues et l'Unité de l'Europe.* Louvain-la-neuve: Peeters.

Ferguson, W. (1998) *The Identity of the Scottish Nation.* Edinburgh University Press.

Fichte, J. (1905) *Reden an die Deutsche Nation.* Munich: Goldmann, 1905.

Fietz, M. (1995) Neuer Streit um Staatsagehörigkeit. *Die Welt*, 15 August.

Fishman, J. (1972) *Nationalism in Europe.* Rowley MA: Newbury House.

Fishman, J. (1977a) *Bilingual Education: An International Sociological Perspective.* Rowley MA: Newbury House.

Fishman, J. (1977b) Language and ethnicity. In H. Giles (ed.) *Language, Ethnicity and Intergroup Relations.* London: Academic Press.

Focus Research and Development (1997) *European Framework Programmes*, European Commission Focus 1997/1.

Fontana, B. (1992) Democracy and the French Revolution. In J. Dunn (ed.) *Democracy, the Unfinished Journey.* Oxford: Oxford University Press.

Forster, A. and Wallace, W. (1996) Common foreign and security policy. In H. Wallace and W. Wallace (eds) *Policy-making in the European Union.* Oxford: Oxford University Press.

Fournol, E. (1931) *Les Nations Romantiques.* Paris.

Gaffney, J. (ed.) (1996) *Political Parties and the European Union.* London: Routledge.

Gardner, R. and Lambert, W. (1972) *Attitudes and Motivation in Second Language Learning.* Rowley, MA: Newbury House.

Geertz, C. (ed.) (1963) *Old Societies and New States: The Quest for Modernity in Asia and Africa.* New York: Free Press.

Gellner, E. (1983) *Nations and Nationalism.* Oxford: Blackwell.

Gesquiere, Y. (1996) Potentialities and opportunities of the Euro as an international currency. *Economic Papers* 115.

Giddens, A. (1990) *The Consequences of Modernity.* Cambridge: Polity.

Gilpin, R. (1986) The richness of the tradition of political realism. In R. Keohane (ed.) *Neorealism and its Critics.* New York: Columbia University Press.

Giordan, H. (1992) *Les Minorités en Europe.* Paris: Kimé.

Gomez, R. (1998) The EU's Mediterranean policy: Common foreign poicy by the back door? In J. Peterson and H. Sjursen (eds) *A Common Foreign Policy for Europe?* London: Routledge.

Gorman, M. (1989) *The Unification of Germany, Documents and Commentary.* Cambridge University Press.

Gorter, S. de (1979) Speech at the International Symposium, Langues et coopération. Palais de l'Europe, Strasbourg, 17–20 April.

Gowland, D., O'Neill, B. and Reid, A. (1995) *The European Mosaic.* London: Longman.

Greenfeld, L. (1992) *Nationalism – Five Roads to Modernity.* Cambridge MA: Harvard University Press.

Gripaios, P. (1995) The role of European super regions. *European Urban and Regional Studies* 2 (1): 77–81.

Grundmann, R. (1999) The European public sphere. In D. Smith and S. Wright (eds) *Whose Europe? The Turn Towards Democracy.* Oxford: Blackwell.

Grundmann, R., Smith D. and Wright S. (in preparation) *Fighting Words: The Discourses of the Kosovan War.*

Guillou, M. (1995) Un défi majeur pour la Francophonie. *Le Sommet de la Francophonie.* No. 896/1995.11.03. Alexandria.

Guizot, F. (1826) *Histoire de la Révolution de l'Angleterre.*

Habermas, J. (1981) *Theorie des Kommunikativen Handelns.* Frankfurt: Suhrkamp.

Habermas, J. (1984) *The Theory of Communicative Action* (trans McCarthy). Massachusetts: Beacons.

Habermas, J. (1989) *Structural Transformation of the Public Sphere: An Inquiry Into a Category of Bourgeois Society (Strukturwandel der Öffentlichkeit)* (trans. Burger). Cambridge: Polity.

Habermas, J. (1992) *Faktizität und Geltung: Beiträge zur Diskurstheorie des Rechts und des Demokratischen.* Frankfurt am Main: Suhrkamp.

Habermas, J. (1994) *The Past as Future (Vergangenheit als Zukunft)* (trans. Max Pensky). Cambridge: Polity Press.

Habermas, J. (1996) *Between Facts and Norms: Contributions to a Discourse Theory of Law and Democracy* (trans. William Rehg). Cambridge: Polity.

Habsburg, O. von (1968) *Politik für das Jahr 2000.* Vienna: Verlag Harold. (Translated as *Bientôt l'an 2000.* Paris: Hachette, 1969)

Hagège, C. (1987) *Le Français et les Siècles.* Paris: Odile Jacob.

Hall, S., Held, D. and McGrew, T. (eds) (1992) *Modernity and its Futures.* Cambridge: Polity.

Halliburton, C. and Hünerberg R. (1993) *European Marketing, Readings and Cases.* Wokingham: Addison-Wesley.

Hallin, G. and Malmberg A. (1996) Attraction, competition and regional development in Europe. *European Urban and Regional Studies* 3 (4)

Ham, P. van, The EU and WEU: From cooperation to common defence? In G. Edwards and A. Pijpers (eds) *The Politics of European Treaty Reform.* London: Pinter.

Hargreaves, A. (1995) *Immigration, 'Race' and Ethnicity in Contemporary France.* London: Routledge.

Harris, P. and Moran, R. (1987) *Managing Cultural Difference.* Houston: Gulf Publishing.

Harvey, D. (1989) *The Condition of Postmodernity: An Enquiry into the Origins of Cultural Change.* Oxford: Basil Blackwell.

Hawthorn, G. (1993) Sub-saharan Africa. In D. Held (ed.) *Prospects for Democracy.* Oxford: Polity.

Hayes-Renshaw, F. (1996) The role of the Council. In S. Andersen and K. Eliassen (eds) *The European Union, How Democratic Is It?* London: Sage.

Hechter, M. (1975) *Internal Colonialism: The Celtic Fringe in British National Development 1536–1966.* University of California Press.

Held, D. (1980) *Introduction to Critical Theory.* London: Hutchinson.

Held, D. (1984) *Political Theory and the Modern State.* Cambridge: Polity.

Held, D. (1991) Democracy, the nation state and the global system. *Economy and Society* 20: 138–72.

Held, D. (1993) *Prospects for Democracy.* Oxford: Polity.

Held, D. (1995) *Democracy and the Global Order.* Cambridge: Polity.

Held, D., McGrew, A., Goldblatt, D. and Perraton, J. (1999) *Global Transformations.* Cambridge: Polity.

Held, D. and Pollitt C. (1986) *New Forms of Democracy.* London: Sage.

Herder, J. (1770) *Über den Ursprung der Sprache.* Berlin.

Herodotus (1996) *Histories* (trans. Rawlinson). Ware: Wordsworth Classics.

Heynold, C. (1995) *A Multilingual Community at Work.* EU Commission Translating Service.

Hiden, J. and Salmon, P. (1994) *The Baltic Nations and Europe: Estonia, Latvia and Lithuania in the Twentieth Century.* London: Longman.

Highfield, R. (1988) Funds delay puts brake on race for fusion energy. *Daily Telegraph,* 20 June, p. 17.

Hill, C. (1996) *The Actors in Europe's Foreign Policy.* London: Routledge.

Hillmore, P. (1998) You want Room 03HO250v. Through the atrium, take a lift, right, follow the purple carpet. Welcome to Europe. *The Observer,* 15 February.

Hirst, P. (1995) The European Union at the crossroads: Integration or decline? In R. Bellamy *et al.* (eds) *Democracy and Constitutional Culture.* Lothian Foundation Press.

Hix, S. (1996) The transnational party federations. In J. Gaffney (ed.) *Political Parties and the European Union.* London: Routledge.

Hobsbawm, E. (1990) *Nations and Nationalism since 1780.* Cambridge University Press.

Hobsbawm, E. (1994) *Age of Extremes.* London: Michael Joseph.

Hobsbawm, E. and Ranger, T. (eds) (1983) *The Invention of Tradition.* Cambridge University Press.

Hoffmann, S. (1995) *The European Sisyphus*. Boulder, CO: Westview Press.

Holsti, K. (1985) *The Dividing Discipline*. Boston: Allen and Unwin.

Hoggart, R., and Johnson, D. (1987) *An Idea of Europe*. London: Chatto and Windlass.

Hoof van, R. (1978) Report presented at Bruges Week, College of Europe, 16–18 March.

Horkheimer, M. and Adorno, T. (1972) *Dialectic of Enlightenment* (trans. Cumming). New York: Herder and Herder.

Hornblower, S. (1992) Creation and development of democratic institutions in ancient Greece. In J. Dunn (ed.) *Democracy, the Unfinished Journey*. Oxford: Oxford University Press.

Horrocks, D. and Kolinsky, E. (eds) (1996) *Turkish Culture in German Society Today*. Oxford: Berghahn.

Hotton, R. and Turner, B. (1989) *Max Weber on Economy and Society*. London: Routledge.

Huntington, S. (1996) *The Clash of Civilisations and the Remaking of World Order*. New York: Simon and Schuster.

Hutchinson, J. (1987) *The Dynamics of Cultural Nationalism*. London: Allen and Unwin.

Hutchinson, J. and Smith, A.D. (eds) (1994) *Nationalism*. Oxford: Oxford University Press.

Huyghe, F.-B. (1993) Français malgré tout. *Le Monde des Débats*, July–August.

Hymes, D. (1967) Linguistic problems in defining the concept of tribe. In *Proceedings of the 1967 Annual Spring Meeting of the American Ethnological Society* (pp. 23–48). Seattle: University of Washington Press.

Ignatieff, M. (1994) *Blood and Belonging*. London: Vintage.

INRA/Eurobarometer 1996 (1997) cited in *L'Opinion des Européens sur les Droits de l'Homme, la Démocratie et les Libertés Fondamentales*. Programme d'information du citoyen européen, Leaflet DG X.

INSEE (1996) *Annuaire Statistique de la France*.

Jacobs, E. (1973) *European Trade Unionism*. London: Croom Helm.

James, E. (1982) *The Origins of France, From Clovis to the Capetians 500–1000*. London: Macmillan.

Jameson, F. (1985) Postmodernism and consumer society. In H. Foster (ed.) *Postmodern Culture*. London and Sydney. Pluto.

Jandt, F. (1995) *Intercultural Communication*. Thousand Oaks, CA: Sage.

Jennings, J. (1995) French constitutional tradition. In R. Bellamy *et al.* (eds) *Democracy and Constitutional Culture*. Lothian: Foundation Press.

Jernudd, B. and Shapiro, M. (eds) (1989) *The Politics of Language Purism*. Berlin: Mouton de Gruyter.

Jessop, B. (1994) Post-Fordism and the state. In A. Amin (ed) *Post-Fordism*. Oxford: Blackwells.

Johnson, D. (1993) The making of the French nation. In M. Teich and R. Porter (eds) *The National Question in Europe*. Cambridge University Press.

Johnson, K., Williams R. and Barron P. (1997) *Funding From the European Union*. Representation of the European Commission in the UK.

Jorna, M. (1993) A democratic deficit but don't tell the people (interview). *The Guardian*, 30 July.

Julliard, J. (1985) *La Faute à Rousseau*. Paris: Seuil.

Keating, M. (1988) *State and Regional Nationalism*. New York: Harvester Wheatsheaf.

Kedourie, E. (1960) *Nationalism*. London: Blackwell.
Kedourie, E. (ed.) (1970) *Nationalism in Asia and Africa*. New York: Meridian.
Kendall, W. (1975) *The Labour Movement in Europe*. London: Allen Lane.
Kennedy, P. (1993) *Preparing for the Twenty-first Century*. London: Harper Collins.
Klíma, A. (1993) The Czechs. In M. Teich and R. Porter (eds) *The National Question in Europe*. Cambridge University Press.
Koch, H. (1991) Legal aspects of a language policy for the European Communities. In F. Coulmas (ed.) *A Language Policy for the European Community*. Berlin: Mouton de Gruyter.
Koenigsberger, H., Mosse, G., and Bowler, G. (1968) *Europe in the Sixteenth Century: A General History of Europe*. London: Longman.
Kohn, H. (1946) *The Idea of Nationalism*. New York: Macmillan.
Kolinsky, E. (1996) Non-German minorities in contemporary German society. In D. Horrocks and E. Kolinsky (eds) *Turkish Culture in German Society Today* (pp. 71–113). Providence: Berghahn.
Krejci, J. and Velimsky, V. (1981) *Ethnic and Political Nations in Europe*. London: Croom Helm.
Kristeva, J. (1993) *Nations Without Nationalism* (trans. Roudiez). New York: Columbia University Press.
Kubchandani, L. (1983) Multilingualism in India. In C. Kennedy (ed.) *Language Planning and Education*. London: George Allen.
Kundera, M. (1984) *The Unbearable Lightness of Being*. London: Faber.
Labrie, N. (1993) *La Construction Linguistique de la Communauté Européenne*. Genève: Champion.
Lafont, R. (1993) *La Nation, l'Etat, les Régions*. Paris: Berg.
Lafont, R. (1971) *L'Occitanie*. Paris: Seghers.
Lamassoure, A. (1994) Speech to Assemblée Nationale, 2nd sitting, 29 June.
Lane, J.-E. and Ersson, S. (1996) *European Politics*. London: Sage.
Laponce, J. (1987) *Languages and their Territories* (trans. A. Martin-Sperry). University of Toronto Press.
Larzac, J. (1971) *Le Petit Livre de l'Occitanie*. St Pons: 4 Vertats.
Latouche, S. (1996) *The Westernization of the World*. Cambridge: Polity.
Latter, R. (1994) *European Security and Defence*. London: HMSO.
Laursen, F. (1996) The role of the Commission. In S. Andersen and K. Eliassen (eds) *The European Union, How Democratic Is It?* London: Sage.
Lavenir, H. (1994) Combat pour la langue française. In *Le Figaro*, 10 March.
Lavisse, E. (1895) *A Propos de nos Écoles*, Paris: Armand Colin.
Lavisse, E. (1902) *Histoire de France*. Cours élémentaire.
Lebrun, F. (ed.) (1980) *Histoire des Catholiques en France du XVe Siècle à nos Jours*. Toulouse: Privat.
Lenarduzzi, D. (1997) Paper given at Conférence inaugurale du Conseil européen pour les langues, Lille, 3–4 July.
Lenzen, D. (1996) Education and training for Europe. In D. Benner and D. Lenzen (eds) *Education for the New Europe*. Providence: Berghahn.
Le Roy Ladurie, E. and Goy, J. (1982) *Tithe and Agrarian History from the 14th to the 19th Century: An Essay in Comparative History* (trans. Burke). Cambridge University Press.
Lewis, F. (1987) *Europe – A Tapestry of Nations*. London: Unwin Hyman.
Lewis, F. (1991) The 71/2 Directorate. *Foreign Policy* 85: 25–40.

Lieven, A. (1993) *The Baltic Revolution*. Newhaven: Yale University Press.
Lipgens, W. (1982) *A History of European Integration 1945–1947*. Oxford: Clarendon Press.
List, F. (1841) *Das Nationale System der Politischen Okonomie*.
List, F. (1904) *The National System of Political Economy* (trans. Sampson). London: Longmans, Green.
Lively, J. (1975) *Democracy*. Oxford: Blackwell.
Lloyd, G. (1992) Democracy, philosophy and science in ancient Greece. In J. Dunn (ed.) *Democracy, the Unfinished Journey*. Oxford: Oxford University Press.
Lockard, J. (1996) Resisting Cyber English. In *Bad Subjects*, no. 24.
Lodge, J. (ed.) (1993) *The European Community and the Challenge of the Future*. London: Pinter.
Lodge, J. (1996) The European Parliament. In S. Andersen and K. Eliassen (eds) *The European Union, How Democratic Is It?* London: Sage.
Lord, R. and Maher, K. (1993) *Linking Perceptions and Performance*. London and New York: Routledge.
Lyons, J. (ed.) (1970) *New Horizons in Linguistics*. Harmondsworth: Penguin.
Lyotard, J.-F. (1992) *The Post-modern Condition, A Report on Knowledge*. Manchester University Press.
Macey, M. (1990) Education, racism and ideology in Britain: The implications of the 1988 Educational Reform Act. Paper given at the One Europe Research Group Conference, Cracow, Poland 21–27 October.
Macioti, M. (1988) Speech reported in R. Highfield, Britain's research cuts problem for Europe. *Daily Telegraph*. 19 August. p. 21.
Mackiewicz, W. (1997) *Address to European Language Council Launching Conference*, Lille. 3 July.
Mackinnon, K. (1991) *Gaelic Past, Present and Future Prospect*. Edinburgh: Saltire Society.
Manoliu, M. (1994) Language standardization and political rejection, the Romanian case. In M. Parry, W. Davies and R. Temple (eds) *The Changing Voices of Europe*. Cardiff: University of Wales Press.
Marchand, P., and Terrier, D. (1992) *La France des Origines à 1789*. Lille: CRDP Collection Démarches et Outils pour la Classe.
Martin, P. (1990) The pattern of language communication in Brunei Darussalam and its pedagogic implications. In V. Bickley (ed.) *Language Use, Language Teaching and the Curriculum*. Hong Kong: Institute of Language in Education.
Marx, K. and Engels, F. (1848) *The Communist Manifesto*.
Marx, K. (1964) *The Economic and Philosophic Manuscripts of 1844*. New York International Publishers.
Mayeur, F. (1981) *Histoire Générale de l'Enseignement et de l'Éducation en France*. Paris: Nouvelle Librairie.
McLean, I. (1989) *Democracy and New Technology*. Oxford: Polity.
McGrew, T. (1992) A global society. In S. Hall, D. Held and T. McGrew (eds) *Modernity and its Futures*. Cambridge: Polity.
Meigret, L. (1969) *Le Tretté de la Grammere Francoeze, 1550*; with *La reponse, 1550; Defenses, 1550*; and, *Reponse*, 1551 (facsimile reprint). Menston: Scolar Press.
Melin (1895) *Histoire de France*. Cours élémentaire.
Menon, A., Forster, A. and Wallace, W. (1998) A common European defence? *Survival* 34 (3): 98–118.

Mény Y., Muller P. and Quermonne J.-L. (1996) *Adjusting to Europe*. London: Routledge.

Messmer, M. (1991) *Staffing Europe*. Herndon, VA: Acropolis.

Middlemas, K. (1995) *Orchestrating Europe*. London: Fontana.

Milward, A. (1992) *The European Rescue of the Nation-State*. London: Routledge.

Milward, A. and Sorenson V. (1994) Independence or integration? A national choice. In A. Milward *et al.* (eds) *The Frontier of National Sovereignty*. London: Routledge.

Mitchell, J. (1995) Lobbying Brussels: The case of Scotland Europa. *European Urban and Regional Studies* 2 (4): 287 – 99.

Mitterrand, F. (1988) *Lettre à Tous les Français*. Paris: Parti socialiste.

Monnet, J. (1955) Opening address to the Comité d'Action pour les Etats-Unis d'Europe.

Moody, J. (1978) *French Education since Napoleon*. Syracuse: Syracuse University Press.

Mordrel, O. (1981) *Le Mythe de l'Hexagone*. Paris: Éditions Picollec.

Morrell, F. (1996) *Continent Isolated*. London: Federal Trust.

Muller, P. (1989) *Airbus, l'ambition Européenne : Logique d'Etat, Logique de Marché*. Paris: Commissariat général du plan, L'Harmattan.

Muylle, N. (1997) Le plurilinguisme au coeur de l'identité européenne. Paper given at Conférence inaugurale du Conseil européen pour les langues, Lille, 3–4 July.

Nairn, T. (1977) *The Break up of Britain*. London: New Left Books.

Nairn, T. (1997) *Faces of Nationalism: Janus Revisited*. London: Verso.

NATO (1976) *Basic Documents*. Brussels: NATO information services.

NATO (1981) *The North Atlantic Treaty Organisation, Facts and Figures*. Brusssels: NATO Information Service.

Naughton, J. (1997) The Internet. Just what we need. A virtual chat about monetary union (review). *The Observer*, 23 February, p. 13.

Ndebele, N. (1987) The English language and social change in South Africa. *The English Academy Review* 4: 1–6.

Nectoux, F. (1996) The politics of European integration after Maastricht. In P. Barbour (ed.) *The European Union Handbook*. Chicago: Fitzroy, Dearborn.

Newlands, D. (1994) A Europe of the region? Regional convergence and divergence in the European Union. Paper given at Beyond Boundaries? Citizens, cultures and languages in the New Europe Conference, University of Salford, November.

Nostradamus, M. (1969) *Prognostication of Maister Michael Nostrodamus in Prouince for the Yeare of our Lorde 1559* (facsimile). New York: Theatrum Orbis Terrarum, Da Capo Press.

Nyborg, K. (1982) *Report on the Multilingualism of the European Community*. European Parliament Working Documents, Doc1-306/82.

Nyborg Report Working Documents (1982) (in Nyborg Report) (OJ No. C 292). 8 November.

Nyland, K. (1990) English use in business – forming a link with English education in Hong Kong. In V. Bickley (ed.) *Language Use, Language Teaching and the Curriculum*. Hong Kong: Institute of Language in Education.

O'Driscoll, J. (1996) Opting for French: the case of the high flyers. Paper given at the Nordic Intercultural Communication conference, Aalborg University, November.

O'Leary, S. (1996) *European Union Citizenship*. London: Institute for Public Policy Research.

Olbert, J. (1979) Une seule langue de communication ou pluralité linguistique? Paper given at the International Symposium, Langues et coopération, Palais de l'Europe Strasbourg, 17–20 April.

Ozolins, U. (1993) *The Politics of Language in Australia*. Cambridge University Press.

Ozolins, U. (1999) Between Russian and European hegemony: Current language policy in the Baltic States. *Current Issues in Language and Society* 6 (1).

Palsgrave, J. (1530) *Lesclarissement de la Langue Francoyse*. London: Johan Haukyns.

Pattanayak, D. (1969) *Aspects of Applied Linguistics*. Asia Publishing House.

Pattanayak, D. (1981) *Multilingualism and Mother-tongue Education*. Delhi: Oxford University Press.

Pause, D. (1997) Introduction. In *Committee of the Regions, Summary of Consultative Work 1996*. (CdR 99/97.EN).

Pennycook, A. (1994) *The Cultural Politics of English as an International Language*. London: Longman.

Pescatore, P. (1983) The doctrine of direct effect. *European Law Review* 8, 155.

Peterson, M. (1995) Regionalism: Passage to parochialism or platform for universal change. Paper given at the Euroconference on cost and benefits of Europeanization, Vienna. April.

Peterson, M. (1979) *International Interest Organization and Transmutation of Post-War Society*. Almquist and Wicksell International.

Pfaff, W. (1993) *The Wrath of Nations*. New York: Simon and Schuster.

Pfeffer, J. (1992) *Managing with Power, Politics and Influence in Organizations*. Boston, MA: Harvard Business School Press.

Phillipson, R. (1992) *Linguistic Imperialism*. Oxford University Press.

Phillipson, R. and Skutnabb-Kangas T. (1994) Linguistic human rights, overcoming linguistic discrimination. *Sociology of Language* 67.

Picq, J. (1990) *Les Ailes de l'Europe, l'Aventure de l'Airbus*. Paris: Fayard.

Pijpers, A., Regelberger, E. and Wessels, W. (1988) *European Political Cooperation in the 1980s*. Dordrecht: Martin Nijhoff Publishers.

Pinder, J. (1995) *European Community, The Building of a Union*. Oxford Paperbacks.

Political Affairs Committee (1982) *Opinion of the Political Affairs Committee*, adopted 26 February. European Parliament.

Potter, D. (1993) Democratization in Asia. In D. Held (ed.) *Prospects for Democracy*. Oxford: Polity.

Plato (1997) *Republic* (trans. Davies and Vaughan). Ware: Wordsworth Classics.

Posner, R. (1994) Romania within a wider Europe: Conflict or cohesion? In M. Parry, W. Davies and R. Temple (eds) *The Changing Voices of Europe*. Cardiff: University of Wales Press.

Preston, L. and Windsor, D. (1992) *The Rules of the Game in the Global Economy: Policy Regimes for International Business*. Boston: Kluwer Academic Publishers.

Prosser, M. (1973) *Intercommunication Among People and Nations*. New York: Harper Row.

Prost, A. (1968) *Histoire de l'Enseignement en France 1800–1967*. Paris: A. Colin.

Quell, C. (1997) Language choice in multilingual institutions: A case study at the European Commission. *Multilingua* 16/1: 57–76.

Radnai, Z. (1994) The educational effects of language policy. In S. Wright (ed.) *Ethnicity in Eastern Europe: Questions of Migration, Language Rights and Education.* Clevedon: Multilingual Matters.

Rahman, A. (1990) The English language curriculum in Bangla Desh. In V. Bickley (ed.) *Language Use, Language Teaching and the Curriculum.* Hong Kong: Institute of Language in Education.

Rannut, M. (1991) Beyond language policy; the Soviet Union versus Estonia. *Rolig papir* 48/91.

Rannut, M. (1994) Papers for the Round Table on Language Policy in Europe. *Rolig papir* 52/94.

Rawls, J. (1971) *A Theory of Justice.* Oxford University Press.

Rees P. *et al.* (eds.) (1996) *Population Migration in the European Union.* Chichester: John Wiley & Sons.

Reich, R. (1991) *The Work of Nations.* New York: Knopf.

Renan, E. (1882) Qu'est-ce qu'une nation. In *Discours et Conférences, Oeuvres complètes* (Vol. 1). Paris, 1947.

Riffault, H. (1991) Comparative research on national identities. *Innovation* 4 (1), 35.

Robers, J. (1996) *The Penguin History of Europe.* Harmondsworth: Penguin.

Robins, K. (1991) Tradition and translation, national culture in its global context. In J. Corner and S. Harvey (eds) *Entreprise and Heritage, Crosscurrents of National Culture.* London: Routledge.

Rocard, M. (1987) *Le Coeur à l'Ouvrage.* Paris: Odile Jacob.

Rodewald, C. (1975) *Democracy, Ideas and Realities.* London: Dent.

Romaine, S. (1989) *Bilingualism.* Oxford: Blackwell.

Romero, F. (1994) Migration as an issue in European interdependence and integration, the case of Italy. In A. Milward *et al.* (eds) *The Frontier of National Sovereignty.* London: Routledge.

Roper, J. (1989) *Democracy and its Critics: Anglo-American Democratic Thought in the Nineteenth Century.* London: Unwin Hyman.

Rosenau, J. (1990) *Turbulence in World Politics.* Boulder, CO: Lynne Riener.

Rosenau, J. (1989) *Interdependence and Conflict in World Politics.* Lexington, DC: Heath.

Rosenau, J. (1980) *The Study of Global Interdependence.* London: Pinter.

Rousseau, J.-J. (1954) *The Social Contract* (trans. Kendall). Chicago: Henry Regnery.

Rousseau, J.-J. (1967) *Essai sur l'Origine des Langues.* Cahiers pour l'analyse, no. 8. (1781).

Rovan, J. (1993) Imaginer une autre Europe. *Le Figaro.* 3 August.

Rubin, J. (1981) The study of cognitive processes in second language learning. *Applied Linguistics* 2 (2): 117–31.

Rummel, R. (ed.) (1992) *Toward Political Union: Planning a Common Foreign and Security Policy in the EC.* Boulder: Westview.

Rummel, R. and Schmidt, P. (1991) Integration and security in Western Europe. In M. Jop, R. Rummel and P. Schmidt (eds) *Inside the European Pillar.* Boulder: Westview.

Sahlins, M. (1976) *The Uses and Abuses of Biology.* Ann Arbor: University of Michigan Press.

Said, E. (1994) *Culture and Imperialism.* London: Vintage.

Salmon, T. (1996) European Union structures and institutions and their powers. In Barbour (ed.) *The European Union Handbook.* Chicago: Fitzroy, Dearborn.

Salt, J. (1995) Foreign workers in the United Kingdom, evidence from the Labour Force Survey. *Employment Gazette*, January: 11 –19.

Samuel, R. and Hinton Thomas, R. (1949) *Education and Society in Modern Germany.* Westport, CT: Greenwood.

Santer, J. (1995) Address to the European Parliament on the occasion of the investiture debate of the new Commission. *Bulletin of the European Union*, Supplement 1/95.

Santer, J. (1997) Address to the European Parliament, Agenda 2000, 16 July.

Sarason, S. (1972) *The Creation of Settings and the Future Societies.* San Francisco: Jossey-Bass.

Sassen, S. (1994) *Cities in a World Economy.* Pine Forge, CA: Sage.

Sassen, S. (1995) *Losing Control? Sovereignty in an Age of Globalization.* New York: Columbia University Press.

Saussure, F. de (1993) *Troisième Cours de Linguistique.* Oxford: Pergamon.

Schiffman, H. (1996) *Linguistic Culture and Language Policy.* London: Routledge.

Schläpfer, R. (ed.) (1985) *La Suisse aux Quatre Langues.* Genève: Zoé.

Schlesinger, P. (1992) Europeanness: A new cultural battlefield? *Innovation* 5 (1): 12–22.

Schlossmacher, M. (1994) Die Arbeitssprachen in den Organen der Europäishen Gemeindschaft. *Sociolinguistica* 8: 101–22.

Schmidt, W. (1993) The nation in German history. In M. Teich and R. Porter (eds) *The National Question in Europe.* Cambridge University Press.

Schmitter, P. (1994) The political dimensions of European integration. In B. Abegaz, P. Dillon, D. Feldman and P. Whiteley (eds) *The Challenge of European Integration.* Boulder, CO: Westview Press.

Schöpflin, G. (1995) Nationalism and ethnicity in Europe. In C. Kupchan (ed.) *Nationalism and Nationalities in the New Europe.* Ithaca: Cornell University Press.

Schwenke, W. (1980) How to solve the Community's language problems. *EC Magazine* 2/80.

Seliger, H. (1983) Learner interaction in the classroom and its effects on language acquisition. In H. Seliger and M. Long (eds) *Classroom Oriented Research in Second Language Acquisition.* Rowley, MA: Newbury House.

Seton-Watson, H. (1977) *Nations and States.* London: Methuen.

Shapiro, M. (1993) The globalization of law. *Indiana Journal of Global Legal Studies* 1, 37–64.

Sharp, D. (1973) *Language in Bilingual Communities.* London: Arnold.

SIBA (1996) *Statistisches Jahrbuch 1995.*

Siguan, M. (1996) *L'Europe des Langues.* Barcelona: Mardaga.

Sjursen, H. (1998) Missed opportunity or eternal fantasy? The idea of a European security and defence policy. In J. Peterson and H. Sjursen (eds) *A Common Foreign Policy for Europe?* London: Routledge.

Skinner, Q. (1992) The Italian city republics. In J. Dunn (ed.) *Democracy, the Unfinished Journey.* Oxford: Oxford University Press.

Skutnabb-Kangas, T. (1984) *Bilingualism or Not: The Education of Minorities.* Clevedon: Multilingual Matters.

Smith, A.D. (1991a) *National Identity.* Harmondsworth: Penguin.

Smith, A.D. (1991b) *The Ethnic Origin of Nations.* Oxford: Blackwell.

Smith, A.D. (1995) Gastronomy or geology? The role of nationalism in the reconstruction of nations. *Nations and Nationalism* 1 (1): 3–25.

Smith D. (1990) *Capitalist Democracy on Trial: The Transatlantic Debate from Tocqueville to the Present*. London: Routledge.

Smith D. and Wright S. (1999) The turn to democracy. In D. Smith and S. Wright (eds) *Whose Europe?* Oxford: Blackwell.

Smith D. and Wright S. (in prep.) *Devolution, Democracy and Europe*.

Social Trends (1996) 1996 edition, HMSO.

Socrates-Erasmus Council (1996) *Data Report 1995, Erasmus and Lingua Action II*. Canterbury, UK Socrates-Erasmus Council.

Socrates-Erasmus Council (1997) *Student Mobility within the European Union: A Statistical Analysis*. DG XXII, Socrates-Erasmus Council.

Soucy, R. (1972) *Fascism in France: The Case of Maurice Barrès*. University of California Press.

Southern, R. (1995) *Scholastic Humanism and the Unification of Europe*. Oxford: Blackwell.

Stalin, J. (1973) *The Essential Stalin, Major Theoretical Writings 1905–1952* (B. Franklin (ed.). London: Croom Helm.

Stevenson, V. (ed.) (1983) *Words: An Illustrated History of Western Languages*. London: Macdonald.

Stobart, J. (1911) *The Glory That Was Greece*. London: Sidgwick and Jackson.

Stone, A. (1993) Ratifying Maastricht, France debates European Union. *French Politics and Society* 11 (1). Winter.

Stone, I. (1994) Belgium and Luxembourg. In F. Somers (ed.) *European Community Economics*. London: Pitman.

Strubell, M. (1998) Language, democracy and devolution in Catalonia. In S. Wright (ed.) *Language, Democracy and Devolution in Catalonia*. Clevedon: Multilingual Matters.

Swann, D. (1995) *The Economics of the Common Market: Integration in the European Union*. London: Penguin.

Swedish Language Council (1998) *Draft Action Programme for the Promotion of the Swedish Language*.

Szépe, G. (1994) Central and eastern European language policies in transition. In S. Wright (ed.) *Ethnicity in Eastern Europe, Questions of Migration, Language Rights and Education*. Clevedon: Multilingual Matters.

Taveneaux, R. (1980) *Le Catholicisme dans la France Classique*. Paris: Société d'Éditions d'Enseignement Supérieur.

Taylor, A.J.P. (1945) *The Course of German History: A Survey of the Development of German History Since 1815* (reprinted 1988). London: Routledge.

Taylor, K. (1995) Local and regional government in Europe. *Political Quarterly* 66 (1). Jan–Mar.

Taylor, P. (1996) *The European Union in the 1990s*. Oxford University Press.

Teich, M and Porter R. (eds) (1993) *The National Question in Europe*. Cambridge University Press.

Thompson, K. (1992) Religion, values and ideology. In R. Bocock and K. Thompson (eds) *Social and Cultural Forms of Modernity*. Cambridge: Polity Press.

Thompson, D. (1970) *The Democratic Citizen*. Cambridge University Press.

Thucydides (1997) *The History of the Peloponnesian War* (trans. Crawley). Ware: Wordsworth Classics.

Tocqueville, A. de (1946) *Democracy in America* (trans Steele). Oxford University Press.

Touraine, A. (1997) *What is Democracy?* (trans Macey). Boulder, CO: Westview Press.

Tournier, J.-C. (1999) *Le Traité d'Amsterdam: De l'Euro à l'Europe.* Paris: Editions de l'Organisation.

Treanor, P. (n.d.) *Structures of Nationalism,* Sociological Research Online, 2 (1). www.socresonline.org.uk.

Trevor-Roper, H. (1983) Inventing traditions. In E. Hobsbawm and T. Ranger (eds) *The Invention of Tradition.* Cambridge University Press.

Trim, J. (1979) The Council of Europe's modern languages project. Paper given at the International Symposium, Langues et coopération, Palais de l'Europe, Strasbourg, 17–20 April.

Truchot, C. (1991) Towards a language policy for the European Union. In *Language Planning* 3: 87–104.

Tsakoloyannis, P. (1997) The EU and the common interests of the South. In G. Edwards and A Pijpers (eds) *The Politics of European Treaty Reform.* London: Pinter.

US Department of State (1994) *Estonian Human Rights Practices, 1993.* 31 January.

Van den Berghe, P. (1978) Race and ethnicity, a socio-biological perspective. *Ethnic and Racial Studies* 1 (4), 402–11.

Varsori, A. (1992) Italian and Western defence 1948–1955. In B. Heuser and R. O'Neill (eds) *Securing Peace in Europe 1945–1962.* New York: St Martin's Press.

Verwaerde, Y. (1990) Question écrite No 11/90, *Journal Officiel* C 328/5. 9 April.

Voltaire, F. (1756) *Essais sur l'Histoire Générale, et sur les Moeurs et l'Esprit des Nations, Depuis Charlemagne Jusqu'à nos Jours.* Geneva.

Waever, O. (1989) Conflicts of vision; vision of conflict. In O.Waever, P. Lemaître and E. Tromer (eds) *European Polyphony, Perspectives beyond East-West Confrontation.* London: MacMillan.

Waever, O., with Herder and Habermas (1990) Europeanization in the light of German Concepts of State and Nation. *Arbejdspapirer* 16. Copenhagen: Centre for Peace and Conflict Research.

Wallace, H. and Wallace W. (1996) *Policy-making in the European Union.* Oxford University Press.

Wallace, W. (1990) *The Transformation of Western Europe.* London: Pinter.

Wallace, W. (1994) *Regional Integration, The Western European Experience.* The Brookings Institution.

Wallerstein, I. (1984) *The Politics of the World Economy: The States, the Movements and the Civilisations.* Cambridge University Press.

Walter, H. (1988) *Le Français Dans Tous les Sens.* Paris: Robert Laffont.

Weale, A. (1995) Democratic legitimacy and the constitution of Europe. In R. Bellamy *et al.* (eds) *Democracy and Constitutional Culture.* Lothian: Foundation Press.

Weatherill, S. and Beaumont P. (1993) *EC Law.* London: Penguin.

Weber, E. (1979) *Peasants into Frenchmen.* London: Chatto and Windus.

Weber, M. (1948) The Nation. In H. Gerth and C. Wright-Mills (eds) *From Max Weber.* London: Kegan-Paul.

Weiler, J. (1997) Legitimacy and democracy of union governance. In G. Edwards and A. Pijpers (eds) *The Politics of European Treaty Reform.* London: Pinter.

Weinreich, H. (1993) Trois cordes à nos arcs. *Le Monde des Débats.* July–August.

Weiss, T. and Gordenker L. (eds) (1996) *NGOs, the UN and Global Governance.* Boulder, CO: Lynne Riener.

Wentzlaff-Eggebert, C. (1997) Paper given at the conférence inaugurale du Conseil européen pour les langues, 3–4 July.

WEU (Western European Union) (1992) Council of Ministers, *The Petersberg Declaration*, 19 June. Bonn.

Whittaker, D. (1995) *The United Nations in Action*. London: University College London Press.

Wierzbicka, A. (1997) *Understanding Cultures through Key Words: English, Russian, Polish, German and Japanese*. Oxford: Oxford University Press.

Williams, G. (1992) *Sociolinguistics: A Sociological Critique*. London: Routledge.

Williams, P. (1980) NATO and the Eurogroup. In K. Twitchett (ed.) *European Cooperation Today*. London: Europa.

Winkler, H. (1993) Nationalism and nation-state in Germany. In M.Teich and R. Porter (eds) *The National Question in Europe*. Cambridge University Press.

Wilson, K. and Dussen, J. van den (eds) (1993) *The History of the Idea of Europe*. London: Routledge.

Wood, G. (1992) Democracy and the American Revolution. In J. Dunn (ed.) *Democracy, the Unfinished Journey*. Oxford: Oxford University Press.

Woolf, S. (1996) *Nationalism in Europe – 1815 to the Present*. London: Routledge.

Wright, S. (1986) *Report on Language Use and Language Training in Lucas Aerospace*. Birmingham: Lucas.

Wright, S. (1993) Patterns of language use among young bilinguals in Birmingham. *Primary Teaching Studies* 7 (1), 22–6.

Wright, S. (1996) Language in the European Parliament. Paper given at conference on Language Rights, Hong Kong Polytechnic University, June.

Wright, S. (1997a) Crossing boundaries: Stories in the European press. Paper given at ICCR conference, Vienna, August.

Wright, S. (1997b) One country, two systems, three languages. In S. Wright and H. Kelly-Holmes (eds) *One Country, Two Systems, Three Languages: Changing Language Use in Hong Kong*. Clevedon: Multilingual Matters.

Wright, S. (1999) The Renaissance of Catalan and Welsh: Political causes and effects. Paper given at conference on International Status and Use of National Languages in Europe: Contributions to a Language Policy, Brussels, March.

Wright, S. and Ager, D. (1995) Major and minor languages in Europe: The evolution of policy and practice in the European Union. *European Journal of Intercultural Studies* 5 (3): 44–55.

Yentob, A. (1997) Speech to BBC television executives, 20 September, reported in the *Sunday Times*, 21 September, BBC bosses to rethink handling of royal deaths, p. 5.

Zapp, F.-J. (1979) Pour une diversification contrôlée. Paper given at the International Symposium, Langues et coopération, Palais de l'Europe, Strasbourg, 17–20 April.

Zwarts, F. (1997) Paper given at the conférence inaugurale du Conseil européen pour les langues, 3–4 July.

Newspaper and audio-visual references

AFP (Agence France Presse) (1994) France Germany – 800 Eurocorps soldiers to parade on Bastille Day, Paris, 7 July.

BBC Radio 4 (1996) From our own correspondent, 10 February.

BBC Radio 4 (1999) *Today* News Programme, 25 June.
BBC 2 (1998) *Compass*, 9 March.
Courrier International (1996) L'Eurocorps: Ni grande armée ni troupe théâtrale. 4–10 January.
Die Zeit (1996) (Bourdieu interview), 1 November.
Economist (1994), 18 June.
European (1996), 19 July.
Financial Times (1988), 26 July, p. 44.
Financial Times (1998), 27 March.
Financial Times (1998), 2 September.
Financieele-Dagblad (1988) DSM claims European chemical industry lacks EC support. 7 June.
Flight-International (1992) Nato: Spinning compass – does the North Atlantic Treaty Organisation have a future? 9 September, p. 63.
Guardian (1997), 30 January.
Guardian (1997), 23 May.
Guardian (1997), 7 June.
Guardian (1997) Off tae Cyberspace. 2 September, p. 4.
Le Figaro (1994) Participation allemande: La polémique. 14 July, p. 14.
Le Figaro (1994) . . . et cinq langues de travail au lieu de onze? 22 December.
L'Humanité Dimanche (1995) L'Offense à la mémoire. 16 July, pp. 10–13.
Le Magazine de Midi-Pyrénées (1997) September, no. 48, p. 47. Toulouse.
Le Monde (1993), 18 November.
Le Monde (1994) Voir et complimenter l'Eurocorps. 14 July.
Le Monde (1996) (Tietmeyer interview). 22 December.
Le Monde (1997) L'anglais colonisateur. 1 December, p. 15.
Le Monde, Dossiers et documents (1991), no. 190, July–August.
Le Monde Dossiers et documents (1997) Mondialisation.
Libération (1993) Offensive linguistique flamande au sein de l'Eurocorps. 19 November.
Libération (1995) La Grèce s'accroche au statut de sa langue au sein de l'Union européenne. 4 January.
Libération (1995) Prise de langues. 2 February.
Libération (1999) Abstention en hausse. 11 June, p. 21.
Observer (1996), 9 June.
Observer (1997), 23 February.
Observer (1997), 22 June.
Observer (1998), 15 February.
Reuters (1988) Italy: deficit will force Italian state to reduce role. 30 August.
Sunday Telegraph (1987), 18 October, p. 4.
Today News Programme, BBC Radio 4 (1999), 25 June.
WDR (Westdeutscherrundfunk) (1998) Ausländer der dritten Generation, 27 March.
Die Zeit (1996), 1 November.

Index

Subject Index

275

Author Index